CREATING A LEAN CULTURE

Tools to Sustain Lean Conversions

SECOND EDITION

"David Mann has provided an excellent review of one of the most common implementation issues in a lean transformation—the essential day to day work practices of team leaders/supervisors/value stream managers that enable the lean system."

—George Koenigsaecker, President, Lean Investments, LLC

"The purpose of lean systems is to make problems glaringly obvious. If implementation does not include standard leadership and cultural support systems to constantly address problems, the point of the system is missed. Many books address lean tools and initial conversion, but if you want the system to stick, read David's book."

**—Robert W. Hall, Editor-In-Chief,
Target, Association for Manufacturing Excellence**

"Mann's book is an excellent start toward Lean Leadership as 'process-dependent' rather than 'person-dependent' in style. The idea of leader standard work is simple and valuable."

**—Ross E. Robson, Executive Director,
Shingo Prize for Excellence in Manufacturing, Utah State**

"At last! A book that bridges the huge gap between the lofty visionary outcomes of Lean Leadership books—and the practical thinking and tools needed to put competitive outcomes in place. This practitioner approach spells out real work needed. All of us should use Mann's first five chapters to crystallize a 'Lean Management System' with the following five chapters to inspire us to roll up our sleeves".

—David Hogg, President High Performance Solutions, Inc.

CREATING A LEAN CULTURE

Tools to Sustain Lean Conversions

SECOND EDITION

DAVID MANN

CRC Press
Taylor & Francis Group
Boca Raton London New York

CRC Press is an imprint of the
Taylor & Francis Group, an **informa** business

A PRODUCTIVITY PRESS BOOK

Productivity Press
Taylor & Francis Group
270 Madison Avenue
New York, NY 10016

© 2010 by Taylor and Francis Group, LLC
Productivity Press is an imprint of Taylor & Francis Group, an Informa business

No claim to original U.S. Government works

Printed in the United States of America on acid-free paper
10 9 8 7 6 5 4 3 2

International Standard Book Number: 978-1-4398-1141-2 (Paperback)

Library of Congress Cataloging-in-Publication Data

Mann, David (David William), 1947-
    Creating a lean culture : tools to sustain lean conversions / David Mann. -- 2nd ed.
        p. cm.
    Includes bibliographical references and index.
    ISBN 978-1-4398-1141-2 (acid-free paper)
    1. Organizational effectiveness. 2. Industrial efficiency. 3. Organizational change. 4. Corporate culture. I. Title.

HD58.9.M365 2010
658.4'01--dc22   2009043561

Visit the Taylor & Francis Web site at
http://www.taylorandfrancis.com

and the Productivity Press Web site at
http://www.productivitypress.com

Dedication

To my wife, Jan, and our daughters, Kate and Elizabeth.

Without your love, support, patience, and encouragement
I could not have written this book.

Contents

Acknowledgments

I owe much to many people with, for, and from whom I have worked and learned—bosses, clients, colleagues, sensei. I will try to acknowledge them here, and apologize to any I miss. Any shortcomings in this book are fully and exclusively my own responsibility.

The Association for Manufacturing Excellence (AME) gave me access to a wider professional audience than I could otherwise have had, and provided vehicles for reaching the larger manufacturing community.

Steelcase, Inc. gave me the opportunity to experiment with and develop many of the ideas and approaches to lean management contained in these pages. At Steelcase, I had the good fortune to work for several executives who supported the idea that there had to be more to lean production than the application of Henry Ford's and Toyota's industrial engineering techniques. Among them were Adolph Bessler, Rob Burch, and especially Mark Baker. I am grateful to all of them.

Mark Baker, Mark Berghoef, John Duba, and Scott McDuffee read early drafts of the manuscript and provided helpful critique and suggestions. I appreciate their willingness to take on this task and their thoughtful comments.

I have had some terrific clients to work with while developing (actually, co-developing) and testing the concepts and tools of lean management. Among them are Shanda Bedoian, Mark Berghoef, Dave Greene, Dave McLenithan, John Mancuso, Kevin Meagher, Didier Rabino, and Jane Velthouse.

I learned a lot about lean thinking from sensei Tom Luyster and Marek Piatkowski and am thankful they shared their knowledge and perspectives with me.

My colleagues on our lean journey have been important in helping develop and refine much of what is in this book. Scott McDuffee, Pat Nally, Bob O'Neill, and Dave Rottiers all contributed to what has emerged as lean management. John Duba and Ken Knister have been constant sounding boards and valued collaborators over the years.

Maura May of Productivity Press took a chance on the basis of a presentation at the AME conference in 2003 and provided welcome and needed encouragement throughout the writing process. Ruth Mills edited the manuscript and made refinements that make the book more accessible to readers.

Finally, I want to acknowledge and thank my first and primary editor, my spouse Jan, who taught me that everybody needs an editor, but probably does not recognize that few ever get one as gifted as she.

Introduction

Creating a Lean Culture addresses a gap in the literature on lean production and the Toyota Production System (TPS). This book introduces a lean system for management, first in concept and then in concrete detail. Lean management is a crucial ingredient for successful lean conversions. Yet, the standard books on lean either don't cover it or only hint at implementing new ways to manage in a lean environment. *Creating a Lean Culture* provides the rationale and then a practical guide to implementing the missing link you'll need to sustain your lean implementation—a lean management system.

Lean production, based on the much admired Toyota Production System, has proved to be an unbeatable way to organize production operations. The key concepts of lean are easily grasped, and relative to most technical engineering projects, lean designs are easily implemented. Yet the majority of attempts to implement lean production end in disappointing outcomes, and declarations like: "Lean won't work here," or "with our people," or "in our industry," or "with our product/process," and so on.

Why, when it seems so simple, are successful lean implementations so difficult to achieve? The answer is in an overlooked but crucial aspect of lean. It requires an almost completely different approach in *day-to-day and hour-to-hour management*, compared to anything with which leaders in conventional batch-and-queue environments are familiar or comfortable.

I'm a social scientist, an organizational psychologist. By conventional measure, I've been in the "wrong" place for someone with my training and background for the past 15 years. It has turned out to be the right place though, to be immersed in manufacturing operations and directly involved in supporting more than 30 brownfield lean conversion projects, large and small. Through much trial and error in these experiences, I've come to recognize a common, but typically overlooked, element in batch-to-lean conversions. This element is a lean management system. Not only is it necessary to sustain new lean conversions, it accounts for the differences between failed and successful implementations.

The book lays out the components of lean management, how they work together, and how to implement the process. *Creating a Lean Culture* maps a course for leaders implementing lean management to guide them through the cultural minefields in batch-to-lean conversions.

Lessons Learned Since the First Edition

I have been fortunate since the 2005 publication of this book to have worked, visited, and corresponded with many people and organizations that have taken ideas in the original edition and run with them. An informal community of practice has developed around the recognition that to be sustained, lean tools need the support of a new approach to management—a lean management system.

The approaches people have taken to lean management turn out to be quite varied. One conclusion I have come to is that there are many "right" or effective ways to do lean management. As with any experiment, there are also many ways that do not work so well. In the best cases, organizations have followed the classic advice of Dr. W. Edwards Deming: Plan, Do, Check (or reflect), and Act (or adjust). They have kept what works for their circumstances and revised or replaced what does not, whether in leader standard work, visuals, or accountability.

I have learned a great deal from comparing notes with lean management practitioners, and have incorporated many of these lessons in this second edition. A primary lesson from application experience has to do with the sequence of implementing the elements of lean management (see "Implementing Lean Management: Where to Begin?" in Chapter 2). The next section briefly describes the new material in this edition. Just as "lowering the water" really *does* expose the next set of rocks, these lessons have brought home again for me the reality of lean as a journey. At our lean best, we are all students.

I heard once about this advice given to an aspiring but struggling singer-songwriter: Write what you know! I had come to know something about discrete manufacturing, and that's what I wrote about in the first edition. I was surprised to learn about lean management applications in process industries, healthcare, and in business processes completely separate from physical production operations. Just as lean applications have in recent years brought benefits far afield from lean's roots in the auto industry, so has the application of lean management

In my last five years at Steelcase, from which I retired in 2009, I developed and led an internal lean consulting team charged with bringing lean applications into the company's enterprise business processes. We facilitated project teams that completed 100 lean business process ("lean office") value stream projects, and learned a great deal from the experience. Some of those lessons appear as a new chapter in this edition, Chapter 6.

What's New in the Second Edition

The changes to this second edition come as a result of my experience implementing lean management systems since the publication of the first edition in 2005. Since writing the original edition, I've had the opportunity to work directly with many lean applications far from the factory floor.

Some of the key changes in this edition include:

- More attention is given to applications of lean management in administrative, technical, and professional environments. In particular, Chapter 6, new to this edition, focuses on that arena.
- New guidance on how to begin implementing lean management in discrete manufacturing, office, and process manufacturing environments is provided in Chapter 2.
- Specifics on how to engage executives through gemba walks have been added in Chapter 7.
- Key information on process versus results measures is included in Chapter 8.
- Information on approaches to implementing lean training are now included in Chapter 10.
- Several new case studies have been added throughout.
- The lean management assessment, or standards (see the Appendix), has been expanded and improved based on actual use, and now appears as two separate versions: one for manufacturing and one for administrative, technical, and professional settings. The assessment is also available in downloadable spreadsheet format at http://www.crcpress.com/product/isbn/9781439811412 and verified at www.dmannlean.com.

How This Book Is Organized

The book is organized into two sections. Part I answers the question: What is the lean management system? This section details the principal elements of lean management and includes Chapters 1 through 6, as summarized in Table I.1.

Part II consists of Chapters 7 through 11 and covers how you learn lean production and, especially, how you learn lean management. The approaches to each are nearly identical. Nine attributes are described for leading a lean conversion project and the important role played by these attributes in slightly—but importantly—different form when leading an ongoing lean production area. Part II also covers some supporting elements in the lean management system, including the aspects of lean management that focus on people-related issues. Table I.2 lists these and coordinates them to specific chapters. Finally, Part II focuses on what to do to sustain the lean management and lean production systems you have worked so hard (or will work so hard) to implement. In addition to guidance for leaders, this includes an audit of the lean management system that can be readily adapted for use in your workplace.

Table I.1 Principal Elements of Lean Management

Element	Key Characteristics	Chapter Details
Leader standard work	Daily checklists for line production leaders—team leaders, supervisors, and value stream managers—that state explicit expectations for what it means to focus on the process.	3
Visual controls	Tracking charts and other visual tools that reflect actual performance compared with expected performance of virtually any process in a lean operation—production and nonproduction alike.	4, 6
Daily accountability process	Brief, structured, tiered meetings focused on performance with visual action assignments and follow-up to close gaps between actual results vs. expected performance.	5
Discipline	Leaders themselves consistently following and following up on others' adherence to the processes that define the first three elements.	3–6

Table I.2 Supporting Elements in the Lean Management System

Supporting Element	Key Characteristics	Chapter Details
The leadership tasks in an ongoing lean operation	Subtle, but important, differences between leading lean conversion projects and leading ongoing lean operations.	8
Learning lean management	Work with a sensei; use the production area as the classroom through gemba walks.	7
Root cause analysis	Standard, basic tools to focus on eliminating the causes of problems rather than settling for workarounds that leave causes undisturbed.	9
Progressive discipline in a lean environment	Applying discipline for performance as well as for conduct as a source of support for expected performance in a lean environment.	10
Rapid response system	Procedures and technology for summoning quick help from support groups and management is important in finely balanced lean operations. New relationships between support groups and production areas are an often-overlooked critical factor for successful "911" systems.	9
Improvement process	How are improvement activities managed when they exceed the scope of the daily task assignment boards?	9
Appropriate automation	IT networks can be powerful tools in support of lean production and lean management. Much of the power in IT for lean consists of knowing when *not* to apply it.	8
Labor planning	A suite of four visual tools for planning the next day's work assignments, rotation plan, and unplanned absences.	10
HR policies	Changes to pay plans, expectations for rotation, applying discipline for problem performers, break schedules, communication processes, pay grades and classifications, and other "people" issues that help or hinder a lean operation.	10
Assessing the status of lean management	A five-level assessment on nine dimensions of lean management (eight dimensions for office processes) to highlight areas needing attention to bring lean management practices up to a self-sustaining level.	10, Appendix

Throughout the book are dozens of highlighted case studies, to show you how lean management and lean production work—or *should* work. And the book is chock full of sample visual ideas, to jump start your brainstorming for what might work best in your own organization.

Who Can Learn From This Book?

This book is for you if you are a leader at any level in an organization undergoing a lean transformation. You could be an hourly leader of a production team, a supervisor of a department and team leaders, a value stream manager with supervisors and support group staff working in your value stream, or you could be an executive—a plant or site or manufacturing general manager; an operations, division, or corporate executive.

This book is also for you if you or your organization is contemplating a lean transformation. You might not yet know much about lean production. There are several clearly written and readily available books and articles you can turn to for an introduction. See the references section at the end of this book, and if you're unfamiliar with the terminology, scan the glossary too.

You might be an engineer or other technical professional concerned about those pesky humans who are likely to trip up your well-designed system. You will find constructive ways of dealing with these issues here, too. Or, you might be a support group manager with questions about the demands lean production will make on you and your group.

This book is also for you if you are wondering what the heck happened to the last project you worked on, the lean project that seemed to hold such promise, but just did not turn out as you hoped it would.

Perhaps least likely, you might be a social scientist interested in how manufacturing organizations undergo change and the conditions that either support or impede it.

Whomever you are, welcome and let's go!

WHAT IS THE LEAN MANAGEMENT SYSTEM? PRINCIPAL ELEMENTS OF LEAN MANAGEMENT

1

Chapter 1

The Missing Link in Lean
The Management System

Most prescriptions for *lean production* are missing a critical ingredient: a lean management system to sustain it. Lean management practices are like many other aspects of lean: easy to grasp, but difficult to execute consistently. This book spells out the distinction between an organization's *culture* and its management system; provides a framework to see the differences between lean and batch cultures; and details the practices, tools, and thinking for establishing lean management. A *lean management system* sustains and extends the gains from implementing lean production. Lean cultures grow from robust lean management systems, and this chapter shows how.

Developing a Lean Culture

What is culture? Is it real? Should it be among the targets in your lean implementation? As a working definition, consider culture in a work organization to be the sum of peoples' habits related to how they get their work done. You will see several examples in the next few pages. Given that, culture must be "real," right? Well, yes and no.

In scientific language, culture is a *hypothetical construct*. That is, culture is a label or idea—a concept we make up to organize and get a handle on what we have seen or experienced. It has been said that something is real if it has observable effects. Culture certainly fits the bill there. People talk about their company's culture all the time as a reason why they can or cannot do something. Keynote speakers refer to an organization's culture as enabling or inhibiting change or resistance. Annual reports proudly refer to company culture as an invaluable asset, and so on.

Should a company target its culture in its efforts to transform its production processes and all the positions—high and low—associated with it? It is tempting to answer: Yes! But, that would be a mistake.

Culture is no more likely a target than the air we breathe. It is not something to target for change. Culture is an idea arising from experience. That is, our idea of the culture of a place or organization is a result of what we experience there. In this way, a company's culture is a *result* of its management system. The premise of this book is that culture is critical, and to change it, you have to change your management system.

So, focus on your management system, on targets you can see, such as leaders' behavior, specific expectations, tools, and routine practices. Lean production systems make this easier, because they emphasize explicitly defined processes and use *visual controls*.

Don't Wait—Start Now!

Do not wait for the "real work," the physical changes of a lean implementation to be done before turning your attention to implementing the management system. Your lean implementation depends on it to survive! Think of it this way: In successful *brownfield* mass-to-lean conversions, no more than 20 percent of the effort involves the typical "what you see is what you get" physical changes. You install new *layouts* to establish *flow*, begin *pull signaling*, develop ways to pace production, and so on. An advanced version of an initial implementation would also include features such as visual methods to track production, start-up meetings, and *standardized work* posted at workstations. But all that only gets you to the 20-percent level at most, and the likelihood of disappointment with the staying power of the changes you have implemented and disappointment in results the new system produces. You might come to the conclusion that lean production does not really fit with your business model, culture, or industry, or some similar explanation.

Well, of course a lean implementation that's only 20 percent complete is not going to be so hot. You have done only the easiest fifth of the process! The remaining 80 percent of the required time and effort is made up of tasks that are less obvious and much more demanding. After the design/implementation project team finishes and moves on, a very different, more subtle sort of rearrangement remains to be done. As a leader, many things change for you: the information you need to rely on, your deeply ingrained work habits, your day-to-day and hour-to-hour routines, and the way you think about problems, managing work, and productivity. All of these and more have to be transformed for your lean implementation to be a long-term success.

You have probably heard over and over that lean is a journey. It is true, but the journey truly begins in earnest after the production floor has been rearranged. Most of the journey is internal, a mental calibration and adjustment to a lean world. On this journey you learn to impose on yourself the same kind of disciplined adherence to process you now expect of operators in following their standardized work. As you continue on the journey you learn to focus with near obsessive intensity on the processes in your system. You learn to trust that results will take care of themselves when you take care of the process.

Without this internal work, the most typical outcome of lean implementations is to reinforce old habits and ways of thinking. As with any new system, when the lean process is turned on, a variety of problems suddenly appear. Without a lean management system in place to support the new physical arrangements, people are left to rely on their old tricks for fooling the system, using familiar workarounds to get themselves out of trouble. This is as true for leaders as it is for operators. It is a path that leads swiftly away from a successful lean conversion. Worse, once you have realized your mistake, it is an uphill battle to convince people that you are serious this time and will stick with the change. Most often, the result is merely a different layout. The promising lean system becomes one more sad entry in the roster of failed change projects.

Why is it that so many attempts to convert to lean end in retreat and disappointment? It is a paradox: So many lean implementations fail because lean is too easy! That is, it is too easy to implement the physical trappings of lean production while failing completely to notice the need for a parallel implementation of lean management. It is too easy just to keep on managing the way we always have. Instead, for the new physical production process to be a success, managers must change from the habitual focus on results to quite a different and less obvious focus on process and all it entails (see the case study "Successful Implementation of Lean Management," below).

CASE STUDY: SUCCESSFUL IMPLEMENTATION OF LEAN MANAGEMENT

The testimony of a former leader of a plant's lean team underscores this point. He had been involved from the outset of a lean transformation initiative in one of the "mother ship" plants located within sight of his organization's corporate headquarters. He provided the technical lean vision for transforming a classic batch-and-queue production process with 13 schedule points into a flow and pull value stream with only a single schedule point. The design was elegant and effective, though not without controversy. It was a radical departure not only in the way production flowed, but also in the way it was scheduled and in expectations for leaders' and operators' performance. He ended up taking a job to lead operations in one of the company's divisions located in a distant part of the country.

He was recruited there to bring the lean focus he had learned in his previous assignment, and he did so with the full support of his division executive. In a relatively short time, roughly 24 months after arriving on the scene and working with the staff he inherited, his team had pulled off three waves of changes in the factory:

- First, they picked up, moved, and rearranged every product line's production operations.
- Second, they conducted *kaizens* on all of the rearranged operations to increase their level of leanness.
- Third, they transformed the scheduling process from one based on inventory transactions and multiple MRP (material requirements planning) schedule points to a manual, visually controlled *heijunka* process for all but the handcrafted 15 percent of the plant's output.

These were major changes in physical arrangements and technical systems. In the previous batch-and-queue system, the time from releasing a manufacturing order to the floor completing a product took 20 working days. In the new flow and pull system, this total throughput time has been reduced to 2 days. In addition to the changes in manufacturing, it took equally significant changes throughout the supporting processes—HR and finance, database and production control, and others to make this happen.

Clearly, this operations leader knew lean philosophy, how to implement it, how to teach it, and how to lead it. Yet he is emphatic that, as important as all the physical and technical changes have been, the operation did not experience much measurable benefit until the implementation turned to the management system. He described it this way:

> The new layouts really enabled the management system. It wasn't until we began focusing on it (the management system) that we began to see big increases in productivity. That came from paying attention to the process, implementing hour-by-hour production tracking, defining standard work for team leaders and supervisors, and following up on accountability for action on *flow interrupters* and improvements. We've seen a 36-percent increase in annual sales dollars per full-time equivalent employee, once we had the management system in operation. Much of that is attributable to lean management.
>
> *Note that this increase in productivity came during a sleep industry downturn in which this division saw a 35-percent decline in sales.*

Lean Management Focuses on Process

The lean management system consists of the discipline, daily practices, and tools you need to establish and maintain a persistent, intensive focus on process. It is the *process focus* that sustains and extends lean implementations. And the practices of lean management produce process focus. Here is how this happens:

1. The visual controls called for in a lean management implementation represent lean's emphasis on process. Timely maintenance of visuals provides physical evidence of leaders' discipline. As important, visuals are designed to capture process performance data, including information on misses, defects, interruptions, system failures, and abnormalities.
2. The visuals with their process data are brought to a standard, often daily accountability meeting. At the accountability session, misses are

reviewed and where appropriate converted into task assignments. The assignments may call for cause analysis, implementing a temporary countermeasure to protect the process from failure, or putting in place a root cause solution.

3. Follow-ups on the actions resulting from accountability assignments become items added, at least on a temporary basis, to leaders' standard work. Is the countermeasure working; has the root cause fix remained in place? Adding these items to leader standard work supports the integrity of the change made in response to the miss or failure first noted on the visual process control.

The data on the visual control, when brought to the accountability meeting, results in the process change. The follow up through leader standard work provides the mechanism to systematically sustain the change. That prevents the process change from fading and disappearing, which happens so often when follow through is lacking.

If this sounds circular, it is designed to be. That is, this virtuous circle starting with visual process data, leading to accountability task assignments for process changes, with follow up incorporated into leader standard work represents a closed-loop system that produces process focus and results in process improvement (Figure 1.1).

As lean management, with its closed-loop focus on process, becomes habitual, little by little—almost unnoticeably at first—a lean culture begins to grow. The new lean culture emerges as leaders replace the mindset to hide problems and bury their causes—a mindset learned in our careers in conventional processes and organizations.

Let us step back for a moment to provide some context for the conversion to lean production and the differences in management system between batch and lean. Lean manufacturing is an idea whose time has come.

Figure 1.1   Lean management as a closed loop system produces process focus and process improvement.

Manufacturers the world over have recognized the advantages in lead time, productivity, quality, and cost enjoyed by lean competitors in industry after industry. And lean is now spreading rapidly beyond the manufacturing sector, in office process of all descriptions, healthcare, government, product development, and IT. One of the attractive features of lean is that it is so easy to understand. Customer focus, value stream organization, standardized work, flow, pull, and continuous improvement are readily grasped. Second, lean is typically not capital intensive. In fact, lean adherents prefer simple, single-purpose equipment with minimal automation. Lean scheduling systems are equally simple and inexpensive, rarely requiring much, if anything, in the way of incremental IT investment. Here, too, leansters typically say less is more. In office, technical, and professional processes where the product is information, increasingly lean improvements are turned to before making IT changes, with value stream maps used to define and document requirements for IT system changes. Finally, lean layouts and material flows are relatively straightforward to design and implement, whether through redesign of entire value streams or more narrowly focused kaizen events.

Parallel Implementations of Lean Production and Lean Management

So, lean production confers many advantages. It is easily grasped, requires minimal capital for equipment and IT support, and is relatively straightforward to implement. Yet, as I have just suggested, the experience of many—indeed, most—companies that have attempted to convert to lean production has been failure and retreat. Again, this is as true in office processes as in manufacturing. It seems so easy, yet success is so difficult! What is it about lean that makes successful implementation so rare as to be newsworthy? Something, some crucial ingredient, must be missing from the standard list of steps in lean conversions. The missing link is this: a parallel lean conversion effort that converts management systems from mass production to lean.

The physical changes in a lean conversion are easy to see: equipment gets moved, inventory is reduced and redeployed, and notable changes occur in material supply, production scheduling, and standardized methods. In an office, changes take place to processes, procedures, and forms. The change in management systems is not so obvious. An orienting question about the lean management system might be: change *from* what, *to* what?

Changing from Conventional Mass Production

Think about management in a conventional batch-and-queue production operation. First and foremost, the focus is on results, on hitting the numbers:

- Did we meet the schedule for this day or this week?
- How many defective units were caught by quality inspections?
- Did we hit our targets for material cost and production labor?

Managers in conventional systems track key indicators like these through monitoring and analyzing reports that summarize the previous period's (day, week, or month) data.

Managers attend many meetings to review production status and troubleshoot problems. These meetings typically revolve around computer-generated reports that line managers and support group specialists pore over in conference rooms. Disagreements are common about which departments' reports to believe. In fact, it is not unusual to spend substantial time in meetings like these arguing about whose report is accurate! ("Your report says the material got here; my report says I never received it.") Sometimes you actually have to go to the production floor to look for or count what the computer says is supposed to be there—an extreme measure in an IT world.

The focus is usually retrospective, looking at what happened last reporting period, determining who or what messed up, and deciding how to recover. With more sophisticated IT systems, these data are accessible more or less in real time. Looking at a computer monitor, managers can see a numerical or even graphic representation of what the IT system presents as the precise state of their production process. This seems like an improvement, and often can be—if the data are accurate (not just precise), and you can sift through all the available data to identify the critical numbers to watch, and you know which are the critical questions to ask of the database.

Getting Rid of the "Do Whatever It Takes!" Approach

When problems arise that threaten schedule completion in batch-and-queue systems, the common practice is "do whatever it takes" to meet the schedule. Expedite internal parts, pressure suppliers, airfreight late materials, put on more people, pressure the inspectors, reorder missing parts with a fudge factor to make sure you get the few good ones you need, authorize overtime. Just meet the schedule! Tomorrow or next week, it is a new day with a new schedule and new challenges. Things that went wrong yesterday are typically dropped in the press to meet today's demands. After all, today's schedule must be met!

In fact, most managers—in offices and manufacturing alike—have learned how to be successful in this kind of system. They know the work-arounds and tricks to ensure success in an uncertain environment where the bottom might fall out in one of several areas on any given day. The tricks of the trade include "secret" stashes of extra material, people, and even equipment to be called on in time of need. Never mind that all this is costly in the long run. In the short run, results are what matter and the numbers do not lie—you either met the schedule or you did not.

Lean Processes Need Lean Management

In lean systems the results certainly matter, but the approach to achieving them differs sharply from conventional management methods. The difference in a lean management system is the addition of a focus on process, as well as a focus on results. The premise is this: Start by designing a process to produce specific results. If you have done a good job of designing the process and you maintain it, you will get the specified results. In concept, this is simply a matter of maintaining production at takt time. If you do, you meet demand. As you make improvements in the process, you should expect improved results.

A critical point is to think about the lean management system as an integral element of the lean process. Here is why. If the process were a perfect system, it would always run as designed and always produce consistent results. A real-world system requires periodic maintenance and occasional intervention and repair to continue producing results. The more complex the system, especially the more automated it is, the more maintenance and repair it requires. It may not seem like this should be true, but it is. A more reliable and flexible solution usually is to rely less on automation and more on people and simpler equipment.

Relying on people brings its own set of issues. People require all sorts of "maintenance" and attention. Left to their own devices, people are prone to introduce all kinds of mischief—variation in the system that can take things far afield from the original design. If anything, lean production is more vulnerable to these effects than mass production, because of the tight interdependence and reliance on precise execution in lean designs. That is why discipline is such an important factor in lean processes. Without a high degree of discipline in a lean process, chaos ensues in short order. That is where the lean management system comes in.

Focusing on the Process Produces Results

Putting it plainly, if you want a process to produce the results for which it was designed, you have to pay attention to it. One of the first rules of process focus in lean production is to regularly see the process operating with your own eyes. This is as much the case with office processes as in manufacturing. The closer your position is to the production floor (value stream manager, department supervisor, team leader as opposed to plant manager, manufacturing director, or VP), the more time you should spend watching the process, verifying execution consistent with design, and intervening when you observe nonstandard or abnormal conditions. Production team leaders should spend virtually all of their time either training operators in the process, monitoring the process, or improving it. Taking time to monitor the production process applies all the way up the chain of command, though with decreasing frequency and duration. That is why lean manufacturing executives meet with their plant managers on the production floor, to spot-verify that processes are defined, visually documented and controlled, and are being followed. It also allows executives to verify that plant managers know what is going on with their lean processes. Meeting in offices to discuss reports becomes a secondary activity in management reviews.

Another way of thinking about this, and another paradox in lean management, is that lean managers are so focused on results that they cannot afford to take their eyes off the process they rely on to produce their results. Looking at what happened yesterday is way too late to do anything about yesterday's results. On the other hand, looking at what happened last hour, last *pitch*, or even better, last takt cycle, gives the chance to recover from an abnormal or nonstandard condition. But, that is only true if trained eyes (like a team leader's) are there to see the abnormality; the pertinent processes are well defined, clearly documented, and operating in a stable environment; and resources are available to respond in *real* real time. That is, someone must be available *right there*, to respond *right now!*

Further, this means focusing on the process as it operates from beginning to end, not only at the completed component or finished goods end. That is why lean designs require so many team leaders to maintain the process, to spot problems in upstream intermediate or subprocess areas, and to respond right away to prevent or minimize missing takt at the outlet end of the process. An integral part of the lean management system is having the appropriate number of team leaders on the floor to focus on the process. It requires a leap of faith not to scrimp on this crucial part of the system; having enough leaders available to monitor the process, react to problems, and work toward *root cause* solutions is an investment that pays off in business results. But at first, and from a conventional perspective, team leaders just look like more overhead.

Measuring the Process against Expected Outcomes

Unlike managing in a results-focused system, process focus implies frequent measurement against expected intermediate outcomes. As necessary, interventions can be started before the end results are affected. A corollary of frequent measurement at multiple intermediate steps in a lean process is that data are readily available to aid quick diagnosis of problems, spur immediate remedial action, and eventually eliminate root causes of problems. This is one aspect of continuous improvement. Rather than waiting for problems to develop, you are constantly monitoring for early signs of developing troubles, and you are primed to take quick action to eliminate the causes of problems. Contrast this with the conventional mass production culture in which most supervisors expect various unpredictable problems and have earned their spurs by being able to work around them to get out the day's schedule.

A new management system is called for in lean conversions, because lean processes are much more tightly interdependent than conventional systems. Lean processes are designed not to rely on the extras stashed away in conventional systems to bail things out in a pinch. Even so, things go wrong in lean systems just as they do in mass systems. By design, a lean process has little unaccounted-for slack in the system to fall back on. Because of that, lean processes require far more attention to disciplined cycle-by-cycle operation to ensure the process stays in a stable state. Otherwise, the process will fail to hit its goals and fail to deliver the business results so important in any kind of production system. Paradoxically then, in many ways, simpler lean systems require more maintenance than conventional systems. That is why they require a specific management system to sustain them.

How Can You Recognize Culture?

Remember that we can define culture in a work organization as the sum of its individuals' work habits. A related way to think of culture is that it is the knowledge an adult needs of how things are done to stay out of trouble as a member of a group. One of the interesting things about culture is that for group members, culture is invisible. It is the things that are given, or "the way we do things around here." It is typical not to question this kind of thing, or even to realize there are alternatives to it. Yet, it is easily possible to "see" work culture in a production environment by asking basic questions about common practices, such as:

1. What are inventory practices around here?
2. How often does management look at the status of production?
3. Who is involved in process-improvement activities in this area?
4. What is the typical response when problems arise?

Asking these questions would reveal some of the distinctions between the cultures in conventional and lean production environments.

The examples in Table 1.1 give a partial picture of the pervasiveness and everyday manifestation of culture in mass and lean production, as well as how they differ from each other. It is made up of myriad habits and practices that make it possible for all of us to go through the work day without having constantly to think about who, what, where, when, how, and so on.

Culture allows us to operate more or less on autopilot during the workday. By the same token, a distinct culture also makes it easy to identify countercultural behaviors, practices, or events. In most groups, these tend not to take root without many other things changing.

Overcoming Cultural Inertia

One implication of culture as a collection of habits and practices is that it has incredible inertia and momentum going for it. Cultural inertia is like a body in motion tending to stay in motion in the same direction unless acted on by an external force. Conventional mass production systems include a culture. So do lean production systems. When you change the physical

Table 1.1   Visible Attributes of Different Cultures in Mass and Lean Production

Cultural Attribute	Mass Production Culture	Lean Production Culture
Inventory practices	• Managed by computer system • Ordered by forecast • Stored in warehouse areas or automated storage and retrieval facilities • Held in bulk containers • Moved by lift truck • Many hours' worth or more per delivery • Delivered by the skid or tub by forklift to vicinity of use	• Managed visually • Ordered to replenish actual use • Stored in *FIFO* racks or grids addressed by part number • Held in point-of-use containers • Container quantity and number of containers specified per address • Precise quantities (often less than an hour's worth) delivered to point of use • Deliveries by hand cart or *tugger*
Production status	• Checked at end of shift, beginning of next shift, or end of week • Checked by supervisor, higher level managers	• Checked by team leaders several times an hour • Checked by supervisors four or more times a shift • Checked by value stream managers once or twice during the shift • Updated for all involved in a sequence of brief daily reviews of the previous day's performance
Process improvement	• Made by technical project teams • Changes must be specifically "chartered" • No changes between "official" projects	• Can be and routinely are initiated by anybody, including operators • Regular, structured vehicles encourage everyone from the floor on up to suggest improvements and perhaps get involved in implementation • Improvement goes on more or less all the time, continuously

continued

Table 1.1 (continued)   Visible Attributes of Different Cultures in Mass and Lean Production

Cultural Attribute	Mass Production Culture	Lean Production Culture
Problem Solving	• Do whatever it takes to hit today's numbers! • Work around the problem; just meet the daily/weekly production/productivity goal	• Record immediate circumstances of the miss, interruption, or breakdown • Put temporary countermeasures in place if needed to serve the customer • Assign task to identify and then to eliminate causes of problem

arrangements from batch to lean, however, the culture does not make a similar change unless specific action is taken to replace one management system with another. That's the parallel lean implementation noted earlier, implementing the lean management system.

Conventional habits and practices live on, even if the layout, material, and information flows have changed. In one example, operators whose area switched from *MRP* schedules to *pull signals* were quite inventive in figuring out how to get access to a copy of the MRP schedule, which they then followed regardless of the pull signals. In this case, the fabrication operators regularly overproduced according to the discarded schedule they retrieved every day from a trashcan near the dispatch office. It was not until they were found out, and the schedule paperwork began to be regularly shredded, that they had to follow the pull signals. Another common occurrence is for operators in newly converted flow lines transformed from batch build to go right on building. When the line fills up, it is typical to see the overproduction stacked on the floor, overstacked on conveyors, overflowing containers, or sitting as piles of unused documents, or as specifications "completed" before the full requirements were defined—and which now need to be reworked.

New Settings with Old Habits Won't Work

It is typical to see supervisors and *team leaders* in a newly rearranged area rushing off here and there to chase parts or jump onto the line to run production. In some cases, it is nearly impossible to convince supervisors or team leaders to make the hourly entries on production tracking charts because they are "too busy" to get to this task. Then, once the tracking charts are actually filled out, it is not unusual to see them simply pile up on (or under) a supervisor's desk with no attention at all to the interruptions documented on the charts. If the schedule has been met, there is no interest in what is on that "paperwork." And if the schedule hasn't been met, there is "real work" to be done; no time to waste with these records of interruption! That will not get the schedule out today, and in the old—and ingrained—culture, that is all that counts.

In conventional mass production, it is seen as important to be busy doing something directly physically linked to production. Waiting for a *production instruction card* to arrive before starting to produce simply seems wrong. Standing and waiting for the next piece to come down a *progressive build line* is definitely countercultural in the mass production world. In such an environment, these interruptions in the rhythm of production are not considered to be valuable diagnostic information, signaling an abnormal condition in the production system; that is for sure! Relying on the reduced inventory of parts called for in a *pull system* seems sure to lead to stock-outs down the line. There is no perceived value in recording data that documents the operation of the process. Action is what counts, and if it is based on gut feel and experience, it must be right, because "...that's the way we get things done around here!"

These are only a few habits of thought, interpretation, and action that people absorb as part of the culture in a mass production environment. They are at clear variance with the kinds of habits and daily practices necessary for the precise and disciplined execution lean systems need in order to meet their promise for productivity, quality, and ongoing improvement. Table 1.2 compares a few of the ways in which mass and lean cultures differ. Many mass production cultural practices are strikingly tied to longstanding ways of relating to others at work. In contrast, many lean practices are related to disciplined adherence to defined processes.

How to Change Your Culture

We usually refer to changing habits with the word "break," as in "That's a hard habit to break." Similarly, many talk about "kicking" habits. In each case, these words imply that changing habits is a one-time thing,

Table 1.2   Differences in Habits and Practices between Batch and Lean Cultures

Mass Production: Personally Focused Work Practices	Lean Production: Process Focused Work Practices
Independent	Interdependent, closely linked
Self-paced work and breaks	Process-paced work, time as a discipline
"Leave me alone"	"I work as part of a team"
"I get my own parts and supplies"	In- and out-cycle work are separated and standardized
"We do whatever it takes to get the job done; I know whom I can rely on at crunch time"	There's a defined process or procedure for pretty much everything; follow the process
"I define my own methods"	Methods and procedures are standardized
Results are the focus, do whatever it takes	Process focus is the path to consistent results
"Improvement is someone else's job; it's not my responsibility"	Improvement is the job of everyone
"Maintenance takes care of the equipment when it breaks; it's not my responsibility"	Taking care of the equipment to minimize unplanned downtime is routine
Managed by the pay or bonus system	Managed by performance to expectations

a discontinuous step-change from one state to another, which once accomplished is an event that is over and done with, and no going back.

Many habits that come to mind are personal and physical in nature: smoking, nail biting, various forms of fidgeting—jingling pocket change, fiddling with an ID badge, a pen, or glasses, etc. At some level, each habit provides a form of comfort. We tend not to think of our work habits in these terms because many of them are part of the particular culture at work, and that is effectively invisible. Nevertheless, these habits arise because they bring a form of comfort, too. In a conversion to lean production, some of these habits will be a hindrance, and some will be a help.

Consider these examples of management habits in conventional mass production operations—some of them are things you want to stop doing under lean management:

- Keep a quantity of extra material stashed away at all times; you might need it.
- Take time to listen to what people want to tell you.
- Always maintain a minimum 10-percent surplus labor and plenty of WIP; something could go wrong.
- Speak to everybody in the department every day.
- Jump onto the line or expedite parts when things slow down, or throw in more people; meet the schedule!
- Always reorder more than the actual need when handling shortages, just to be sure you get enough.
- Use an informal gauge of queue size; always keep the line full in case something goes flooey.
- Approach people who are standing idle and ask them to get back to work.

You can think of many more once you start to see work habits and practices as something you do without thinking about it. There is nothing wrong with habits as such. We need them to make the workday more efficient. What is important to remember is this: *work-related habits are just as difficult to change as personal habits!*

Extinguishing versus Breaking Habits

It is helpful to think in terms of the technical language from behavioral science used in connection with changing habits. The term is not "break." Instead, psychologists use the term "extinguish" when talking about changing habits. Extinguish implies a process, something that occurs gradually over time rather than an event producing a suddenly changed state. Because of that, extinguish also implies a change that can be reversed under certain conditions. Think of Smokey the Bear's rules: Douse a campfire with water, stir the coals and turn them over, then douse again. If you do not follow these rules you run the risk that the fire can rekindle itself from the live embers you failed to extinguish.

So it is with habits. They linger, waiting for the right conditions to assert themselves again. We have seen this kind of thing just days following implementation of new lean layouts. Here are some actual examples of old habits reasserting themselves in areas newly converted to lean layouts—again, examples you want to avoid:

- Build up some inventory.
- Allow longer or extra breaks.
- Send people off a balanced line to chase parts or do rework.
- Start a task early, even if all the information is not available from the upstream department.
- Work around the problem today and let tomorrow take care of itself.
- Leave improvement to "the experts" rather than wasting time on employee suggestions.
- Do not bother with the tracking charts—we never actually do anything about recurring problems anyway.

Make Sure You Don't Slip Back into These Old Habits!

To sum it up, you do not need a different management system for lean because it is so *complex* compared to what you have done before. You need it because lean is so *different* from what you have done before. Many of the habits in your organization, as well as your own, are likely to be incompatible with an effectively functioning lean production environment. You have a conventional mass production management system and culture. You need a lean management system and culture. The next chapter shows how to go about making that change.

Summary: Technical and Management Sides Need Each Other

Because lean production is a system, it does not matter where implementation starts. Eventually you will get to all of the elements. But sequence does matter when implementing lean technical elements and the management system. We have learned that technical change must precede cultural change. Technical changes create the need for changed management practices. More than that, lean management does not stand on its own. Without the physical changes in *flow and pull* and the takt-based predictability they permit, production will continue to operate in an environment of daily crisis. How would you track flow interrupters when there is no takt-balanced standardized work, no flow? How would you assess material replenishment performance without standard *lot sizes* or resupply times?

So, start with the physical changes to the production process, but do not implement them by themselves. Just as changes to the management system do not stand well by themselves, neither do technical changes. Every technical change requires support from changes in the management system—the support of new management practices—to maintain integrity over time. If that is not a law of nature, it is darn close to it! Each time you implement an element of the lean production system, implement the elements of the management system right along with it. The elements of the management system give you the tools to help you sustain the newly converted lean process, close the loop on process focus, and drive further improvement. Those elements and the conditions for successfully establishing lean management are what this book is about.

Chapter 2

The Lean Management System's Principal Elements

The lean management system, like the lean production system, consists of only a few principal elements. Lean management is a system in which the elements are interdependent (as in the lean production system). That means all of the elements have to be present for the system to work. A third similarity with lean production is that none of the elements is complex or complicated. And finally, lean management and lean production themselves are interdependent; one does not stand for long without the other.

So, what are the principal elements of the lean management system?

Chapters 3, 4, and 5 go into detail on the principal elements in lean management. The point to emphasize in this chapter is the way the elements combine to form a system. An automotive analogy provides a helpful illustration (see Figure 2.1). Think of three principal elements as representing major parts of a car: the engine, transmission, and controls. The fourth element is the fuel.

Figure 2.1   Making lean management go.

The Principal Elements of Lean Management

In lean management, *leader standard work* (element number 1) comes first. It is the engine. Leader standard work is the first line of defense for the focus on process in lean management. When the leader follows his or her standard work effectively, the rest of the lean management system has a good chance of operating effectively, powered by the engine of leader standard work.

The transmission in lean management is its *visual controls* (element number 2). The visuals translate performance of every process into expected versus actual, throughout the production and management systems. These data are recorded regularly and frequently, often many times a day. They are displayed in highly visual, widely accessible, readily reviewed formats. In these ways, the visuals convert the driving force of leader standard work into traction. Visuals give leaders the ability to quickly spot and move to action where actual performance has not met what was expected.

The controls in lean management, the steering wheel and gas pedal, come with the daily accountability process (element number 3). Through daily accountability the leader can steer, setting direction for improvement activity in the area: Which of the gaps between expected and actual captured by the visual controls should we work on? Daily accountability also allows the leader to control the pace; how much gas to give for improvement; how quickly should we expect improvement to be completed; how many resources should we assign to this task?

At first blush, none of this sounds like a big deal to accomplish. Assembling a daily checklist for leaders certainly is not difficult. Whipping up a bunch of visual tracking charts is also a simple matter. Lots of people can produce those in Excel in no time at all. The basics for daily accountability merely involve scheduling the appropriate daily recurring 15-minute meetings: one for the team leaders to get together with their supervisor and the other for the supervisors and support group representatives to get together with the value stream manager. In fact, you could consider most of these tasks as fairly straightforward administrative details. Why should this merit discussion, much less a whole book?

The answer, of course, is in the fourth element of lean management. Think of *discipline*, leaders' discipline especially, as the fuel that powers the engine that makes the entire system go. Establishing leader standard work, visual controls, and a daily accountability session will not amount to any ____ ___ without the discipline to execute these elements as designed and intended.

This is particularly true as you are starting out on your lean journey. Remember, establishing new habits requires extinguishing the competing old ones. That takes constant positive reinforcement of the new and negative reinforcement of the old, a course that experience shows is easier to avoid than to follow.

Lean Elements Need to Work Together

You will find there is little "coasting" in lean management. If you stop following through on any of the three principal elements because things seem stable and in control, it is certain that you will soon face unstable and out-of-control processes that require you to reinstitute the very elements you thought you could do without. Remember the law of entropy, in which organized systems tend to move toward states of increasing disorganization? Lean production and lean management are not physics, but this law of nature nevertheless seems to apply. Ease off on focus or discipline and your lean systems will quickly deteriorate along with their hoped-for results.

Returning for a moment to the automotive analogy for the lean management system, imagine you were fortunate enough to win a new car in a fund-raising raffle. Consider your shock when on going to pick it up you find an engine in a crate, a transmission sitting on a bench, a speedometer and steering wheel in boxes, and a can of gasoline. If the parts are not assembled and working together, they will not take you where you want to go (see the case study "How Lean Management Fails When the Elements Don't Work Together").

CASE STUDY: HOW LEAN MANAGEMENT FAILS WHEN THE ELEMENTS DON'T WORK TOGETHER

For the lean management system to operate effectively, its elements must work together. In one case, leader standard work had been in place for team leaders and supervisors for nearly a year. The area in question produced several lines of upholstered chairs, most of which had been in production for many years. The chairs were made to order.

Demand for them had declined to the degree that they were only produced sporadically. On the occasion in question, a day's worth of production was called for on one of these aging lines. An experienced assembly operator from elsewhere in the seating department was assigned to build the day's order. He was not experienced with the specific line but the supervisor had reason to be confident. She had an experienced chair builder, standardized work for the build process, and a team leader in the area.

As it turned out, the operator did little more than nod to the standardized work and then began building the chairs approximately according to the standard sequence. By failing to follow standardized work, he missed a critical step in the standard sequence of work elements that involved spraying glue onto the foam substrate to which upholstery fabric was then applied. This caused a known flaw once the product was in use in the field, a flaw the standardized work had been revised specifically to prevent.

The team leader's standard work called for verifying the operator's adherence to the production standardized work. The supervisor's standard work called for spot-checking the team leader's adherence to his standard work. Both were carrying their standard work documents with them that day, but neither exercised the degree of discipline to look beyond the surface. (Instead, the situation was probably assessed as, "The operator is in the workstation building the chairs and they look OK from here. The production-tracking chart is being filled out and the pace is good.") What was required was to actually observe the operator following the standardized process, element by element, in sequence. Those sequenced elements called for using a template to mask off glue overspray from the troublesome areas.

Once the customer complaint was registered, it was clear beyond a doubt that the cause was failure to follow standardized work—on the part of the operator, team leader, and supervisor. Two layers of defense for the integrity of the process had failed because of "coasting" through the discipline of standard work. The checklists were in place and the boxes had checks in them, but the disciplined in-depth observation implied in leader standard work was missing. Engines as a rule do not function without fuel; leader standard work without discipline is no exception to this rule.

Execution Is Key to Lean Management

Making checklists is easy. Developing and posting operator standard work is straightforward. Filling out production-tracking charts is not a demanding routine. In the absence of leaders' disciplined adherence to their standard process, all of this was of no value in preventing a known defect from being produced and shipped. Not only do the elements of the lean management system have to be in place, each has to be scrupulously observed for the system as a whole to work. This case also illustrates, in a small way, the dependence between results from lean production and an effectively functioning lean management system. Lean management acts as the eyes and ears of diligence. Lean management monitors whether the lean production system is being faithfully executed and sounds the alarm when execution deviates from design.

On a more positive note, as you get better and better at executing the elements of lean management, your job as a line production leader will become easier and easier, increasingly free of the "fire alarms" you used to chase all day long most days. In fact, one value stream leader spontaneously remarked to me that his area had become so stable and predictable that he now looked forward to uncovering flow interrupters and other abnormalities.

Those things gave him something "fun to focus on," he said, with the opportunity to lead a kaizen to attack the source of the problem, make his work more interesting, and make his area run that much better. His daily routine includes scrutinizing the daily production-tracking data for ways to make improvements in the process. He has reduced the interval of observation for production tracking by a third (to 20 minutes) to be able to catch smaller interruptions. In a longer interval, these interruptions might not cause a miss, and thus would go unnoticed. His team leaders are Pareto-charting reasons for misses in two different areas, looking for the most frequent problems in order to attack them, and so on. This is an example of what lean management can look like and the ways it can sustain and extend the gains in lean production.

Implementing Lean Management: Where to Begin?

Leader standard work (covered in detail in Chapter 3) is the highest leverage element in the lean management system, the engine that powers the system.

But in many cases, leader standard work may not be the element to start with when implementing lean management. Here's why.

Standard lean advice calls first for stabilizing a process, followed by standardizing it, and then simplifying—or improving it. This advice also often applies to the sequence for implementing the elements of lean management.

Organizations that attempt to start their lean management implementation with leader standard work often find it difficult and confusing. Their difficulty makes sense when you think about the unstable state of many conventional operations before a lean conversion begins. Leaders spend their days firefighting and expediting, especially in areas closer to the floor in factory or office processes. It is tough to create a stable, standard routine under those circumstances. Organizations find they cannot make leader standard work effective because the leaders are constantly being pulled into a crisis or emergency. The leaders asked to try it say that leader standard work does not make sense, that it is not meaningful to them.

Start with Visual Controls

In most cases, technical lean changes create stability. Think of a production or order processing work cell with steady, paced work replacing the previous stop-wait-search-start condition. Or, consider a pull system that controls production or orders between operations, rather than an MRP push system in a plant or no systematic scheduling at all in an office process. In a lean production system, you use capacity to produce what is needed. No more overproducing one component while the needed item is out of stock; no more drowning in unneeded supplier deliveries but still being short of what you need *right now*. With these stabilizing technical changes in place, the need for cultural change—for changed leadership practices and behaviors—comes into focus. It now makes sense to implement a lean management system in order to sustain the new stability and identify opportunities to improve on it.

Begin your lean management implementation by linking it to the technical lean implementation, whether it is a kaizen or a complete value stream makeover. As the last step in the technical implementation, put visual controls in place as described in Chapter 4. The visuals reflect frequent readings of the health of and adherence to the lean design. And, of course, the visuals record misses in the newly transformed process. Establish a standard accountability process through which the misses are converted into actions that sustain and improve on the transformation, as described in Chapter 5.

Now you have elements of standard work for leaders that make sense and sustain the lean conversion:

1. Go to the visuals regularly to verify they are being completed consistently, in a timely manner, and with appropriate specificity.
2. Conduct the standard accountability meeting with the visual tracking charts or their data brought into the session:
   - Ask about the misses recorded on the visuals.
   - Make assignments to understand and act on the causes of process misses and system breakdowns, as well as assignments based on your and others' observations in the area.
   - Follow up on current and overdue assignments.
3. Add to leader standard work as appropriate to monitor changes from completed accountability tasks.

For most organizations the best advice is to begin with stability-producing lean projects and use them to prepare the ground for lean management. With the area operating in a more stable state, the leader has time to pay attention to visual controls and to act on the feedback they provide on the health of the process. This closes the loop on process focus, sustains improvements from the lean project, and drives further improvement. With these steps, the lean management implementation grows from the technical lean changes. The technical changes create the conditions in which lean management makes sense to those asked to follow its new direction.

When Implementing Leader Standard Work First Can Work

I have seen the occasional situation where starting lean management with leader standard work can be effective, in each case involving highly automated manufacturing environments. The critical characteristic is the relative lack of repetitive hand labor in the manufacturing process.

Leader Standard Work in Automated Production Environments

In highly automated operations, relatively few operators tend multiple, often widely separated, pieces of automated production equipment. Some examples are operations that produce discrete units such as precision machined automotive components, microelectronic devices, alkaline batteries, or paperboard pressware, or continuous process operations producing materials such as steel, films or membranes chemicals, or some types of food products. With high automation, few people actually operate a production process. Those who are on the floor often spend their time moving from asset to asset, determining whether to stock them up, changing components, checking process parameters, making adjustments, performing routine in-process maintenance or inspection tasks, and so on.

Floor Time for Leaders

Just as with conventional repetitive manufacturing operations, production leaders in conventional high-automation operations are often occupied off the floor with a variety of tasks. Much of what these floor leaders do was once the responsibility of support groups such as human resources, finance, product development, quality, production control, engineering, marketing, or maintenance. In effect, other functional groups in the plant or business have over time shifted parts of what used to be their work to production floor leaders. Some examples are tasks related to payroll, attendance and FMLA leaves, inspections, calibration, cycle counting, product trials, customer relations, and a variety of record keeping and reporting tasks.

Gradually, this work comes to occupy the majority by far of floor leaders' time. The cumulative effect of these transfers on the value-adding processes in the plants typically goes unexamined. The support groups justify these moves as cost savings, optimizing support departments' productivity measures. But the net effect is to sub-optimize the value-adding production processes by robbing line leaders of their time on the floor.

One such high automation plant began its lean management implementation with leader standard work. As a first step, the plant production leaders and lean team members took inventory of leaders' current tasks. In doing so, they were able to see the accumulated distractions filling leaders' days and how little time leaders actually spent on the floor. Instead, too much of what leaders knew about their processes day to day came from reports, or flurries of floor activity caused by material shortages, quality problems, and equipment breakdowns.

From "Check the Box" to "Improve the Process."

As leader standard work developed, the work of support groups was either sent back to the departments from which it came or found to be no longer necessary and dropped altogether. The result was that leaders were able to spend much more time in their processes. The newly developed leader standard work allowed the leaders to focus on the equipment tracking charts, which the plant had already established but which had not been driving improvement. Recording process data had been a going-through-the-motions activity. Leaders had not had the time to focus on what the data were showing.

Now, with distractions stripped away, the leaders' standard work led them to focus on these data and otherwise develop a much clearer picture of what was going on in their areas. From this closer focus, they began to see steps they could take to stabilize and improve their processes. When the plant implemented the other two main elements of lean management, accountability processes and revisions to leader standard work, the closed loop, process focused improvement picture in this plant was completed.

Does Lean Management Apply in Process Industries?

The lean management system identifies a set of practices and behaviors to close the loop on process focus and drive improvement. Process focus in a manufacturing environment assumes comparing actual versus expected production of discrete units of physical products. The key measures of process focus are based on takt time as the pace for production. These two assumptions—discrete production and takt pace—work well in repetitive production environments producing discrete units of output, whether in factory or office settings. These assumptions, however, do not work so well in process industries or high volume, equipment-intensive manufacturers. If the assumptions do not fit, do lean and lean management apply in process industries?

For example, consider these two types of operations: First, continuous process operations such as a steel mill or high volume extrusion plant; second, high volume, automation-intensive operations such as an alkaline battery plant producing over 1.5 billion units annually, or a fuel systems plant shipping 75,000 fuel injectors a week. In either case, it certainly is possible to measure actual versus expected output in weight, linear feet, or discrete units. And operations like these do use these measures, not as measures of process, but rather as appropriate measures of results. "How many feet, pounds, or units did we produce today?" is a natural question to ask. What if the answer comes back as less than plan, requirement, or expected for any period of observation, such as an hour, a shift, or a day? In a process operation, as in discrete production, less than expected output begs the question: "Why? What happened that cost us production?"

In a discrete production operation, you can usually answer this kind of question in terms of flow interrupters in assembly or problems upstream that starved later production steps. Investigation might take you to breakdowns in fabrication, problems in a finishing operation or with incoming materials, components out of spec, or operator performance issues. In a process operation, assuming good control of incoming material, the problems are much more likely to be related to the process assets. In the battery plant, the high speed inserting, filling, or sealing equipment might have gone out of adjustment or broken down. In the steel mill, the shroud may have misaligned, exposing the melt to the contaminating atmosphere as it was being poured into the continuous casting operation. Either problem would result in defective product being produced, though the defect might not be detected until the finished goods stage, or worse, by the customer.

Process Focus in Process Production

In these cases, close focus on process does not mean close focus on assembly or fabrication operations as they produce finished units, subassemblies, or raw components. In fact, there usually are few people to watch in process operations because of the high level of automation. Instead, close focus on process means focus on and tracking the status of the critical assets. These are attributes like temperatures, pressures, flow rates, chemical composition, and critical characteristics of the outputs at a given point. Standardized work for production people and leaders will usually have more to do with making standard rounds of equipment, logging key values, perhaps verifying the next lot of materials is where it should be, looking for unusual patterns in operating characteristics, and doing or following up on in-process quality checks and machine wellness tasks.

Many if not all the tasks followed up in leader standard work lend themselves to visual controls. The visuals should provide clues to the best places for root cause improvement or temporary remedial countermeasures. These clues can be converted to small or larger-scale assignments in standard accountability processes. The countermeasures or improvements can be recorded in operating and leader standard work and can thus be monitored and sustained, closing the loop on process focus.

You might think about a continuous or high volume automated process as someone who is hospitalized. In the hospital, patients are monitored for the status of many systems: blood pressure, pulse, blood oxygen, blood chemistry, the heart's EKG signals, and more. This is close focus on process, just as it is in the continuous process operation. In both cases the results are important, absolutely. Also important, and with far more leverage, is the information that explains the direction of the developing result. When you monitor the health of the constituent elements of your process, you understand what is happening with it—its health. This allows you to understand why it is producing the current outcomes. And, this equips you to intervene, either immediately or in the longer term, to address an observed incident or pattern of abnormality or ill health.

CASE STUDY: PROCESS FOCUS BEYOND TAKT TIME

An automotive fuel system plant was committed to going lean. Its production process had to meet tight tolerances at high volumes. It was a capital-intensive, precision machining operation that ran around the clock, five days a week. Demand varied by the needs of the automakers' engine plants, its customers. The automakers released monthly schedules to the fuel system plant, with level weekly requirements. So, demand was known a month in advance and was stable within any given week.

The fuel systems plant's first foray into lean was a Total Productive Maintenance (TPM) program focused on reducing machine downtime. Breakdowns had been a chronic problem in this operation, and they became the focus of the new lean initiative. TPM took hold and the glaring equipment reliability problems were progressively resolved. As equipment reliability stabilized, the plant's lean team and operations leaders recognized there were far fewer major equipment breakdowns, but the plant was still losing production time.

Their next step was to further tighten their process focus. They began measuring overall equipment effectiveness (OEE) for their key production equipment. OEE measurement is based on tracking the so-called six big losses in OEE: minor stoppages, major stoppages, waiting for operator, waiting for material, yield or defects, and speed losses. The data are used to compute the OEE coefficient (see glossary).

The plant began tracking losses in each of the six categories every hour for each of its critical assets. Not only did OEE give a clearer picture of how production was being lost, it anticipated the questions a purely takt-based measure would prompt. That is, a takt-based measure would lead you to ask why we lost production last hour. In this automated equipment-intensive environment, the answer would almost certainly involve one of the six big losses.

"Why did we lose production this hour?"

"The finish machining cell was down."

"Why was the cell down?"

The answer, which would prompt further investigation, would likely be a major or minor stoppage, or waiting for material or an operator. With OEE six losses monitoring in place, the questions can begin with: "Why were we waiting for material?" No backtracking is needed to uncover the details of a problem that happened yesterday or on the previous shift. The data are right there, recorded and preserved on the OEE tracking chart.

In high volume, equipment-intensive automated or process industries, close focus on process means close focus on equipment. In these cases, takt-based measures are actually further from the process, further from the sources of variation than a measure like overall equipment effectiveness (OEE). Lean management is about close focus on process to highlight misses and drive improvement. This principle operates as clearly in process industries as in discrete production environments.

Your process does not have to resemble an automotive assembly operation to benefit from a lean transformation, and to be sustained by implementing lean management. Every lean application is an invention, one you derive from a small set of lean principles: Understand value from the customer's perspective. Find the value stream that produces value. Focus on the processes in the value stream to identify and eliminate sources of waste from it. Strive to make the value stream responsive to your customers' demands. And keep repeating these steps until non-value-adding steps are completely eliminated.

You can derive what process focus means in your operation from these few lean principles based on an in-depth understanding of your operation. The key ingredients are your understanding of what makes your process tick, and your judgment. Then, it is a matter of converting process focus into improvement no matter what the nature of your process. Nobody can do it for you, but fortunately you are in the best position to focus on process and use it to drive improvement.

So, gas up the Lean Management Express and take it for a spin. You will find the road in front of you gets smoother and takes you to places you could previously only dream about.

Summary: Four Principal Elements of Lean Management

The lean management system consists of four principal elements:

1. Leader standard work
2. Visual controls
3. Daily accountability process
4. Leadership discipline

Even considering its additional supporting elements, lean management is not a complex system. In this respect, it is similar to the lean production system; a handful of principles define both approaches. The principal elements are illustrated in depth in Chapters 3, 4, and 5. Supporting elements are the subject of Chapters 6 through 9, with a lean management assessment instrument included in Chapter 10 and the Appendix.

Another similarity between lean production and lean management is the high level of interdependence among the elements in each one. Not only must the elements be put in place, they need careful, daily attention. Left untended, the management system quickly deteriorates and loses its effectiveness, just as with the production system. But, when lean management becomes "the way we do things around here," the benefits are considerable. Lean management that is well and consistently implemented helps bring the foundation of stability to lean production conversions, a foundation on which ongoing improvements can be built. Establishing and building on this foundation are the subjects for the remainder of the book.

Chapter 3

Standard Work for Leaders

Standard work for leaders, the engine of lean management, is the highest leverage tool in the lean management system. As mentioned in Chapter 2, leader standard work is the first principal element of lean management; this chapter describes it in detail.

Leader standard work provides a structure and routine that helps leaders shift from a sole focus on results to a dual focus on process plus results. This change in focus is crucial to the success of a lean operation. Moreover, it is perhaps the most difficult thing to accomplish in a leader's personal conversion from batch and queue to lean thinking. Leader standard work aids this conversion by translating the focus on process, an abstract concept, into concrete expectations for the leader's own specific job performance. Just as standard work elements in a production workstation provide a clear and unambiguous statement of expectations, the same is true of standard work for leaders. (The main difference is that virtually all of an operator's time at work is defined by standardized work. For team leaders, the proportion is still about 80 percent. The proportion drops to about half for supervisors and about a quarter for value stream leaders.)

Keep in mind as you consider the potential leverage of leader standard work that it may not be the element with which to begin your lean management implementation, as noted in Chapter 2.

Leader Standard Work Is Process Dependent

Leader standard work also provides a foundation for continuity in lean management in a unit. Each time a new team leader or supervisor starts work in a lean area, things should continue to operate much as they have, assuming the process has been in a satisfactory and stable state. In batch operations, in contrast, one often sees a "new sheriff in town" mentality accompanying change from one supervisor to the next. That is, in these circumstances the management system depends on the person. With leader standard work, the lean management system is process dependent, not person dependent. Instead, key aspects of the management system are captured and presented in leader standard work as a well-defined process in which core tasks and routines are explicitly called out.

There are several benefits to this approach. One benefit is continuity of basic practices across changes in incumbents, which minimizes variability that might destabilize the production process. But perhaps more important is a second benefit, especially for organizations involved in a transformation from batch and queue to disciplined lean operation.

This second benefit is that leader standard work quickly allows an organization to raise the game of the existing leadership staff, or highlight those unable to make the transition. Leader standard work does this by presenting a clearly stated recipe—the standards for expected behaviors for leaders in a newly lean environment. This is superior to the alternative of waiting and hoping for So-and-So to "come around," or to "get it." Leader standard work is first focused on "doing it," rather than "getting it." It allows a much speedier separation of those who are willing and able from those who are not. Experience in lean conversions suggests between 10 and 20 percent of leaders are unable or unwilling to make the transition. Glossing over certain leaders' failure to understand or support the lean initiative carries a high risk of seriously slowing or degrading the effectiveness of a lean conversion. Leader standard work makes these cases clearer, sooner. A lean initiative is like any other program in raising questions about management's commitment to back up its words with actions. Management can act to address these questions more quickly based on the clearly documented expectations in leader standard work.

As the transition proceeds, leader standard work captures the cumulative to-date essence of an organization's best practices in lean management. This provides a solid starting point for those in leadership positions. As such, standard work for leaders provides a leg up for leaders to improve their performance, building on the preserved experience of others. In this way, leader standard work is a specific means through which average leaders can consistently turn in above-average performance. If you think of the lean management system as a kit of parts, leader standard work provides the instructions for how they fit together. It reduces ambiguity and sets the conditions under which an individual leader's success is more likely.

Leader Standard Work as Interlocking Layers

Leader standard work is layered with a degree of redundancy built in, linking the layers. Think of a job responsibility for team leaders, such as filling out the production-tracking form every 20 minutes and noting reasons for misses when the team misses the goal for a pitch. Here's how the layers work for this task:

- The team leaders' standard work specifies this task.
- The supervisor's standard work calls for spot-checking the pitch-tracking chart four times a day, initialing it each time. Further, the supervisor's standard work calls for leading a brief daily meeting of his or her team leaders to review the previous day's pitch charts to understand any misses in performance and ensure action has been initiated as appropriate. These are constant reinforcements for the team leaders to focus on their processes.
- The value stream manager's standard work calls for initialing every pitch chart in the value stream once a day, and leading the top tier of the daily accountability process every day. A key feature of these meetings is a review of yesterday's production-tracking charts. The value stream manager scrutinizes the reasons for misses on the charts. The supervisor knows to be prepared to explain what happened.
- When appropriate (typically where the supervisor needs more resources or more encouragement to resolve the problem), the value stream manager assigns follow-up action items to the supervisor or support group representatives and posts the assignments on a visual daily task accountability board for review the next day.
- All of this is prompted by the specific requirements in leaders' standard work from value stream manager to team leader.

Could any of these three levels of leaders find ambiguity in the requirement to maintain and monitor production-tracking charts, paying careful attention to reasons for missed pitches, and initiating appropriate corrective action? It is unlikely, because these steps appear as routine daily items in their standard work (see Table 3.1). With this kind of readily audited daily direction, establishing focus on process is simply a step-by-step routine. It makes lean accessible and actionable to even the most inexperienced leader, to the most unreconstructed batch thinker.

Leader Standard Work Shows What to Do—and What Not to Do

The case study Leader Standard Work's Role in Creating and Maintaining Stability shows how standard work can help a leader see what needs to be done. Standard work for leaders also works in the converse; that is, it can also show what should not be done. Another case illustrates this point (see "Standard Work Requires Sticking to the Plan").

Leader Standard Work Should Be Layered from the Bottom Up

The most important activity in a production operation is production. In a lean environment, carefully designed and monitored processes define production activity. When the process operates as designed (and refined), it meets its goals for safety, quality, delivery, and cost.

One of the two primary responsibilities of leaders in a lean production environment is to see to it that the processes run as designed. (The second is to improve the processes.) The process is most likely to run as designed when operators doing the actual production and related jobs are following their standardized work. If they are, things should run predictably.

For these reasons, standard work for leaders is built, or layered, from the bottom up, usually based on standard work or standard procedures at the value-adding level:

- Develop team leaders' standard work based on maintaining production at *takt time* (or the equivalent takt-derived pace) and ensuring that standard work is being followed in the production process.
- Build supervisors' standard work based on monitoring and supporting team leaders in carrying out the responsibilities in their standardized work.

Table 3.1 Typical Items in Leader Standard Work

Frequency	Team Leaders (TL)	Supervisors (Supe)	Value Stream Mgrs (VSM)	Plant Manager (PM), Execs (When in Plant)
Once daily, typically repeated each day (or each occasion for plant managers and executives)	Check call-ins Adjust labor plan	Shift change coordination Daily admin tasks	Daily admin tasks	Review performance trend charts
	Lead team start-up (tier 1) meeting (5–10 min)	Attend a TL start up meeting	Night shift gemba walk	Spot check, sign-off pitch charts, other visual controls
	Floor check production start-up	Floor check production start up	Lead value stream task/ improvement (tier 3) meeting (10–20 min)	Lead weekly plant performance/ improvement review meeting (PM)
	Supe-TLs (tier 2) meeting (5–15 min)	Lead (tier 2) meeting w/ TLs • Misses, issues, improvements • Daily task board due and new items	Daily gemba walk w/ one supe	Spot-review process and product improvement work
	Gemba walk w/ supervisor	Attend weekly recurring plant-level meetings	Formal audit of one area	Verify leaders' standard work
	Supe-TLs meet accountability, improvement (5–15 min)	Gemba walk w/ TLs one on one	Attend weekly recurring plant-level meetings	Verify TL, supe on floor or why not?
	Daily (weekly) continuous improvement meeting w/team	Spot-check buzzer-to-buzzer work		

continued

Table 3.1 (continued)   Typical Items in Leader Standard Work

Frequency	Team Leaders (TL)	Supervisors (Supe)	Value Stream Mgrs (VSM)	Plant Manager (PM), Execs (When in Plant)
	Next day planning • Labor plan • Prep for team start-up meeting	Spot-check, sign-off each pitch chart Review status of all other visuals		Gemba walk each VSM, staff manager weekly (PM)
Many times daily, often specified by time of day or number of times	Monitor buzzer to buzzer work before, after breaks	Spot check standardized work in each TL's area	Spot-check buzzer-to-buzzer work	Floor time
	Verify pitch by performance • Record reasons for variation • Note, act on flow interrupters	Floor time	Spot-check, sign off pitch charting in each department. Spot-check other visuals	
	Monitor standardized work in each station • Check compliance • Reinforce, correct performance as needed		Spot-check standardized work in each department	
	Revise production standard work as needed		Floor time	
	Train operators as needed			

Figure 3.1 The lean management system supports and sustains lean implementations and their standardized lean processes in both manufacturing and enterprise business processes.

- Similarly, build *value stream managers'* standardized work to monitor and support supervisors for following the responsibilities in their standard work.
- The same holds true for executives. Build their standard checklists for time on the production floor to verify the chain of standard work is being upheld and the production process is being supported for stability and improvement.

This network of support for the integrity of the production process is represented in Figure 3.1. The network serves as a bridge to keep lean production and management moving. In addition, each of these layers is discussed in more detail in the next section of this chapter.

The interlocking and somewhat overlapping set of leaders' standard work is directly comparable to the quality checks built into successive workstations on a lean assembly line, process steps in order management, or standardized procedures in a hospital. On the line, the standard work elements for each station typically include checks on the quality of some aspect of the work performed in the previous station. These redundant quality checks are a strength in a lean process. They often contribute to eliminating the need for a separate inspection position in which no value added work is performed. And so it is with leader standard work. Each successive level of leader standard work includes checks for the tasks that culminate in supporting the integrity of the most important work in the operation—the standard execution of the production process. That is the purpose of leader standard work: maintaining the integrity of the standard lean process, whether in an office, a factory, a healthcare facility, or any lean process.

CASE STUDY: LEADER STANDARD WORK'S ROLE IN CREATING AND MAINTAINING STABILITY

An illustration comes from the case of a supervisor's return from vacation. He had been using standard work to structure his workday routine for several months before leaving for a few days off. His area, a sub-assembly and final assembly operation with about 35 people, was running smoothly when he left. Not so upon his return. He returned to find purchased part shortages, shortages of some parts made in-house, and other in-house parts out of specification and unfit for use. The area was behind schedule, and the team leaders had been spending all of their time trying to expedite the various missing parts.

The supervisor immediately jumped into the fray, joining the team leaders in expediting, calling suppliers, and going to his in-house suppliers to attempt solutions to the out-of-spec problems. The assemblers continued to build whatever they could, robbing parts from one order to complete another, offloading partially built units wherever there was space on the floor, and generally keeping as busy as they could doing whatever work presented itself no matter when it was due out.

After two days of exhausting, but largely fruitless efforts, his area remained behind schedule and in a state of jumbled confusion. At that point, his value stream manager who had been observing the situation suggested to the supervisor that he might try returning to his standardized work. The supervisor listened and beginning the next morning took his boss's advice. Instead of running here and there, he and his team leaders stayed with their process. As shortages interrupted production, they directed their crew to other tasks while documenting what had caused the stoppage. They transmitted this information to the appropriate support groups, in this case engineering and materials management as well as the value stream leader. These situations were also topics at the value stream's daily accountability meeting. Within a day, the missing parts began to be delivered and the problem with out-of-tolerance components was resolved. The assemblers concentrated on completing the oldest orders first and were on their way to working up to the current day's schedule. A sense of calm returned to the area.

By the time I saw the supervisor, on Thursday afternoon of the week he returned from vacation, he swore he would never deviate again from his standardized work. At the same time, he acknowledged the powerful pull of past practices (supervisor as firefighter) though he was also struck by the comparison in effectiveness of the old and new approaches. He has been a faithful adherent of standard work, both for himself and his team leaders ever since.

CASE STUDY: STANDARD WORK REQUIRES STICKING TO THE PLAN

A new team leader had been on the job only a few weeks and had no precedents to follow. Her area, which covered two assembly lines that were building two different sizes of the same family of products, had not had team leaders before. She was the first.

The area had been well and carefully designed by a bright, technically oriented value stream leader and his staff. Standard work was posted for all the area's production-related operations, in-cycle and out-cycle as well. Even so, there were repeated interruptions, usually because in-house or purchased parts were not available when needed, or because the computer algorithm used to schedule the finishing processes was unable to produce an even flow of units into assembly.

I had encouraged the value stream manager to establish standard work for his new team leader and later suggested some edits to a draft she had produced. A few weeks later, I saw her in her production area and asked how it was going with her standard work. She pulled the page of standard work out of her back pocket and held it up in front of her like a school crossing guard with a stop sign. "It's great," she exclaimed, going on to say it was useful in reminding her what she needed to do. But better than that, she added, it was a terrific way to explain to the many people making requests of her why she could not do what they asked. "I have to stick to my standardized work," she said she told them.

Since then, more team leaders have been added to her value stream, each with well-defined standard work. Now, every operator in the value stream has someone whose standard work includes responding to his or her questions and requests.

What Does Leader Standard Work Cover?

Most of an operator's day—over 95 percent of his or her time—is accounted for by standardized work. In a lean environment where work is paced by takt time, most production and related work is timed and balanced. Leaders' work is rarely timed this closely. Even so, it is important to pay attention to the total work content called for in leaders' standard work to be sure they can perform it effectively and thoroughly. In positions at increasing distance from production, leaders' standard work usually becomes less structured. And as organizational level increases, less time is specified in standard work with more time for discretionary tasks. In the same way, as organizational level increases, fewer elements need to be performed in a specific sequence or at specific times of day.

Leaders' standard work includes coverage of visual controls and executing the daily accountability process. That is the source of its high leverage. Follow leader standard work and you maintain the principal elements of the lean management system. Maintain the lean management system and you maintain the health of your lean production system and enjoy its results.

Leader standard work includes some tasks that are specifically sequenced to happen at indicated times. Others occur once a day, once a week, or as the need arises. Some tasks repeat several times every day. Again, the closer to the production process, the more structured the standard work. Because leader standard work is derived from the standard work that defines the production process, leaders' standard work will vary depending on the nature of each leader's area. For example, the specifics of what a leader in a fabrication area focuses on and tracks will differ from the specifics in an assembly area. In the same way, what leaders track in an office, technical, or professional area will differ from one another, and from a manufacturing production area.

Team Leaders

These are the first line of defense for the integrity of the lean production process. They should be on the floor in their area paying attention to their processes virtually all of their time. As such, their standard work typically accounts for most of their time—80 percent plus of their day. Team leader standard work includes many items sequenced to the start and end of production, and many items periodically repeated to monitor and maintain the production process. Their standard work also includes discretionary time to respond to abnormalities, work on daily improvement tasks, and perform periodic tasks such as training operators. To accommodate this variability in their work, their time is specifically not filled to 100 percent.

Supervisors

Supervisors' standard work accounts for about half of their time. Most of the items in supervisors' standard work repeat daily or weekly. They involve:

- Getting the shift started and staffed appropriately.
- Reviewing yesterday's production-tracking documents to understand and take any further required actions to follow up misses or other issues.
- Reviewing team leaders' task assignments due that day and making new assignments.

Periodic tasks during the day call for the supervisor to work with the team leaders as well as to monitor and verify execution of the team leaders' standard work.

Value Stream Managers

Value stream managers' standard work accounts for approximately a quarter of their time (not including regularly scheduled off-the-floor meetings). Theirs includes leading a brief structured daily accountability meeting as part of the daily accountability process, just as for team leaders and supervisors. The value stream manager's standard work includes weekly *gemba walks* with each supervisor for teaching and inspecting the "homework," just as supervisors' standard work includes gemba walking their team leaders. The balance of the value stream manager's shop floor standard work calls for verifying execution of supervisors' standard work tasks. In this way, the value stream manager maintains his or her link in the chain of support for the integrity of the production process.

Form and Format for Leader Standard Work

Leaders' standard work differs markedly from operator standard work in one important respect. Leader standard work documents should be working documents. Leaders should have their standard work with them virtually all the time, whether on a clipboard, printed on a card, in a daily planner, or in a PDA. The leader should note completion of the indicated tasks on the standard work form. When they are unable to complete a task in sequence, on time, or at all, they should specifically note it and record why. This is exactly equivalent, and as important, as noting reasons for misses on production-tracking charts. Their notes should also reflect when misses occurred in their areas and what action they took.

Leaders should use the standard work document to record daily notes, observations, requests for follow-up, and the like. If a leader uses a PDA to hold standard work, he or she should print out the record of the day's events at the end of the day. Leaders' standard work documents also serve as a communication vehicle with the leader's supervisor (hence the PDA printout). The leader turns in each day's document to his or her supervisor who quickly reviews it to pick up any actions requested by the subordinate and note the nature of the subordinate's response to abnormalities in his or her areas. Often, "turning in" standard work means filing it in a visual display. This signals completion of standard work for that day and makes the documents readily available in a single location for the supervisor to scan quickly.

As part of the weekly gemba walk, the supervisor pulls the subordinate's previous week's standard work for a brief review, looking with the subordinate for patterns in misses (time of day, specific task, etc.) that might reveal a systematic source of interruption, something either or both might attack depending on what it is. Gemba walking is, first and ongoing, a teaching and learning model; the main teaching method to learn lean. The learning model implicit in gemba walking is a master-apprentice model. In this model, the master shows the apprentice how, gives the apprentice the opportunity to practice, observes the result and gives feedback, often critique mixed with encouragement.

For example, if meetings off the floor cause missed items in the subordinate's standard work, the superior might have to intervene with those calling the meetings. If the interruption is to attend to defective equipment, the subordinate might get a task assignment to determine the cause of the downtime and initiate or recommend action to prevent it.

Periodically during this review of the previous week's standard work documents, supervisor and subordinate should consider whether the content of standard work should be updated to reflect changes in the production process or on lessons learned in the preceding period. As with operator standard work, do not think of leader standard work as static. As things change in the process and as individuals learn and develop, integrate those changes in standard work. Standard work is not like the virtually unvarying set-it-and-forget-it atomic clock at the U.S. Naval Observatory. Standard work for operators and leaders alike is merely the best we know how to do things for now.

The Role of Training for Lean Implementation

It is not unusual in presentations about lean implementation initiatives to hear how important a lean training program has been, what was covered, how long it lasted, and how many people went through it. It is also not unusual to hear in the same kinds of presentations how much time and effort was spent in lean training and what a waste it turned out to be; that back on the job nobody knew how the training translated into what they were supposed to do. Or, as is too often the case, superiors had not been included in the training program and so were still asking their subordinates for the same old things.

Without a doubt, there are conditions under which lean training can be quite effective as an ingredient in a lean conversion. It can help to drive change, develop buy-in, and move the conversion in the hoped for direction. Often in these cases, one of the expressed objectives is to help drive a change in culture. I think this misses the point about what drives cultural change, namely expectations for different behavior and a process for supporting it.

If I had to choose between lean training for a new recruit to lead a lean area or providing him or her with a copy of clearly written standard work, I would choose standard work every time. Especially starting out, lean is more about what you do than about what you know, and the latter (knowing) grows from the former (doing). Training is not something bad or to be avoided; on the contrary. Developing familiarity with the principles of lean through classes or reading assignments is valuable. But, as far as preparing anyone to step into a lean area and keep it operating and improving, training by itself is an inadequate, as well as expensive and time-consuming, substitute for specific expectations and processes for following up on them.

Training pays off far more when delivered in gemba walks through the master-apprentice learning model. Training delivered in this fashion means the lessons can be individually tailored to the student's level. The teaching can be illustrated with specific situations in the student's area of responsibility; reinforced through assignments for hands-on application implemented over the course of a week; and followed up in the next week's gemba walk by inspection and critique. The lessons are further reinforced by the "what-to-do-when" practices called out in leader standard work to maintain and improve lean production and lean management.

Summary: Leader Standard Work Is Element Number 1 of Lean Management

Leader standard work provides the greatest leverage in the lean management system because it captures the expectations for executing the principal elements of lean management. In the best of circumstances, leader standard work eliminates guesswork for floor managers and team leaders. It is typical for standard work to stabilize the leader's day. Standard work not only specifies what the leader should do. It also, by implication, identifies what the leader should not be doing. Focus on your own work and call on others to focus on theirs. The alternative is to climb back onto the fire truck. It may be a gratifying and comfortable place to be, but it drives lean backwards. Many leaders in production operations are oriented toward doing: getting things done, crossing things off a to-do list. Leader standard work fits well with this orientation. For those with a more creative bent, standard work allows them to get the routine things taken care of with less mental energy, leaving them free to focus on making changes and improvement.

Lean management does not come about only from having its pieces in place. The lean management system works for you when you work for it. That means coming to think differently about what might appear to be many small things, but which add up to a big thing. The big thing is discipline on your part as a leader to follow your standard work faithfully and in depth. That will entail scrutinizing the entries on visual controls, focusing on gaps revealed there between expected versus actual, and holding people accountable to complete daily improvement task assignments to address and close these gaps. All of this—closing the loop on process focus—follows from your standard work as a leader. Fueled by your disciplined adherence to it, leader standard work becomes a powerful engine for the lean management system.

Chapter 4

Visual Controls

The status of virtually every process should be visible in lean management. If takt time is the heart of lean production, visual controls and the processes surrounding them represent the nervous system in lean management. Visual controls are even more important in office processes; work in offices moves in the IT network where it cannot be seen. Chapter 2 introduced visual controls as the second principal element in lean management; this chapter offers examples of visual controls for a variety of processes. Table 4.1 lists all the visual controls that are included in this chapter and throughout the book. In addition, several photographs show what several actual in-use examples of these visual controls look like.

The intent is not to present an exhaustive survey of visual controls; instead, the purpose is to illustrate that the variety and type of visuals are as broad as the variety of production processes. The form of the visuals is limited only by your imagination, guided solely by the purpose of making easy and widely accessible the comparison of actual versus expected performance. That is the reason this book doesn't include a CD of visual control forms. The best forms are those you develop and revise yourself to show the information you need to quickly see the status of your processes.

Finally, the chapter concludes with a description of the benefits of using simple visual controls over more sophisticated IT technology.

Visual Controls Focus on Process and Actual Performance

The purpose for visual controls in lean management is to focus on the process and make it easy to compare expected versus actual performance.

Table 4.1   List of Illustrated Visual Controls

Figure	Title
4.1	Production pitch tracking chart
4.2	Monthly pitch log
4.3	Job by job tracking chart
4.4	Priority board color coding
4.5	Priority board hourly status chart
4.6	Completion heijunka
4.7	Late load log
4.8	Detail illustration of tracking board for "re"-processes
4.8a	Photo of reorder board
4.9	Example of visual control board for noncyclical processes
4.9a	Photo of a visual control board for 5S tasks
5.1	Daily accountability board
5.1a	Photo of a daily task accountability board
5.1b	Photo of a daily "run the business" board
6.1	Visual control for progression of work through an office process.
9.1	A-3 project plan form
9.1a	Photo of an A-3 project plan board
10.1	Attendance matrix
10.2	Labor and rotation plan
10.2a	Photo of a labor planning board
10.3	Sample skills matrix entries
10.4	Suggestion system idea board
10.4a	Photo of an idea board

Lean is an improvement system. These comparisons highlight when the process is not performing as expected and thus where improvement might be needed.

Comparing expected versus actual performance is a central theme in lean management's emphasis on process focus. In some lean conversions with an

---

CASE STUDY: USING VISUAL CONTROLS
TO IMPROVE PERFORMANCE

In one company, visual display boards for cells were put up to satisfy the dictate of the division general manager. The general manager insisted that the information on the boards be kept up to date. When he was in the plant, which was a half-day drive from the majority of his responsibilities, he inspected the boards carefully to make sure they were current.

At first, the boards were current only during his visits and allowed to lapse as soon as the GM left the plant. The division's lean *sensei*, seeing this during one of his trips to the plant, asked a value stream manager to try actually using the boards for a few weeks to test the proposition that he might find them useful. During a subsequent gemba walk with the sensei, the value stream manager exclaimed that by simply noting misses and making the visual assignments (part of the daily accountability process) to respond to them, things had actually improved. Several problems of long standing were eliminated. Performance and results had stabilized. Visual controls are important, not because they satisfy executives' demands for visual displays, but because they bring focus to the process and, in doing so, drive improvements.

---

exclusively technical focus, visual controls such as performance-tracking charts are often little more than wallpaper. Indeed, great attention may have been devoted to developing a cosmetically consistent look for forms and displays, missing the point that lean management is not about the forms or the appearance of the visual tools. It is important that leaders understand why they track performance and that they commit to action in response to performance data and follow through, so that action assignments turn into improvements. It may take a while before this sinks in with leaders, though sometimes it happens quickly.

A Variety of Tools to Visually Monitor Processes

Performance tracking charts, such as hour-by-hour production-tracking charts, are among the most commonly seen visual process monitoring tools

---

CASE STUDY: PROBLEMS ARISE WHEN YOU HAVE CHARTS BUT DON'T USE THEM

In a lean conversion project early in a company's lean journey, I found hour-by-hour charts tossed onto a bottom shelf of a supervisor's desk on the production floor. The charts were literally covered with dust. No reasons for misses were noted on them (though plenty of misses appeared); no action had resulted from them. Not coincidentally, this particular lean conversion project stalled and did not get restarted until the product line was transferred to a different plant.

Despite early disappointments, other transformation projects were begun. As implementation and understanding of lean management have taken hold, the same charts are posted and current, highlighted color codes readily distinguish hours where goals are met from those that missed, while well-documented reasons for misses are reflected in posted "Top 3" weekly lists of interrupters and actions to eliminate their causes. The production-tracking charts are now scrutinized daily by the area supervisor and later by the value stream manager. Periods of missed production are treated as a big deal rather than with a shrug. Support groups and line leaders are mobilized to respond to them. Overall, there is a much-heightened sense of accountability for action to understand the causes for misses and to resolve them.

---

in lean production areas. When visual monitoring tools are implemented as part of a process that includes mechanisms to sustain them, such as leader standard work, the tracking tools have a good chance of being used effectively. Visual monitoring tools are part of a new way of managing an operation. Most production leaders are pragmatic people. If a tool works for them, they are likely to use it. But without a process that defines how the tools are used and sustains their use, the tools are likely to fall by the wayside.

Hour-by-Hour Production Tracking Charts

These basic tracking tools measure expected versus actual output hour by hour (or more frequently) during the day (see Figure 4.1). These charts are appropriate in areas with the expectation for a steady, takt-paced rate of output, such as assembly or subassembly areas in which flow production has been implemented.

Area: B211 Assembly TL: Tina T.	Production Tracking Chart			Date: 4/27/10 Takt: 60 sec.
Pitch	Goal Pitch/ Cumulative	Actual Pitch/ Cumulative	Variation Pitch/ Cumulative	Reason for Misses
7–7:30	20/20	18/18	–2/–2	10 min. startup mtg. Meeting long 2 minutes–safety issue
7:30–8	30/50	30/48	0/–2	
8–8:30	30/80	30/78	0/ –2	
8:30–9	30/110	32/80	+2/0	TL helped at station 5 for 6 cycles to catch up before break
9–9:30	20/130	20/130	0/0	10 min. break
9:30–10	30/160	30/160	0/0	
10:30–11	30/190	27/187	–3/–3	Container short three P/N 46230721-notified PIC
11:30–12	/190	/187		30 min. lunch
12–12:30	30/220	30/217	0/ –3	
12:30–1	30/250	30/247	0/ –3	
1–1:30	30/280	30/277	0/ –3	
1:30–2	20/300	20/297	0/ –3	10 min. break
2–2:30	30/330	30/327	0/ –3	
2:30–3	30/360	30/357	0/ –3	
3–3:30	20/380	21/378	+1/–2	10 min. cleanup washup TL helped sta 5, 3 cycles–want on-time finish
3:30–4		2/380	+2/0	Overtime: Minutes, why? 2 min., made up for part shortage @ 10:30 pitch
Totals	380/380		0/0	Pretty good shift–external failure and recovered– minimal OT

Note: Color codes used to indicate at, below, or above goal. In this black and white example, white background represents green for on goal, black represents red for below goal, and gray represents blue for above goal.

Figure 4.1   Production pitch-tracking chart.

The chart (Figure 4.1) shows the expected production in number of units each hour. Entries record the actual number produced and the nature and reasons for interruptions in the process. Even before a rate can be calculated, for example, in new product production areas, interruptions in flow can be documented every hour (or other interval). This is important for establishing process discipline and the habit of documenting abnormalities in the process, as well as addressing the interrupters. Reasons for misses are the most important entries on the form, regardless of the maturity of the process.

CASE STUDY: TAKING IMPROVEMENT TO A NEW, MORE FOCUSED LEVEL

On a gemba walk with a value stream manager, I noted from their production-tracking charts that two of the cells in her area reliably met and often exceeded their hourly goals. In talking with her about possible opportunities to improve in these cells, we discussed shortening the interval of observation from an hour at a time to half an hour at a time. This seemed especially appropriate in this instance.

Both cells produced a daily-varying, made-to-order mix of models with a variety of work elements and *cycle time*. Units with less work content could be produced faster than average; those with more content took longer than the average time. If a series of lower-work-content units followed an interruption, time made up on them could cover interruptions that occurred earlier in the sequence. (The sequence was physically set in advance, so there was no opportunity to "game the system" to make results look better.)

The value stream manager decided to take that step. Her thinking was that by reducing the interval by half—in effect, looking more closely at the processes—problems would show up as interruptions that in a longer interval of observation were hidden by the cells having enough time to catch up and still meet their hourly goals.

With the smaller interval of observation, more missed pitches did show up. Interestingly, many were the result of database inaccuracies. That is, the database showed cycle times for the different units that were accurate for some models, too low for some, and too high for others. This meant the capacity for these two cells was randomly misstated depending on the units for any given day's production. This was reflected in the weekly trend chart for pitch attainment. Before the change in observation period, the percentage of pitch attainment was regularly in the high 80 percents to mid 90 percents. After the change in interval, these percentages dropped by some 20 points.

The value stream manager with the supervisor carefully looked at the daily tracking charts for the week after the measurement change. The supervisor pointed out the problem in the database and backed it up with documentation, identifying units that clearly ran faster or slower showing virtually the same work content allowance in the database. The value stream manager then looked again at the tracking charts. She asked why the reasons-for-misses column was blank, both for pitches where the cells had beaten or missed their goals as an artifact of the database problems. Rather than living with an inaccurate database that misstated the actual capacity of the two cells, the value stream manager wanted to see the model numbers for units with inaccurate run times recorded in the reasons-for-misses column. That would allow her to assign the value stream engineers the task of correcting the database model by model, a little at a time, rather than in a single overwhelming batch request.

The supervisor was unhappy that her performance numbers had arbitrarily deteriorated, even though previously they had been arbitrarily inflated. But the value stream manager had more confidence about being able to drive further improvement in these cells. Now that she knew the capacity of these two cells more accurately, she and the supervisor had an improved basis on which to compare expected versus actual performance. Because the value stream manager understood why she was having process performance data visually tracked, she saw the need to increase the level of resolution of the observations to provide a clearer picture of the true operation of the processes. This step led to a more accurate picture of variability in the cell and set the stage for changing from a time-based pitch to a load-by-load method of tracking. This method is more appropriate for the variable work content jobs in these cells and has proved helpful in identifying interruptions and imbalances in them.

As the process stabilizes, the interval of observation should shrink from an hour to a shorter interval, perhaps a half or quarter hour, or an interval defined by a pitch. The interval can be as brief as 5 minutes or even less, depending on the process, its maturity, and the way output is packed and shipped. The reason for reducing the interval of observation is to provide a closer, more finely grained picture of flow interrupters. When a process is newly established, it is not unusual to experience breakdowns upstream of the process (e.g., equipment failures no longer covered up by inventory, supplier problems, scheduling snafus) not to mention problems internal to the process that cause failures. As these gross interruptions are resolved, the observation interval should progressively shrink to more precisely capture the next levels of interruption and so define the next focal points for improvement. In other words, to catch smaller gremlins, use a net with finer mesh! The case study "Make Sure Your Employees Know the Charts Are Not Micromanaging Them" illustrates this point.

CASE STUDY: MAKE SURE YOUR EMPLOYEES KNOW THE CHARTS ARE NOT MICROMANAGING THEM

Consider the case of machine operators who produced job by job in defined lot quantities to replenish parts kept on display in a supermarket. They complained to their team leader and supervisor about being micromanaged when these charts were introduced. They felt the company was saying they could no longer be trusted to put in an honest day's work. The supervisor responded by telling them the charts were, in effect, a way for the operators to assign jobs to him! He went on to explain that his job was to resolve problems that interfered with the operators' ability to run smoothly all day. The charts would tell the story of where the supervisor needed to step in and get the problems solved. In short, he said, this was micromanagement of the production *process*, not of the people in it.

The operators began to use the tracking charts to document long-standing problems that repeatedly caused them downtime and frustration. This may well have been to test the supervisor's word that he would respond to issues the operators documented on the charts. The supervisor was true to his word. He and the area team leader responded by focusing on these problems and getting them fixed. The outcome was progressive elimination of many recurring frustrating situations that interfered with operators being able get into a rhythm and feel they had had a productive day at work.

The problems surfaced by the operators were plain to see to even moderately trained eyes, but they had simply never gotten attention in the previous batch environment, because the area had been buffered by large stocks of inventory. Now that it was running to a precise supermarket pull system, with carefully calculated on-hand quantities and replenishment times, the interrupters needed to be resolved.

Many of the issues emerged with the departure of the few experienced hands, taking with them the undocumented "tribal knowledge" of how the area ran. The result was at times near chaos, featuring things like mixing storage for active and obsolete tooling, without identification, on the same racks or even jumbled together in cabinet drawers. There were no step-by-step work instructions for complex operations, resulting in much trial and error for the new operators trying to set up and run the jobs. Raw materials were delivered in a way that required time-consuming handling to get them to the point of use. Gauges on the equipment needed alignment. Stockouts and defective, out-of-spec parts were common, given these sources of instability in the process. None of these were particularly complicated problems.

With the tracking charts as the vehicle, the operators were able to shine a light on these situations. The supervisor and team leader got them taken care of permanently, winning respect for themselves and for the tracking process as well. Stockouts and defects from this area are now rare occurrences, operators rotate through the area without a hitch, and productivity in the area has never been as good. This is a good illustration of where micromanagement of the process can produce outstanding results for all involved.

How Visual Controls Enforce Discipline

This case illustrates the connection between the leader's discipline and the effective use of visual controls. Visuals are an important enabler for disciplined focus on and adherence to lean processes. This focus on process is absolutely essential for establishing and maintaining a lean management system. And carefully designed lean processes require this kind of disciplined attention and support. We have ample evidence they do not sustain or improve themselves. That is the reason for lean management's emphasis on leadership discipline and follow-up, so you do not leave lean processes on their own to fend for themselves.

Visual controls amount only to wallpaper without the discipline to insist they are taken seriously and used as a basis for action. Without disciplined follow-up by leaders, visuals are destined to take their dust-covered places behind equipment and under staircases along with the other boards and banners of past failed programs. It certainly is not a pretty picture, but it is just as certainly a common one in North American factories where leaders did not have the discipline to stay with programs they launched.

This case showed one way to use pitch tracking charts. The same example—instances where cells could frequently beat their pitch goals—would show up more clearly when pitch attainment information was displayed for more than a single day. It is often useful and a good practice to record the summary data in a format that makes it possible to see trends. Are Fridays more productive than Mondays, for example? Or does productivity dip after break times? The same display also allows operators in the area to see how they are doing over a period of time: Are we getting better? It is a simple matter to produce such a chart.

When the team leader is filling out the pitch chart, with the highlighter in hand he or she can color code the pitch on a 31-day summary pitch performance chart, one that stays in the area all month. The daily pitch charts are typically taken down and moved to the location for the daily value stream accountability meeting and kept there. The summary chart remains a local record of performance (see Figure 4.2).

Job-by-Job Tracking Charts

"Flow where you can, pull where you can't, never push" is a maxim in lean production. In lean management, the task of visually tracking production in pull areas differs quite a bit from the expected even rate of operation in flow areas. That is because processes operating in pull (or *kanban*) replenishment areas are those where shared or constrained resources supply *supermarkets* (i.e., buffer inventories of work-in-process materials or components waiting for the next downstream customer processes to withdraw them for use).

The rate of resupply or replenishment depends on several factors. Among them is the rate of consumption by downstream processes and ultimately by the takt-paced final segment (often assembly) of the production process. Lot sizes and often setup times vary from job to job and part to part for single workcenters that produce several or many different parts. In short, there is no even flow to measure against an expected even rate of output per hour (or other period of observation). Yet pace is an important element in lean production. How does the lean management system make pace visible in pull production areas? That is, in an area producing by the lot or

Month: May					Monthly Pitch Log															Area/Line: 854														
% Attained:	80	80	80	95																															
Pitch																																			
4:30–5																																			
4–4:30																																			
3:30–4																																			
3–3:30																																			
2:30–3																																			
2–2:30																																			
1:30–2																																			
1–1:30																																			
12:30–1																																			
12–12:30																																			
11:30–12																																			
11 11:30																																			
10:30–11																																			
10–10:30																																			
9:30–10																																			
9–9:30																																			
8:30–9																																			
8–8:30																																			
7:30–8																																			
7–7:30																																			
6:30–7																																			
6–6:30																																			
5:30–6																																			
5–5:30																																			
Date	1	2	3	4	5	6	7	8	9	10	11	12	13	14	15	16	17	18	19	20	21	22	23	24	25	26	27	28	29	30	31				

Note: Color codes are used to indicate at or below goal for a given pitch. In this black and white example, black shading represents red for below goal, gray shading represents green for at goal.

Figure 4.2 Monthly pitch log.

batch instead of a piece at a time, how can expected versus actual performance be readily seen and responded to?

The answer is surprisingly straightforward, fortunately. When pull systems are set up, it is necessary to know the batch or lot size and the time allowed both to set up the equipment and to produce the specified quantity for every part produced by each machine or workcenter. That information is the basis for establishing *machine balance charts* and setting up the supermarkets and replenishment cycles on which pull or kanban systems are based. It is easy to see that this information should also be the basis for expected versus actual for these workcenters.

A chart that captures expected and actual set up and run times for each job produced during a shift in a workcenter clearly shows when the work is on pace and when the pace is impeded. The expected setup and run times for each job should be printed on the production instruction signal. The signal is usually a card but sometimes might be a dedicated rack or other specialized container. Having this information on the production instruction signal makes the expected times readily available for the operator to record on the job-by-job chart. On this chart as on most others, the reasons for misses are the most important information on it (see Figure 4.3).

Priority Board Hourly Status

Priority boards are a regular part of pull system operations. Priority boards provide the schedule for operators running the equipment that replenishes what has been consumed in a pull system. Production instruction cards or equivalent signals represent the schedule. These kanbans (cards or other signals) list the planned length of time to set up and run the job, the lot size, container type, and other pertinent information for the operator for each job. When the production instruction signals come back to the producing workcenter, they are typically put on the priority board (or rack, track, or wire) in the sequence in which they arrived. An hourly status chart for the priority board shows the queue of jobs waiting to run for each workcenter. It translates the number of jobs waiting into stoplight colors.

Color codes—green, yellow, and red are typical—are applied to segments of the physical queue that holds the kanbans. The queue could be a lane marked on the floor for carts or racks leading to a workcenter, or a matrix of pockets or slots on a board or taped off on the side of a machine.

Date: _____	Job-by-Job Tracking			
Operator: _____				
Asset: _____				

Part Number	Setup Minutes		Run Minutes		Reason for Misses
	Goal	Actual	Goal	Actual	

Setup and run time goals from production instruction card.

Met goal = green, longer than goal = red.

Figure 4.3   Job-by-job tracking chart.

The color codes are based on information from the machine balance chart. The physical segment of the queue that is closest to "next up" is colored green. Jobs in this part of the queue will normally be able to run in plenty of time to resupply the supermarket. It may not even be necessary to run the equipment just yet when the queue is in the green. The yellow part of the queue signifies a heavier load where the jobs can be replenished in time with normal work hours, providing nothing goes wrong. Otherwise, jobs will be late or it will take overtime to avoid stockouts. The red part of the queue means a heavy load as a percent of machine capacity that will require overtime and/or the last jobs will be late, unless action is taken to prevent it (see Figure 4.4).

Next up	2	3	4	5
10	9	8	7	6 Order material here
11	12	13	14	15
20	19	18	17	16

Note: Color codes used to indicate load status. In this black and white example, white background represents green for capacity OK, gray background represents yellow for capacity warning, and black background represents red for capacity action required.

Figure 4.4   Priority board color coding.

The tracking chart's entry for the hour is the color code for the last job in the queue, the one with the longest wait before its turn to run comes up. The chart provides a snapshot of priority board load conditions each hour. It is easy to tell at a glance how the area is running compared to how it should be (see Figure 4.5).

When this method of displaying the status of the queue waiting at a bank of equipment was first implemented, the value stream manager was delighted. "Finally," he said, "I can tell where we are in this area without having to find the supervisor and ask him how we were doing. Now, all I need is to walk by the board and I can tell at a glance whether I can move on to the next thing or whether I need to start asking questions. It's great!" Such is the pleasure visual controls can bring by simplifying the tasks of running the business day to day!

Completion Heijunka

When jobs of varying lot sizes and expected run times go through a single workcenter, job-by-job tracking is the tool to use for visually representing expected versus actual pace and identifying anything that interferes with expected operation. When jobs of varying work content are produced in a cell or line, the situation is a little different.

The completion *heijunka* identifies when the last piece of a job or load is due to be completed. It is maintained at the end of the line or cell as a pigeonhole box or any similar array of slots or pockets with the openings

Priority Board Hourly Color Status																								Asset:					Month:					
Hour																																			
5 am																																			
6 am																																			
7 am																																			
8 am																																			
9 am																																			
10 am																																			
11 am																																			
noon																																			
1 pm																																			
2 pm																																			
3 pm																																			
4 pm																																			
5 pm																																			
6 pm																																			
7 pm																																			
8 pm																																			
9 pm																																			
10 pm																																			
11 pm																																			
midnight																																			
1 am																																			
2 am																																			
3 am																																			
4 am																																			
Date	1	2	3	4	5	6	7	8	9	10	11	12	13	14	15	16	17	18	19	20	21	22	23	24	25	26	27	28	29	30	31				

Color = Color code for priority board row of the last production instruction card in line.

Figure 4.5 Priority board hourly color status chart.

Figure 4.6 Completion heijunka.

labeled with clock times. When the load is introduced to the process, the expected duration of processing (from the job's total work content) gets converted to the expected due-out time for the last piece. That information gets sent to the end of the line. There, the kanban (or shop paperwork) for each load is put in the slot corresponding to its expected time of completion. When the load is complete, its card is pulled from the heijunka opening. A heijunka status-tracking chart lists each load and records its completion status; green for on time, red for late. The reasons for misses are entered on the heijunka tracking chart for loads that finish late, just as they would on any other production-tracking chart (see Figures 4.6 and 4.7).

When time sequencing is needed to level volume and/or mix, a release-pacing heijunka box can be used at the beginning of the line, with expected times for starting each job defining the time slots. A job tag or kanban for each job is loaded into the slot corresponding to the load start and end times. In both cases, in addition to the heijunka tracking charts, glancing at the heijunka box and the clock tells whether you are currently meeting the expected pace.

Between-Process Tracking

Were subassemblies available when they were expected? Did the units come out of a separately housed process when they were due? Did parts arrive on time from the "re" processes—refinish, rework, repair, or reorder? Are suppliers delivering on time? In each of these cases, how many instances are there of overdue performance over a period of time and what are the causes? These are the usual questions you would ask from the perspective of lean management, of course. What is unusual is that with visual controls, practically anybody can tell performance and performance history at a glance.

Late Load/Job Log			
Date	Time Due	Time Done	Reason for Overdue

Figure 4.7 Late load log.

Start with an array of slots or pockets on a board labeled with clock times and/or days of the week or month depending on expected turnaround time. Place a tag or the actual order paperwork in the opening that corresponds to when the item is due out. If the paperwork or tag appears in a "late" spot, or if the overdue item's tag remains on the array for Tuesday at 11:00 am and it's now Tuesday at 4:00 pm, it is late.

Presto! With a glance at the board the status of performance (and reasons recorded on the accompanying log sheet) are immediately clear to all. No interpretation is required, nobody needs to make barcode scans (or maintain the barcode system) or log onto the network and look up status or a specific order, no reports need to be run, consulted, or reconciled. Late is late, on time is on time. The reasons are there to be seen, subjected to analysis and action right away where needed, and for root cause solution later. Note that the tracking charts for on-time performance percentages and reasons for misses are not unique to heijunka applications; they apply equally well in tracking performance between processes.

Noncyclical Process Tracking

Production is the most important process in a production operation. But without attention to its supporting processes, production will be uneven, unpredictable, and unreliable. In a lean operating environment, production is expected to operate at an even, predictable pace, running directly or indirectly at takt time. That means many things are predictable:

■ Material arrives at the point of use in a predictable manner when it is needed.

■ Quantities in containers and number of containers in supermarkets are as defined.

■ Routines for handling kanban cards or other signals are accurately followed.

■ Equipment is available to run when expected, operates predictably without unplanned down time, and produces components to specification without defects.

■ The tools, equipment, and supplies needed at any workstation are easily verified as being in their designated places unobstructed by clutter or debris.

CASE STUDY: A TALE OF TWO NETWORKS—IGNORING INFORMATION VERSUS VISUALLY DISPLAYING

Consider these contrasting cases. In the first, units were assembled and then sent into a finishing department by conveyer through an opening in the wall and then out again for final assembly and pack, and then to shipping. Nominal turnaround time for finishing was four hours. As units entered the finishing room, they were scanned in. When they were released, they were scanned out. Their length of stay in the finish room was routinely reported on a report from the IT system.

I was talking with the fabrication manager one day when we were interrupted by an urgent reorder request. It seems a unit had been in the finish room for over a week, apparently undergoing repeated attempts to rework the finish. Finally, with the ship schedule looming, finish called fabrication with the reorder. Production for that unit had to start all over again from raw materials, and be expedited through the entire process. The fabrication manager, between groans, was able to tell me exactly to the minute when the unit had first gone through the wall into the finishing room.

In the second case, an assembly supervisor was complaining to me about the lack of response to his department's request for refinished parts when the original finish was defective. The reorder requests were logged into a sophisticated software application that controlled and tracked the finishing process. The software transmitted the request to the area where parts were loaded onto the conveyor to the finish room. There, replacement parts were to be picked and put on the line or the originals reworked and then sent through the process again to be refinished. The finishing process was located, as with the first example, on the other side of a wall and fed by a loop of overhead conveyor.

Despite the sophisticated software network, orders frequently got lost somehow, usually because of human data entry error at the ordering or load stations. The outcome was that incomplete units languished in the assembly area's repair bay. Worse, they sometimes were forgotten in the press of other work, until their ship dates had passed. All involved had repeatedly been admonished to be careful when keying information into the system, but mistakes kept happening.

Converting a Problematic Computer System to a Simple Visual System

The supervisor never knew when to expect his reorders. Whenever he thought about it and was nearby, he would find the unload/reorder person and ask him or her, "How are we doing on refinish?" The operator would dutifully query the database. Sometimes the information was accurate, and sometimes it was not. After listening to the supervisor about this specific frustration, I asked him to think about how a visual control might help. He told me he already had a slick computer system, but it did not seem to be doing him much good. We walked around the area for a few minutes and noticed paperwork taped to racks holding kits of parts in the so-called "bone yard," the area where kits missing pieces were parked to wait for arrival of reordered parts, so they could be moved into the assembly process. The finish line software printed the paperwork for each reorder. The operators taped it to the appropriate kit rack so they would know where to put the reordered parts when they came down the line.

In a few minutes, the supervisor figured out that he could print duplicates of the reorder paperwork, write on it the date and time of the reorder, and place it on a board with a row for each day of the week. He implemented this process the following day using adhesive-backed clear plastic pockets* mounted on a board at the reorder station. At our next gemba walk, he was grinning from ear to ear as he showed me the visual reorder tracking board. At a glance he could tell what parts his area was waiting for, when they had been reordered, and whether they were overdue. He no longer had to bug his unload/reorder person for status of his reordered shortages or worry about losing track of units awaiting parts in the repair bay.

Soon after that he bought a two-way radio so the person working the unload/reorder station could check with the load station on parts that were close to overdue. The original board had a row of pockets for each day of the week. If parts got delivered by the next day, that was a big improvement. In its current version, the board's array of pockets reflects an expected four-hour turnaround. The label on the pocket for reorders placed between 7:00 am and 7:59 am, for example, shows its orders should be delivered by 12:00 noon. If the reorder paperwork is in the pocket after 12:00 noon, it is easy to tell it is late! (See Figures 4.8 and 4.8a.)

---

* Two sources for a variety of plastic pockets are Storesmart.com and Associatedbag.com.

Refinish Reorder Board

Monday

In 5:00–5:59	In 6:00–6:59	In 7:00–7:59	In 8:00–8:59	In 9:00–9:59	In 10:00–10:59	In 11:00–11:59	
Due by 11	Due by 12	Due by 1	Due by 2	Due by 3	Due by 4	Due by 5	etc.

Figure 4.8　Detailed illustration of tracking board for "re" –processes.

Figure 4.8a　Photo of a refinish-reorder board. On this refinish and reorder tracking board orders are expected to be returned complete in four hours. The photo is from October 27. For the day October 26, an order was put in the system between 11:00 am and 12:00 pm. A duplicate copy of the order was printed and put on the board in the slot indicating it was due back complete by 4:00 pm that day, but the board shows it is late. Two reorders are on the board for October 27. Reorder performance is visible with a glance at the clock and at the board.

This kind of tracking and the feedback it prompted throughout the process is what resulted in the dramatic improvement in turnaround time. The improvements were not difficult to make; they simply had not previously been identified and documented.

As to the computer networks involved in these two examples, I do not intend to make them out to be the bad guys. In the first case, we had not learned to use the information in the network. The mere presence of precise information in a database that could generate reports seemed to be all anyone was interested in. The multiple reports enabled managers in different (interdependent) departments to argue with and point fingers at each other when things were not going well. In the second case, we learned to get the information out of the network and visually display it in a way that made it far more useful for comparing expected versus actual and focusing on the process. Those steps ultimately drove significant improvement in the reorder process.

This kind of visible tracking of performance between two processes applies as readily to processes within the same building or in the same company as it does to expected delivery times from suppliers. In many cases, the ability to distribute information across a computer network is valuable. But remember, just because information is held in databases does not mean it cannot also be simultaneously visually displayed and managed. That is always a desirable option from the point of view of the lean management system.

These are examples of some of the processes that must operate effectively for production to run in a stable state. In lean management, each process should have a primary visual control, such as a visible signal that daily maintenance and cleaning tasks or longer-interval preventive and predictive maintenance procedures were performed. In addition, each of these processes should also have a secondary check, or verification that what was to be done was actually performed. Secondary checks are often items in team leaders' or supervisors' standard work or items reviewed in regular weekly audits of, for example, pull system wellness, 5S, TPM, or safety to name a few.

These important chores are unglamorous, to be sure. Nevertheless, they are similar in importance to the saying: "An army marches on its stomach." No matter how well trained the troops are, they must be well fed over time to perform well. The same is true by analogy in lean production. No matter how well designed the production and replenishment systems are, if they are allowed to deteriorate (a certainty if they are not looked after and maintained) the production system will run only by fits and starts.

This looking-after and maintenance are important aspects of the lean management system. Here, too, expected performance versus actual execution should be reflected in visual controls that act as the basis for assessment, assignments for improvement, and accountability for follow-through. As elsewhere, visual controls should be in place even if a database holds and automatically dispenses schedules. Yes, the maintenance department does have a computerized job assignment and tracking system. But how does anyone other than the maintenance dispatcher know that the work is being assigned as agreed and completed on time?

In one rather sad case, a maintenance department facing budget pressure decided to reduce its staff and then stretch the intervals between scheduled preventive maintenance. Because the maintenance tasks and schedules, kept in the computerized maintenance management system, were accessible only to the maintenance department, nobody was the wiser until unplanned down time showed alarming increases and the plant manager began asking questions.

By contrast, consider the difference when the planned maintenance schedule is kept at the equipment with an easily visible sign-off spot for each date and work to be performed, plus "go-see" verification written into the team leader's standard work. Compliance with the maintenance schedule can be readily verified. Proposed changes in the schedule would prompt discussion between those who depend on the equipment and those charged with keeping it reliable (see Figures 4.9a and 4.9b).

Maintaining Visual Trackers and Acting on the Information They Provide

You might ask: "Aren't all these visuals a lot to maintain?" Not if there is a systematic process for maintaining them. In fact, that is one of the main contributions of standard work for leaders. Team leaders either do or do not make entries on the visual trackers as specified by their standardized work. Supervisors' and value stream leaders' standard work directs them to review the visual controls several times daily (or at least once for value stream leaders) for two reasons: one is to verify the visuals are being maintained. The second is to verify that appropriate actions have been initiated when abnormal conditions are identified on the visual controls.

When considered in total, there indeed can be lots of visual controls in a value stream or entire facility. But each visual is singular. A single person is accountable for executing it. One or two or more people have specifically designated responsibility for verifying its maintenance and for taking action

FF1 Support Area 5S Task Board (partial)

1. Task cards' "task" side color coded to match the day, e.g., Tuesday.
2. "Complete" side always green (black in this black and white figure) for at-a-glance monitoring (e.g., Monday).
3. Plastic card slots are color coded and labelled to identify task and specific day's card color (e.g., Wednesday).
4. Cards are handwritten and highlighted index cards in adhesive-backed clear plastic.

(a)

(b)

Figure 4.9 Example of a visual control board for noncyclical tasks.

if it slips. And any of these visual controls is simple, straightforward, can be interpreted at a glance, easily audited, and diagnosed. Put that together with the simple, unambiguous definition of responsibilities for maintaining and using the controls and the system looks much more manageable, as it is in actual application.

Benefits of Using Simple Visual Controls Instead of More Sophisticated Information Technology

From an IT perspective, visual controls might seem like an embarrassing return to the information Stone Age. Visuals are usually not very snappy looking because they are maintained by hand. People are actually counting things (how many pieces do we expect in this load; how many are actually in it?) and writing them down. Have these people not heard of computers and bar code scanners?

It is true that many leansters are almost reflexively anticomputer, perhaps too much so. Why? Are we simply hopeless Luddites who never learned to type or navigate in Access?

Table 4.2 lists comparisons that help explain the advantages of visual displays, and even some advantages of IT solutions. Overall, the lean management system favors hand-completed visual controls because of its bias toward pitch-by-pitch focus on process and the importance of everyone involved in a process having timely information about how that process is performing. When information is available to only a select few, whether managers or specialists, only those few can take responsibility. Indeed, only those few have the information base for thinking about why the process performed as it did, what the causes of that performance might have been, and what might be done to eliminate the causes of interruptions or to improve performance from its current level. The following sections describe these advantages in more detail.

Consider the first two attributes in Table 4.2. Timely information about process is important for two reasons. First, if the information on the visual tracking is filled in, it at least means someone is in touch enough with the process to record its performance. And the information is widely accessible, particularly to those working in the process. Often (and preferably) thanks to color coding, the information is interpretable at a glance from a distance of 10 feet or more. (Chapter 5 includes a case study where the operators at the far end of an assembly process brought binoculars to work so they could see the production tracking chart and know if they were on or behind pace!)

With information captured by an automated process, the information will be timely as long as the automation is working and data entry has occurred on time. But the information is often not readily available to the people working in the process because computer and network access is required to view it. Few may have login privileges or the licenses required by SAP and other software suppliers. Or the computer may be located

Table 4.2 Comparing Manual Visual Controls versus IT Information: Timeliness of Visual Controls

Attribute	Manually Visually Controlled	IT Provided
Info timely?	On the floor, current as of the last pitch (when maintained)?	Current as of the last data entry and last time the report was run
Info accessible?	Right there for all to see, often interpretable from a distance of 10 feet or more	Right there but only for the individual right in front of the screen
Info precise?	Not always; notes sometimes vague, reporting periods occasionally missed	Yes, absolutely, regardless of accuracy!
Info verifiably accurate?	Usually a close-by physical location to go see as verification of the visual display	Often can't assess accuracy; data are often a long way from the physical source and reflect human judgment and execution of data entry
Does it prompt questions?	Yes; often can be asked and answered right where the control is posted	Usually only the question designed into the report can be addressed
Easy to change and customize?	Yes, forms can be easily modified, new ones created as the need arises	Not usually; often takes IT or one with time and specialized knowledge to make changes— assuming desired changes don't crash other applications
Intimidation factor?	Very low; about as difficult as coloring with crayons	Can be quite intimidating to those not literate in the system
Ownership or alienation?	Floor operators create the information that stays in their areas, often in their own handwriting	Information is taken away from the floor, transformed into computer-generated reports that no longer have "fingerprints"
Info simultaneously available many places?	No (with exception of multiple card kanban systems)	Definitely a strength of an IT network
Computational accuracy?	With humans, no computation should be considered "routine"!	Definitely a strength of an IT system

Table 4.2 (continued)   Comparing Manual Visual Controls versus IT Information: Timeliness of Visual Controls

Attribute	Manually Visually Controlled	IT Provided
Overhead required?	Very little beyond people who are already there. Pens and highlighters are cheap!	Thousands and millions for gear, specialized departments, consultants, troubleshooting, etc.

where only the person operating the system can read it. Further, if the information requires manual data entry, such as scanning production paperwork, it may be current only a few times per shift. Finally, the ability to read the all-important reasons-for-misses entries requires one to be right in front of the screen.

Accuracy versus Precision of Visual Information

Computerized information is highly precise, often notoriously so. Results may be reported out to several decimal places, but based on inaccurate entries or relatively old data. Especially where reason codes are the basis for recording reasons for misses, they may convey a false sense of precision. Indeed, they may convey a view of conditions from the perspective only of the person who developed the codes. Coding schemes often lose their bearing on current operations as conditions change, or they are checked off quickly with little consideration for their specific applicability.

When hand-entered reasons for misses are reviewed, it is easy to assess the quality of information presented. Is the reason a well-crafted problem statement, such as "light paint on upper inner surface of drawer handles on series XXX models"? Or is it too vague to interpret, much less to use as a basis for action, such as "handles" or "paint?" Is a reason for interruption missing altogether? This is an instance where a second-level process check can occur, in this case of the quality of the entries on the visual controls. This kind of opportunity is rarely available in automated data collection systems, or on systems that rely on reason codes.

Proximity of Visual Controls

Another advantage of visuals completed by hand is that they usually are (and should be) close to the process whose performance they reflect. That means it is easy to go look at and verify that what is shown on the visual corresponds to physical reality in the production process itself. This ease of verification is another example of assessing quality of the information in the visual control.

Sometimes it is possible to make the same verification with IT systems, but often the relative scarcity of computers in the production area makes it less convenient to perform a go-see verification or quality check. Worse, the computerized system encourages managing the production process from a computer screen in an office somewhere removed from the actual production area. Interestingly, this problem can also occur in supervisor's offices even when these are little more than a stand-up desk and a computer. When you are focused on a screen, you are not focused on the process. Either violates the lean management system's three-part prescription for focusing on process: "Go to the place, look at the process, talk with the people."

Flexibility of Visual Controls

IT systems provide powerful analytical tools, without doubt. However, often the analyses (that is, the questions addressed by the automated systems) are those programmed into the reports that are accessible on the system. Typically, only the questions addressed in the report can be answered by it. In contrast, questions prompted by entries on a visual control chart can often be addressed, at least initially right where the control is posted. When that is not the case, for example, when a new defect has surfaced, a new control can be easily drawn up to track and address it.

For example, when a piece of equipment starts malfunctioning, it is easy to draw up a simple downtime log to record instances, durations, and observable causes or symptoms that can be tallied up or Pareto-charted. Or, when a process starts to produce rejects, it is a simple matter to start tallying them. Pareto-charting the defects and then taking action on the findings come next, with no programming or transcription of data required. By contrast, someone with specialized knowledge is usually required to reprogram an analysis in an automated system. It might mean getting support from IT, often not a quick proposition, or getting help from a technical professional in the area who is already working on a full plate of assignments. Or automated tracking, specifically because it is automatic, can produce nicely printed charts from, say, automated bar code scans of completed units. When actual volume is less than expected, nobody is there to record the miss and reason why. Or it happens at the end of the day, as in:

"Let's see, why did we miss that pitch seven hours ago?" Batching in this way often produces less than accurate and useful information.

Visual Controls and the "Fingerprint Factor"

Perhaps it should not be so, but often people in a production operation look past posted computer-generated reports, even graphic ones, of leading performance problems. That is especially true when the data are reported in table format. Managers often do not realize that it takes a trained eye to read and interpret information presented in these ways, and production operators often have not had that kind of training. It is a very different story when the operators themselves have been involved in recording the data, or working through it in start-up meetings led by their team leader.

Hand-created data, especially when you know whose hands created it, including the real possibility that the hand was or could have been yours, have a much lower intimidation value than the crisp, precise-looking management document someone has posted on your team's information board. This fingerprint factor is important. It helps draw people to the information and conclusions from records they have had a recognizable part in creating. The same is not the case with impersonal, computer-generated materials, even those with the slickest graphics.

CASE STUDY: USING COMPUTERS TO CALCULATE THE NUMBER OF REQUIRED PARTS

Another application where IT shines is where mathematical computation is required. Computers are far more reliable at simple math than humans. Here is a case of a creative, early use of network broadcast subassembly signals similar to those discussed just above. In this case, the need was to signal the number of drawers that would be needed in final assembly of storage cabinets. The cabinets varied in size from two to five drawers and came in three widths. An early solution was to hold the drawer bodies, all of which were a standard interior color, in a supermarket on the assembly floor. The drawback to having all the sizes on display was the amount of floor space they consumed and the large number needed to guard against stock outs. It amounted to a lot of inventory and a lot of floor space.

The broadcast solution was to send the drawer producing area the information on the number and sizes of drawers for cabinets just entering the color application process prior to assembly. Operators would call up the proper screens on the computer and do the math to determine the number of fixed lot quantities of drawers in each size that were called for. They would then put a kanban for a lot quantity of that size drawer on the priority board. In the course of the multiplication and division required, the numbers did not always come out right. Sometimes too few drawer bodies of a given size were prepared, sometimes too many.

The solution quickly became apparent: have the computer do the math and then broadcast the number of fixed lot quantity orders to the drawer prep area, signaling the operators to put the right kanbans on the priority board. It was immediately clear that having the computer compute and broadcast was far superior to having the operators call up screens and do the calculations. The result overall was a significant reduction in inventory and floor space and much improved availability of the right parts at the right time.

The Power of Networks

There are two aspects of information reporting where IT solutions win hands-down. IT networks are excellent tools for broadcasting information to dispersed locations. A network can readily broadcast the sequence of units starting into the final assembly process, so that subassembly operations can produce to the discrete unit in exactly the needed sequence. A version of this is at work every time a customer places an order at Taco Bell. No finished inventory needs to be held; instead, every order is custom-produced in the proper sequence.

This is a particular application of the golf-ball method of signaling developed in Japanese factories. The difference is that instead of color-coded golf balls arriving at a subassembly station to signal the model or type of unit starting into final assembly, an electronic signal arrives on a screen or prints as a label at the beginning of the subassembly process—just like an order for a bean burrito with no cheese. These are flexible and powerful applications, as long as the server does not go down!

There are applications of kanban systems where the same information (what part, how many, which container, etc.) can be broadcast for display at multiple locations, for example, at the ordering and producing locations. But where kanban cards might have to travel a distance (surprisingly short—50 feet—for this risk to surface) there is a real danger of kanbans being lost. In these cases, broadcast transmissions of the kanban information, displaying the kanban at the sending (or ordering) end, and printing a copy of the kanban at the supplying (or receiving) end is the better solution, preserving the advantages of visual management.

Intangible Benefits of Visual Controls

It is probably beyond dispute that asking people to take a few minutes per shift to record performance data requires far less overhead than the cost of hardware, software, and support resources needed to automate data collection to track process performance. Beyond the financial implications is the "soft" benefit no accounting system can calculate. These are the benefits from increasing the level of involvement of operators in observing, analyzing, and improving the processes in which they work every day.

Overall, visual controls not only heighten focus on process and accountability for that focus, they also provide the foundation for a far greater level of employee involvement than could any other reporting system. For lean production to truly be a process improvement system, that kind of involvement is essential.

Summary: Visual Controls and the Data for Lean Management

Visual controls are powerful contributors to lean management. Visuals reflect the human scale of production activity and process focus. They connect people to their processes, and at the same time reflect adherence to the process—or its lack. In doing so, visuals represent an important, simplifying addition to lean management.

Visual controls help transform the abstract concept of discipline in lean management into directly observable, concrete practices. Actual versus expected moves from the realm of an idea to easily interpreted visual tracking tools. Visual controls are the basis for comparing actual versus expected performance in lean management. They do not make the comparison, but they make the comparison possible. Visuals are a principal vehicle for focusing on process, and for verifying this important aspect of lean management. The variety and application of visual controls are limited only by your imagination. Which visuals to use and where to use them are determined by the needs, both stable and emerging ones, in your processes.

The actual appearance of visual controls is relatively unimportant beyond basics of legibility and ease of interpretation. I have seen both plain and fancy ones work equally well or poorly. What is important about visual controls to you, the leader at any level, is that you understand the reason for having them. By insisting through your standard work that the visuals are maintained and current, visuals constantly reinforce the focus on process. This focus makes it easier to see the contrast between expected and actual process performance. By doing this, visuals allow you to identify opportunities to press for improvement.

At first glance, visual controls may look like an afterthought or mere window dressing to the serious business of lean technical design. In fact, visuals provide the basis for much of the "management"—process focus, discipline, and accountability—in the lean management system. Neither aspect of lean, technical design or management system stands well without the other; visual controls contribute substantially to the robustness of lean management and through it, lean production.

Finally, visual controls in lean do not always mean the absence of IT tools, but the immediate, accessible, flexible, inexpensive, and responsive nature of visual controls makes these simpler solutions the preferred ones for most applications in lean operations.

Chapter 5

Daily Accountability Process

A daily accountability process is the third principal element of the lean management system. It provides the steering wheel, that is, the task assignments made by the meeting leader for what improvements will be worked on. It also provides the throttle, or the due date and resources for the improvement task. This chapter shows how to implement daily accountability through daily meetings and visual controls, with case studies to guide the way.

At first glance, this component of lean management seems designed simply to ensure follow-up on task assignments made in response to yesterday's problems or opportunities for improvement. A more significant (though less obvious) purpose of daily accountability is to reinforce the lean management system's focus on process and through it to identify and implement opportunities for improvement.

How Batch Production Differs from Lean

In a batch world, the object is to meet the schedule. Leaders are expected to fashion workarounds to get past problems that threaten schedule completion. There is little follow-up because the task is the same the next day: Do whatever it takes to meet the schedule. In a lean world, the focus is on maintaining and improving the process. Follow-up in lean management calls for understanding the causes of yesterday's problem and then eliminating them.

In a batch system, you ask: "Did you meet the schedule?" That is pretty much the sum total of your daily accountability. In a lean system, you ask: "What caused the problem that interrupted the process, and who will do what to resolve it?" Where batch systems have structured processes to deal with daily shortages, for example, lean management's structured process deals with daily accountability for making process improvements that eliminate the causes of shortages.

Lean management is all about focusing on the process: stabilize it, standardize it, and improve it by exposing problems, eliminating them, and repeating the cycle over and over. Visual controls are a key in making it easier to see quickly the status of your processes and the problems that interfere with them. The design of standard work for leaders, slightly overlapping and redundant, is intended to ensure the visuals are maintained in the first place, and acted on after that. Again, this is lean management closing the loop on process focus and driving improvement.

So in addition to including regular checks on the status of visual controls, leader standard work also includes a process to follow up on the stories told by the visual controls. This is the daily accountability process. In it, leaders assess the meaning in the visuals, assign appropriate responses, and hold people accountable for completing their assigned tasks. This follow-up process occurs largely in the structure of daily three-tier meetings. In this way, the three principal elements of lean management combine to form the essence of the lean management system. Leader standard work, visual controls, and the daily accountability process, plus the discipline by leaders to maintain the integrity of these three, form the heart of what makes lean management go.

Three Tiers of Daily Meetings

The daily accountability process takes place as an interlocking set of three brief, structured, daily meetings, one of which is the familiar, but often misunderstood, team start-up meeting. Each of these meetings is an explicit example of lean management's focus on comparison of expected and actual.

As the name suggests, there are three tiers of meetings:

1. The first tier (first, because it typically happens at the start of the shift) is the production team leader meeting briefly with the team members.
2. The second is the supervisor meeting with his or her team leaders and any dedicated support group representatives.
3. The third-tier meeting is the value stream manager or equivalent meeting with his or her supervisors and support group representatives or staff members.

4. A fourth tier is possible where the plant manager meets with his or her production and support staff members.

Each of the meetings shares these characteristics:

■ Brevity—rarely if ever longer than 15 minutes
■ Posture—standing up
■ Location—on or immediately adjacent to and not physically separated from the production floor
■ Agenda and content—defined by a visual display board

The second- and third- (and fourth- where applicable) tier meetings have a dual focus. The first is on "run-the-business" activities. The second is on activity intended to improve the business. These meetings are among the main occasions where the increased accountability that comes with visual controls can be seen. Accountability and disciplined adherence to process are central to a daily enactment, primarily at the second- and third-tier meetings, of a three-part process:

■ Assessment based on data captured on visual controls
■ Assignment for corrective action and/or improvement
■ Accountability for having completed the previous day's assignments

Far from the daily bureaucratic burden of typical recurring staff meetings, these second- and third-tier daily stand-up sessions are highly structured with the focus on building accountability and taking action to resolve problems and drive improvement. The first-tier team leaders' meetings are, among other things, the primary vehicle for supporting and extending bottom-up participation in improvement suggestion systems. In the case of all three (or four) tiers of meeting, information and accountability for performance are clearly, graphically, and visually displayed.

The daily three-tier meeting structure itself is something of a visual control. The meetings take place on the production floor standing up at the information board for the appropriate tier. The board is the location, agenda, and content for the daily meetings. The agendas and roles are standardized. The meetings are brief, not exceeding 15 minutes for the third tier. The team leader, supervisor, or value stream manager leads his or her respective meeting.

The first agenda item is always the day's labor plan. At the first-tier meeting, this item is addressed as a visual display of the starting positions and other assignments for the day. Did all team members who were expected show up and check in at the team meeting? If not, who goes where to get production started? At the department meeting, if unplanned absences are interfering with the start of production in one of the production teams, how can we shift people among areas quickly to bring production up to the day's planned rate? Similarly at the value stream, has any department been unable to balance labor with the day's planned work? And if so, what redeployment can be made at the value stream level to get things running as planned? Beyond that, the agenda and scope expand going up the tiers, as described next.

CASE STUDY: DISPLAYING ACTUAL FINISHED GOODS IN UNITS OR BY DOLLAR VALUE

In a cabinet assembly area, there were two parts to the main assembly line. The cabinet cases were built up at the head of the line and then moved in FIFO sequence into a queue between case build-up and drawer assembly, insertion, and final assembly. (In a later refinement of this layout, the drawers are assembled and inserted as the cases are built up, all in the same line.) The whole process was designed to run at a takt time of 36 seconds, producing a completed cabinet every 36 seconds. A production-tracking chart was used to keep track of the line's pace every half hour. The team leader took the number of finished units from the counter at the end of the line, wrote that number in the "actual" column for the time period in question, then picked up a highlighter and color coded that period's actual:

- Green signified having met the takt pace.
- Yellow meant missing it by five percent or less.
- Red meant the line had missed the takt pace by more than five percent.

(In the refined design, only red and green are used.)

The drawer assemblers were separated from the head of the line by about 50 feet. The production-tracking chart was beyond the head of the line, far enough away that the drawer crew could not see it. One day the value stream manager noticed a pair of binoculars in the drawer assembly area and asked about it. One of the operators told him they were unable to see the color code on the pitch chart because it was too far away, so an operator brought in the binoculars to be able to tell how the line was performing.

In a similar case, team members in a shipping department used to pay little attention to the posted information about the dollar value of a day's shipments. When the team leader switched to writing the average dollar value shipped per team member and a goal, the operators immediately began to pay attention, becoming interested in tracking their performance at several points during the day.

Few of us would participate in a competitive game without keeping score. Most people who come to work every day have at least a latent interest in knowing how they or their team performed. That interest is a pathway to what motivates them. It is worthwhile to reflect those interests with items on the team's tier-one board.

Tier One: Team Leader and Production Crew

The focus at the production team's meetings is mostly on today's assignments and any items of special note that day. The daily rotation and labor plans for the area (described in Chapter 10) are on display at this meeting, so people can check their assignments before work begins. The team leader updates yesterday's performance, covers any items of note from the previous day, and reviews today's plans and any issues. The team board may display summary project plans (objectives, current and planned future state, indicators of success, timeline, members) for significant externally supported activities going on in the area. And, on designated days of the week, specific topics might receive special focus. These could include, for example, safety, quality, 5S audit results, status of ideas suggested by team members for improving processes in the area, or other topics.

Especially for this meeting, the principle of "pull" communication is important to observe. That is, it is easily possible to provide far more information than team members are interested in or prepared to act on at any given level of system maturity. These meetings are not intended to become one-way "communication" conduits for the organization. They are intended to be a place where team members feel free to raise questions and concerns and where team leaders and others respond or do the investigation necessary to provide a response. Yes, some corporate news is passed along as well, but team members have an active role in putting topics on the information sharing part of the agenda.

Where there are not yet well-defined or well-understood reasons for maintaining team information boards, it is common to see the boards, even elaborately designed ones, festooned with printed copies of emails, often weeks or months old, and hung with Excel output—spreadsheets, charts, and graphs. That is usually a sign of confusion over the purpose of the board. By contrast, employees will make it clear when they are interested in information that reflects their performance. The binoculars case illustrates that as well as any I have seen.

Tier Two: Supervisor and Team Leaders

This meeting, led by the supervisor, focuses on two topics: running the business and improving the business. Information on the departmental team board typically includes status of key processes and equipment as well as week- or month-to-date summary performance data on safety, quality, delivery, and cost. Team leaders bring their production-tracking charts from the previous day and post them on the designated spot on the information board. The board is also likely to display the previous week's top three problems, their magnitudes, and actions underway to resolve them.

The initial items on the meeting agenda are similar to those from the team leaders' meetings: noteworthy items from yesterday and upcoming issues for today as well as updating the trend charts on the board. The focus then shifts to the production-tracking charts. It is important for the supervisor and his or her team leaders to understand each missed pitch reflected on the tracking charts. These will be the subject of further discussion at the third tier, or value stream meeting where the production-tracking charts will be scrutinized again. The supervisor knows to be prepared to describe what happened; what actions, if any, are underway in response; and whether he or she needs support from anyone at the third-tier meeting.

The second topic, improving the business, involves a visual task assignment board. This is a matrix of rows, one for each meeting participant's name, and dates, usually a week or two labeled day by day. The supervisor makes assignments to the team leaders and any support group representatives in response to needs identified from the production-tracking charts and from the other improve-the-business tools that are regular features on the meeting agenda. The supervisor writes these assignments on small cards or Post-it® notes and places them on the board on the due date for the person assigned. The supervisor's weekly gemba walks with the team leaders can result in assignments, as can less formal observations in the area, ratings on regular audits (such as 5S, supermarket status, safety), and actions assigned to the supervisor at the third-tier meeting or on gemba walks with the value stream leader.

The Red Dot, Green Dot Convention

At each day's meeting the supervisor reviews the tasks due that day. He or she works down the column for today's date, asking for each assignment in today's column if the task is complete. If it is, the supervisor puts a green self-adhesive ("sticky") dot on the Post-it® note. If it is incomplete, the supervisor pursues the reason enough to get a clear understanding, asks when the expected completion date will be, negotiates about that if necessary, and puts a red sticky dot on the Post-it® note. The assignment is kept on its original due date. The first assignments to be reviewed in this part of the meeting are always those that are overdue (see the dots on Figures 5.1a, 5.1b, and 5.1c).

The original due dates for assignments are never changed, nor are the assignment Post its® ever moved from the original due date. The red dot/green dot convention is absolute and arbitrary. Complete is complete; overdue is overdue. Period. When tasks are completed, the meeting leader puts a green dot next to the red one. Lots of red dots accumulating on daily task assignment boards invite important questions. Are we overestimating our capacity to get assignments done? Should the meeting leader consider adding more capacity, focusing existing capacity better, or recalibrating his or her estimates of what is entailed in a day's improvement task? Are tasks being kept from completion by impediments external to the area? If so, should the meeting leader or a designated other investigate? External issues sometimes need to be brought to the next higher tier for investigation, support, or resolution.

Think of the red dots on task assignment boards the same way you think of reasons for misses on a production-tracking chart. Their purpose is neither shame nor blame; rather they highlight a gap between actual and expected. In the relatively rare case, red dots will accumulate because someone is either incapable or unwilling to get his or her assignments completed. That becomes a matter for a performance discussion with the individual involved. Most of the time, something unexpected has happened or the planned cooperation of an external group or person has not come through. If the dots form a pattern over a week or more, the meeting leader will definitely want to investigate.

Figure 5.1 Daily accountability board.

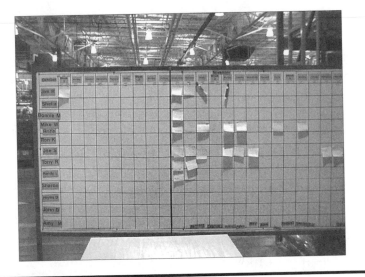

Figure 5.1a   Photo of daily accountability task board. This photo is from October 27, the date marked by the dark index line. The assignments from earlier in October have been removed. The board's magnetic date numbers will be reset for November when the month turns. Green/red coding is done here with markers. The dots are visible on incomplete assignments transferred from October to November. The color coding markers are held on the board by magnetic tape. The names of the value stream manager, supervisors, and support group representatives appear at the left.

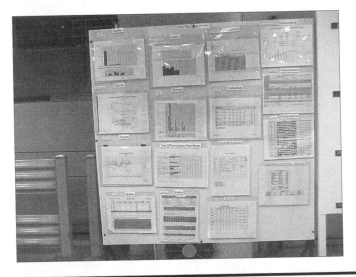

Figure 5.1b   Photo of daily "run the business" board for a focus factory. Boards like this one show yesterday's pitch attainment and other visual controls for performance appropriate to the process. They also display yesterday's entry on trend charts for safety, quality, delivery, and performance. Any of the charts can prompt process improvement assignments. These can include assignments on the daily task board, or result in a problem-solving or project assignment.

Stating that red dots do not represent an individual failure is easier to say than to hear. Even assigning visible, public accountability for completion dates is enough to make many uncomfortable at first. That is why it is important to emphasize the arbitrary nature of the green/red rule. Things do happen that are outside any individual's control; that is the most frequent cause of red dots.

Day-to-Day Project Management

To be effective in the daily improvement segment of the three-tier meetings, the meeting leaders (supervisors and value stream leaders) need at least rudimentary project management skills (a topic touched on in Chapter 8). That is, the leaders must quickly perceive the series of step-by-step actions to attack a flow interrupter or develop an improvement. This skill, the ability to see an implicit work-breakdown structure, is necessary to make appropriate one-step-at-a-time task assignments that cumulatively respond to the interruption or opportunity. Follow-up on these task assignments is straightforward with the visual daily task board on which the assignments are posted.

CASE STUDY: RED DOTS INDICATE INCOMPLETE WORK—BUT THEY DON'T SHOW THE REASON

Consider these cases illustrating the rule of arbitrary green/red assignment. The lean leader in a plant had an assignment on the task board to deliver a lean-related training session to a group in the plant at 2:00 pm on a Monday. At 1:00 pm that day, a fire broke out in the dust collection system for an aluminum grind-and-polish operation. Much of the building filled with white smoke. The plant and offices were evacuated for several hours, thoroughly disrupting the day's planned activities. Needless to say, the lean leader was unable to deliver his training session. What was the result at the next day's task review meeting? He got a red dot!

In another case in the same facility, the operations VP began using a variation on the task assignment board to post and track projects assigned to his staff members. The assignment matrix was ruled off by weeks rather than days, reflecting the meeting's weekly schedule as well as the scope and scale of the projects. The tasks on the Post-its® were the projects' agreed-to weekly milestones.

The staff members liked the system because they could readily tell what all the projects were, and whether and when a project would have an impact on someone else's area. These were longer-term projects that usually extended over 60 to 90 days or more. Recognizing that, project owners were allowed to move milestone tasks from week to week for milestone dates more than a month from a given week's meeting. Milestone dates within 4 weeks of the meeting day were frozen so actual versus expected could be seen.

The staff member in a recently created position, responsible for sourcing materials and purchased parts, had several projects involving suppliers. These responsibilities had gone untended prior to filling the new position. Many of the sourcing staffer's project milestones collected red dots week after week as he pursued negotiations with the supply base on quality, cost, consolidation, lot size, and delivery frequency.

After using the new visual weekly project tracking system for several months, the VP and staff came to the conclusion they had underestimated the time it would take to conclude these projects. They agreed to "refresh" the board using the information gained from the actual versus expected red dots to reset expectations for how long this kind of work was likely to take. The sourcing person had been doing excellent work, the likes of which the company had never undertaken before. The operations staff as a whole was going down the learning curve together in this area. There was never a hint of blame, shame, or recrimination arising from the red dots; instead, all involved treated it for what it was, a valuable learning experience. Coincidentally, this experience of the senior operations staff was a powerful example for calming the anxieties of their subordinates, who were about to begin getting daily task assignments and green/red follow-up coding.

Tier Three: Value Stream Leader with Supervisors and Support Groups

This is the daily value stream meeting at the value stream board. At this meeting, daily performance data are added to trend charts covering the typical dimensions—safety, quality, delivery, and cost—along with any others important to the area.

The value stream manager briefly reviews the day's staffing situation and then touches on yesterday's performance measures. Items of note are covered regarding past performance or upcoming items. Next, the value stream leader turns to yesterday's performance-tracking charts. He or she scrutinizes them for completeness, misses, and the reasons why. Based on the data, he or she makes and posts assignments for action. The last part of the value stream meeting is a review of overdue items still pending and assignments due today. This proceeds in the same way for the value stream as for the department, except all the value stream's support group representatives are regular attendees at the meeting and are potential recipients of assignments.

In an example of process trumping structure, the value stream leader acts as though the support group representatives report to the value stream. In some places, they do; in others, they do not. The leader makes assignments directly to the support group members and holds them directly responsible for getting their assignments completed on time. If issues arise in these relationships, the value stream leader takes them up with his or her peers on the plant staff and the plant manager. As organizations become better educated and aligned about lean as an operating philosophy, the priority of functional projects rarely overrides immediate intervention on matters that threaten the expected flow of production or hold up measurable process improvements in daily operations.

CASE STUDY: SUPPORT GROUPS CAN HELP SOLVE LONG-STANDING PROBLEMS

An outstanding example of *support* groups responding to the needs of the value stream occurred in a case in which a product line was added to a recently formed *mixed-model progressive-build flow line.* (This was the same cabinet assembly line where the operators in the drawer area brought in binoculars.) The product line in question had been fabricated and assembled in a different plant since its introduction a dozen years earlier. In its original plant, individual operators working by themselves assembled units at workbenches, building the cabinet from start to finish. Now, the units were being built on a balanced, takt-paced assembly line. When more than one or two of a particular model of these units came down the line, things stalled badly. The production-tracking chart showed missed pitches for the entire run of these products.

The cause of the flow interruptions was well known to those who had previously worked with the product. A particular style of drawer did not fit correctly and the cabinet's lock mechanism was balky. Each of these problems required extra work to make the units fit and function properly. When the units were bench-built, these models just took a little more time. The individual builders knew how to make the repairs. On a line paced at a 36-second takt time, these deviations caused missed takt cycles every time these problematic units came down the line.

At the value stream meeting the day after this problem emerged, the value stream leader assigned engineering and quality to deliver for the next day a plan to resolve the problems. They did so and were assigned to carry it out. Within two weeks, both problems of a dozen years' standing were permanently solved; the units now run smoothly down the line at takt time regardless of drawer style and whether or not locks are called for.

Daily Accountability Exposes and Solves Problems Quickly

In the case involving drawers and locks, the lean production process exposed problems that used to be covered up by rework occurring at essentially untimed workbenches. The lean management system provided the tools and setting to get the problem resolved in a quick and accountable fashion.

Further Note on Task Assignments and Follow-Up

The supervisor at the department board and the value stream leader at the value stream board are free to make assignments from sources other than reasons for misses on the production-tracking charts (as noted earlier in this chapter). Gemba walks with individual leaders, results of routine audits, and the leader's observations of the area can all result in task assignments. But assignments are not necessarily a one-way street. Subordinates or support members can bring requests for help or support to the meetings. In effect, they ask the supervisor or value stream leader to assign tasks to himself or herself where those tasks are best carried out by one in a position of more authority or with access to more or different resources.

In the third-tier meeting when the value stream manager focuses on yesterday's visuals and asks for explanation, he or she sends a powerful message about focusing on the process. When he or she assigns tasks to respond to misses or opportunities to improve, a powerful message is sent about the importance of cycle-by-cycle performance and improvement. When red-dotted items are asked about in the meeting, it sends a powerful message about taking action, NOW. What happens, or fails to happen in these meetings has widespread effects on what people in a value stream come to think of as important. Two contrasting cases illustrate this point.

It's Not about the Boards!

It is not unusual to hear people say they want the visual elements in the lean management system to have a consistent look, "...so when people move from area to area or plant to plant, everything looks the same." In fact, the appearance of information boards and other examples of visual controls is far less important than how they are used. What's important is leaders' commitment to establishing standards and expectations; using tools to identify expected versus actual; and following through on what they find.

TWO CASE STUDIES: IGNORING TEAM INFORMATION BOARDS VERSUS USING THEM TO IMPROVE

In the first case, team information boards had been established for each team leader's area as part of an important new product's showcase lean production area. The boards were neat and uniform, and lots of emphasis was given to keeping the entries on them current; the area had lots of visitors from VIPs and customer groups. So, the team leaders all learned the importance of maintaining their boards and did a good job of keeping the entries current, including the entries on their production-tracking charts.

As with many new product introductions, the design for the production process had looked good on paper. Once it was installed and operating, it became apparent that several aspects of the process should be changed. Project teams were formed to make the changes, and the area's performance improved. In fact, virtually all of the changes made in the area for its first 18 months of operation came from project teams working on fairly substantial changes to the layout.

Near the end of this time, I happened to ask a team leader what he thought of the information board he so dutifully maintained. He snorted and said derisively that the board was a joke. He had been recording reasons for misses for nearly 2 years, he said, and not a single thing had happened as a result. He still faced the same problems day in and day out regardless of how often he wrote up problems in the reasons for misses section of his production-tracking charts. "I'm going to quit filling the darn thing out," he said. And he did. Nobody said a word to him about it until a new value stream manager and supervisor were named for the area. Until that time, the main focus had been "hitting the number" for schedule completion and cost. Although this plant has performed satisfactorily, there is a sense that it could be doing better than it has.

In a contrasting case, I was touring an assembly area in a plant that had undergone and continued to undergo changes designed to make its layout and processes leaner and leaner. The plant lean team had introduced production-tracking charts and the daily accountability process recently, as part of a lean management implementation.

I stopped and asked an operator (who had no idea who I was) if she had a production-tracking chart. She said she did and showed it to me. It was filled out, noting where production had missed its hourly goal and a reason why.

I asked her what she thought of the chart. Her face lit up as she proceeded to tell me what a good thing it was. "We've written down things that have frustrated us forever," she said, "and they've been taken care of, just like that! It's a lot better around here now with these forms," she said. When I looked at the department's information board, I could see the list of top three flow interrupters and actions underway to resolve them. Clearly this was an area that paid attention to the health and improvement of its processes. This plant has been outperforming its goals at the same time it has been absorbing substantial change.

Every application of the principles that drive visual controls is an invention—for example:

- Forms or charts
- A units-produced counter
- Bicycle flags identifying minimum and maximum levels in a queue
- Audible alarms

- Beads strung on a wire, as in billiards scorekeeping, to represent accumulating demand in a subassembly or feeder area
- Tags on an inclined track or in pigeonholes

Insisting that every visual control should look like every other one misses the point. Yes, processes need to be systematic and standardized and the visuals need to fit these criteria as well. However, what is most important about visual controls is that leaders are committed to using them effectively. Where local process characteristics dictate varying from a visual standard, so be it.

Early on in the use of team information boards, one plant manager saw a board he liked (it had been carefully measured and put together, labels and date numbers had been engraved at a sign shop, and the whole thing was impressive to see). He ordered copies for each of the value streams in his plant and decreed that all value stream leaders begin using them immediately. (It is worth noting that his background included significant responsibilities in national-brand, multi-plant, continuous process operations. In his prior experiences, everything was standardized across sites.)

As it turned out, the design of the board's daily task accountability matrix was a winner, duplicated elsewhere. The rest of the board was very much a first draft, though cosmetically pleasing. Most of it has been revised. The copies that were ordered were soon festooned with paper charts, some of which were there at the direction of the plant manager after he realized the design he ordered did not reflect the data on which he wanted his value stream managers to focus.

Standardization is generally a good thing; standardizing before having had enough experience to work the bugs out of a design is not. If you are able to view as experiments the different approaches to even the same visual controls, you preserve an appropriate sense of learning by experience. In addition, allowing local experimentation gives leaders who have never before worked with visual controls the experience of having to think through what they want to measure and track, and why. That is valuable indeed.

As the experiments proceed, enough of a consensus will emerge about which design elements have proved the most useful to incorporate into a standard along with expectations for how the visuals should be used. That is the time to standardize. Keep in mind, however, that standards reflect only the current best practice. As further experience and insights accumulate, expect, indeed, encourage the standards to change as a reflection of improvements.

The "Vacation Paradox" and Capacity for Improvement

Lean production is fundamentally an improvement system, but getting it to work that way can be difficult. Suppose you have a limited number of engineers and other specialists available for assigning to projects. You may wonder how all these continuous improvements will come about. As it turns out, the answer is in the latent capacity for improvement, developed in the daily task assignments in the second and third tiers of the three-tier meeting structure.

Supervisors who came up through a batch-and-queue system will usually tell you they have no time during the day to do anything but fight fires and expedite. As the lean conversion stabilizes, and especially as supervisors begin to follow their own standardized work, they find themselves spending less and less time fighting fires. In addition, their standardized work not only makes it clear what they are supposed to do, by implication it makes it clear what they are not supposed to do. That is, they are not supposed to be running here and there doing the jobs of quality, material supply, and engineering. Instead, they are supposed to use those cell phones and two-way radios to notify their support groups when things go wrong outside their production area.

Overall, this has the effect of freeing chunks of time in their daily routine. Standard work only accounts for about half of a supervisor's time, and even team leaders have about 20 percent of their time available and unassigned in their standard work. The intent is to put at least some of this time to use on activities to improve the business. The source of these activities comes from the daily task assignments made at the daily three-tier meetings. All of this provides the vehicle for transforming the 100-percent run-the-business focus to a shared one that includes regular work on process improvement.

These small, one-step-at-a-time daily assignments give production leaders the experience of doing more during the day than just running the day-to-day business. Many production leaders have had little or no experience with project management. The daily task assignments represent project management *work breakdown structures* on a small scale. These assignments show how small steps can lead to significant outcomes when disciplined accountability for execution is part of the picture.

Besides that, leaders learn that these steps can easily fit into a daily schedule, especially when an area is operating in a stable state. Further, these cumulative improvements frequently do not require teams of technical specialists. I have a name for this phenomenon of suddenly having the time to do more, to work on improvement steps in addition to run-the-business activities. I call it the *vacation paradox*.

It works like this: When I am about to go on vacation, especially if it is a fishing trip, which means leaving my family behind, I want to be sure there are no loose ends at home—or at work—during the few days or week I am gone. So, I scan my world for things that need to be tied up before I leave. The last thing I want is to return home and face an unhappy family because I forgot to look after a detail that ended up inconveniencing them! The same is true at work. I want to return to no more than the usual accumulation of email and voice messages. I certainly do not want to return to find I left a smoldering situation or untended assignment that burst into a full-fledged problem while I was out on holiday.

In short, during these prevacation times I get lots more done at home and at work than I usually do. I do not transform into a maniacal dervish of activity, but I do use my time more efficiently. That is the vacation paradox: there is a lot more time to get small things done when they are clearly identified and scoped and there is a reason to get to them. Avoiding unhappiness in my family or boss is one reason to get to them before vacation. Another is having tasks done and coded with green dots rather than red.

Imagine the impact of the team leaders and supervisors in a value stream devoting as little as 15 to 30 minutes every day to improvement tasks! The capacity to do this work has been present all along. The unstable, firefighting nature of leaders' roles in a conventional production environment demanded all of their time and energy for meeting the daily production schedule. In an increasingly lean environment, as production stabilizes, it is possible to tap this latent capacity, though it takes time before the extra work ceases to seem like an imposition in an already busy day. When that happens, it is possible to say that an organization has developed the habit of daily improvement.

The power of this process can be surprising. Leaders and operators from the Deep South to Canada and anywhere in between have all commented on the effectiveness of the daily improvement assignments keyed to recurring causes of interruption. Problems that had seemed as much a part of the workday as coming through the door in the morning had been worked into oblivion step by step and were gone. Operators, as in the job-by-job area noted in Chapter 4, were happy to have a vehicle for getting their problems solved. And leaders were initially amazed at the results the visual, accountable, daily focus on correction and improvement produced, as in the drawer fit and lock function case study in this chapter.

Accountability in Office Processes

In repetitive manufacturing, it makes sense to focus on accountability daily. Variations can come at you fast in a high volume factory. That is also true in high volume office processes such as order management/customer service. But where office processes do not cycle so quickly, weekly accountability sessions can be a better fit. The objective is to produce improvement, not to hold meetings for their own sake.

Summary: Daily Accountability Improves Processes

Daily accountability is a vehicle for ensuring that focus on process leads to action to improve it. The structure of the daily accountability process is straightforward, a series of three brief meetings to review what happened yesterday and assign actions for improvement. These are paced, stand-up meetings on the production floor that emphasize quickly resolving or investigating to the next level interruptions in the defined production process. The purpose of these meetings is not communication of information someone somewhere in the organization thought others ought to hear.

Daily accountability is the vehicle for interpreting the observations recorded on the visual controls, converting them into assignments for action, and following up to see to it that assignments are completed. As with the other principal elements of lean management, daily accountability relies on disciplined adherence to its processes on the part of those who lead the *three-tier meetings*. When this discipline is present, leaders follow their standard work. Leading the three-tier meetings effectively is an important part of leaders' standard work, which is to make it clear that maintaining visual controls is vital, expected, will be closely reviewed, and leads to action.

The daily accountability process also provides a vehicle for introducing and modeling the basics of project management for those leaders who came up through the ranks and may not have had exposure to these tools. And, the process definitely reinforces the connection of support groups with the manufacturing process by involving them in daily accountability assignments to resolve manufacturing's issues, and quickly. This is true whether or not support group members have a formal reporting relationship to the value stream.

By reinforcing process focus and driving improvement, daily accountability actually creates increased capacity for improvement via the vacation paradox. Finally, the green dot/red dot convention brings visual accountability for expected versus actual into concrete reality for a value stream's leaders and staff members. The effect is a powerful reinforcement of this theme running through lean management.

Chapter 6

Lean in Administrative, Technical, and Professional Work

Lean is no longer just for manufacturing. The roots of lean are deep in the shop floor of course, beginning with Henry Ford. But, in recent years, lean thinkers have found the principles and many of the tools of lean are just as effective in administrative, technical, and professional (office) processes. And, lean management approaches are needed to sustain and extend lean in office business processes just as in manufacturing.

This chapter illustrates some lean and lean management applications in the office world. It describes relationships among process problems in offices, solutions by application of lean tools, and sustaining the gains with office lean management applications. A second subject is resistance to change. Resistance is a potential issue in any lean implementation, although its background is often different with lean office initiatives. Accountability can spark resistance for office workers; usually, overcoming resistance simply takes consistent execution of lean management. The chapter's third subject addresses the environment in which enterprise business processes operate. Enterprise lean faces particular pitfalls characteristic of its environment, specifically regarding leadership alignment. Lack of alignment can be a problem in any lean implementation; in enterprise lean, it can be troublesome. The chapter concludes with suggestions that an condition, and measures to prevent the problems and bu ment with enterprise lean.

Lean office, or lean enterprise, first spread to administrative functions from the experiences and lessons lean manufacturers learned in their factories. Now lean initiatives can be found in diverse sectors of the economy beyond manufacturing, in organizations whose products are solely knowledge and/or services. Among many examples are finance and insurance, government, healthcare, software, pharmaceutical development, sales and distribution, customer service, and education. An increasing number of organizations are beyond asking, "Will lean work for me even if I don't manufacture anything?" Instead, the question now is, "How do I apply lean to improve my business processes?"

For the practitioner, lean and lean management apply nearly transparently in processes like these, just as in manufacturing. But unlike in manufacturing, disciplined process analysis and intentional design are rarely—if ever—applied to enterprise business processes. Instead, many office processes have been left to evolve over time, usually with little examination. I have never been in a factory that did not have engineers concerned with process design, even if not always a lean design. I have rarely been in an office in which engineers were involved in designing or refining business processes. *

For these reasons, and from experience with over 100 lean enterprise projects, I am convinced there is as much to be gained in improved throughput, quality, productivity, and engagement in offices as in factories. Initial gains from lean enterprise projects commonly reach or exceed 50% reductions in total cycle time, process time, and errors and rework, as well as revealing further opportunity for improvement of the same magnitude, just as in manufacturing.

Lean Management in Enterprise Business Processes

Most things of value, whether a service, a drawing, new knowledge, or a manufactured good, are produced as the result of a process. As a process improvement system, lean applies to any process. For this discussion, consider linear or step-by-step processes.† Some examples are handling a customer service request, establishing a new customer account, replying to an RFP, updating catalogs, making changes to terms and conditions,

---

* It is not unusual for organizations to automate their unexamined processes along with the wastes and inefficiencies that have grown into them.

† Developmental processes are iterative in nature, and while the same lean principles apply, iterative processes appear to be different (see, for example, Schipper and Swets, 2009).

modifying a standard offering per a customer's request, or manufacturing a product. Many problems familiar to lean practitioners crop up in these kinds of processes, and lean principles apply in eliminating them. Table 6.1 shows just a few examples of problems in enterprise business processes and the application of lean tools to improve flow and reduce waste.

Just as with manufacturing, implementing lean tools in enterprise business processes is the easy part; the tools require no more than 20 percent of the effort, often less. Sustaining the lean implementation takes most of the work. As in manufacturing, this work typically remains undone, even in the best examples of lean office tools implementations. For that reason, sustaining enterprise lean implementations requires the parallel implementation of a lean management system. Table 6.2 shows lean management applications that could be used to sustain the lean responses to business process problems.

Resistance: Accountability and Visual Controls

Visual controls are important in any lean management implementation. In office processes, the progression of work typically cannot be seen. For this reason, visuals might be even *more* important than in the factory, where flow and interruption are usually in plain view. In offices, work progresses through the IT network, hidden from easy observation. You can see people at computers or on the phone, but you cannot see the work. It is typical in lean office projects to find that half of the work time is spent on work-related but non-value-adding activities. These are things like doing rework to correct errors or changes in requirements or inputs, making requests for missing information, seeking clarifications, and waiting for approvals or replies.

The amount of rework and non-value-adding activity in office processes may contribute to the tendency for office workers to resist the increased accountability that comes with lean and lean management. Compared with manufacturing, applying time-based expectations for performance (and measuring actual versus expected output) is not as obviously a fit in office settings. Office work often involves considerable variation in the nature and duration of work content from one unit of work to the next. And office workers are simply not as used to being held accountable to the same extent as production workers in manufacturing. Many tasks in office settings are seen as specialized, only to be performed by "specialists." With office work framed this way, expected rates of output and other measures of yield and productivity have not been widely applied, to individuals or to the team.

Table 6.1   Office Process Problems and Lean Solutions

Process Problem	Lean Response
1. Large batches produced between steps in administrative processes increase wait time, slow throughput, and conceal defects.	• Create defined flow lanes to control WIP between processes • Or, link process steps in a cell
2. Uncontrolled release of work into an engineering process causes imbalance, bottlenecks, and backups when separate flow paths are not defined for jobs with substantial variation in work content.	• Implement heijunka logic for releasing jobs into the process based on calculated or estimated work content. • Track actual vs. expected work content to improve accuracy of estimates and calculations
3. Misunderstood requirements between process steps result in rework in the receiving step to correct defects or seek missing information from the supplying step.	• Link processes where possible. • If not, kaizen involving both to understand capabilities, define requirements, design feedback
4. Downstream processes start work early in an attempt to speed up throughput only to rework their "early" efforts when final input to their process differs from what they anticipated.	• Kaizen to create readiness checklist to be completed before work is released to the downstream process
5. Unplanned downtime in the IT network causes lost production, missed delivery dates, and overtime.	• Create user downtime log • Regularly review with IT • Visual status of tickets • Visual status of system improvement work
6. Wide variation in method and sequence among people in same jobs doing similar tasks results in variable quality and productivity.	• Define standard sequence of steps • Document standardized methods • Document expected productivity
7. Many people order supplies, resulting in overstock of some items, stockouts of others, and mystery items nobody seems to use.	• 5S supply areas • Put supplies on kanban replenishment system • Define reorder process and responsibility

Table 6.2 Lean Management Applications to Sustain Lean Responses to Problems in Office Processes

Process Problem	Lean Response	Lean Management Applications
1. Large batches	Flow lanes or a cell	• Define processes • Leader standard work to monitor adherence • Production-tracking chart to identify problems • Accountability processes to understand and address causes
2. Release of work not controlled	Heijunka release	• Define processes • Leader standard work to monitor heijunka release • Production-tracking chart to identify variations from expected work content • Accountability processes to understand and address causes
3. Upstream, downstream needs not understood	Link processes, define needs, feedback	• Leader standard work to monitor adherence to defined process at upstream step • Production tracking to identify problems at downstream step • Joint start-up meeting of both steps • Accountability processes to understand and address causes of problems and variations at both steps
4. Starting too early	Readiness checklist	• Leader standard work to monitor actual use of readiness checklist • Production-tracking chart to identify rework • Accountability processes to understand and address causes of problems and variations at both steps
5. Unplanned downtime	Downtime log with review, visual status	• Leader standard work to monitor use of log • Visuals with pending and current tickets, expected due dates • Joint reviews with IT to rank problems and maintain accountability for timely resolution

continued

Table 6.2 (continued)   Lean Management Applications to Sustain Lean Responses to Problems in Office Processes

Process Problem	Lean Response	Lean Management Applications
6. Variation in method and sequence	Standard sequence, methods, expectations	• Standardized work or procedures • Visual controls for progression of work through standard sequence • Leader standard work to monitor adherence to standard work • Production-tracking chart to identify misses • Accountability processes to understand and address causes of variations and misses
7. Overstocks, stockouts, mysteries	5S; kanban system.	• Defined responsibility for pull system audit with posted results • Accountability processes to understand and address causes for identified misses

Lean thinking changes many of these assumptions and practices. Visual controls in offices as in factories raise the level of accountability for everyone involved in a process. So do expectations for productivity. Cross training and cellular designs shrink the number of "specialists" and bring common standards to many areas of performance. Of course, this allows ready comparison of performance among people and teams, another form of accountability. Any or all of these factors can contribute to lean initiatives facing greater initial resistance in office areas than in factories. What should you do?

Stick with it! Demonstrate by your actions that people are taken seriously when they record problems on the visuals or suggest process changes. Act on the process misses and interrupters recorded on the visual production tracking charts. Work quickly to eliminate real problems and implement constructive suggestions. Explain why some "problems" or suggestions will not be taken up. (These often represent requests to return to the previous mode of operating. As such, they represent teachable moments, opportunities to review a point or two in the rationale for lean.) As you respond to and eliminate problems people have brought to your attention, you will also be eliminating some long-standing sources of frustration for those who do the work. When you follow through on problems and suggestions, people will experience the benefits, and their resistance will fade. Similarly, green-red coding of visually posted assignments and project milestone tasks shows progress being made, and credits people and teams for getting things done. These actions are powerfully reinforcing, and they contribute to eliminating office workers' initial resistance to lean and the tools of lean management.

These experiences can be seen in the marketing, engineering, and manufacturing database case study, My Process, Your Process, Our Process.

A simple but important step in reducing non-value-adding effort in office processes is to make it visible. Value stream mapping the process is often a good first step to show the waste. But it is not unusual to find disagreement on what to map, and on how the process works among those performing the same tasks in the process! In these cases, it is necessary to begin by developing agreement on the steps and sequence that constitute the process. Once agreement is reached, it is possible to map and then visually track the progression of work, and to see opportunities for improvement. For an example of a visual used to track progression of work through an engineer-to-order/database updating process, see Figure 6.1.

When work moves between steps in an office value stream through the IT network, visuals allow you to ask and answer questions like these:

- Where is a given unit of work in the sequence of steps?
- Has each step been completed on time and in the agreed sequence?
- If expected throughput time in a step has been exceeded or missed, what was the reason for the miss?
- If the process is interrupted at a given step, what is the recovery plan?

Just as in manufacturing, visuals in office processes allow you to identify and respond to variations in process performance. Office misses can become the basis of a task on an accountability board, are often documented on a Pareto chart at the end of a week, are frequently the subject of root cause analysis, and might appear as the problem statement in an A-3 project to implement a root cause solution. Leader standard work sustains the building block elements of the lean management system by focusing on executing the visuals, the accountability processes, and the other elements of lean management. But the units of work in office processes can vary from unit to unit (for example, difficult vs. routine requests for post-sales service, or first-time designs vs. minor modification). Because office process work often lacks the repetitive tasks of some manufacturing settings, the percentage of a leader's time occupied by his or her standardized work may be less than that of their counterparts in the factory.

CASE STUDY: MY PROCESS, YOUR PROCESS, OUR PROCESS

A product data group created the marketing and manufacturing data-bases and "smart" product graphic symbols used by customers to create layouts and then order products. Together, this database work was the longest item on the new product development critical path. Standard time from start to release was nine months, often delaying new product commercialization. The process had for years resisted repeated attempts to improve it. As a last resort, the area manager asked for help from the office lean team.

In doing background work, the lean team found marked differences in how the database people did their work. Some seemed to start in the middle, some at or near the beginning, and no two people seemed to follow the same sequence of steps. In a series of intense work-shop sessions with the lean team's help, the database people agreed on a defined set of steps. In following sessions, they hammered out a sequence in which they would work through the steps.

One more workshop session produced on a large whiteboard a matrix of projects (as the rows) by process segments, and steps within segments (as the columns). With steady follow-up, the group came to follow the steps uniformly. Now it was possible for everyone to see the progression of work on each project, and daily stand-up meetings at the board enabled the team to mobilize help and develop an understanding of problems when a project got hung up at a particular step.

A note on resistance: "Hammering out" is not too strong a description of what it took for these technical specialist office workers to agree, however grudgingly, to try the new process. Two factors were at work that led to overcoming their resistance to change, one internal to the department, one from outside.

The outside factor was the failure of all previous efforts over many years to reduce the bottleneck represented by the database process and the costly delays it added to product introductions. Even after complet-ing implementation of a new enterprise resource planning (ERP) soft-ware system that encompassed engineering, marketing, manufacturing, order management, as well as database, there was no improvement in database throughput. Database was now a corporate level problem, with the attendant pressure on management to find a better way. There was no change in the value of treating people with dignity and respect. Now, however, it became clear that finding solutions to the database bottleneck had to go forward even if people did not like it—and that did not constitute disrespect for the database group. So, the department manager pushed for change more insistently and with greater firmness than his predecessors.

The internal factor was the power of value stream mapping. The mapping sessions revealed a veritable spaghetti-bowl of rework, over-processing, disconnected schedules and priorities, starting some work too early and other work too late; the map was nightmarish. It is said that reasonable people, given the same information, will reach generally the same conclusions. That ultimately was the case here.

Supported by the department manager, the lean team facilitators firmly but respectfully forced the database group to face the reality of their work processes. It was clearly reflected on a current state value stream map the database group had created, supported by the lean team members. As part of the workshop, the database people had gone through lean training. Now, in the value stream mapping sessions, the lean team facilitators reinforced and interpreted the lean lessons. Between their manager's insistence and the lean facilitators' support, enough of the database people realized they simply could not continue asserting their process could not be improved. They agreed, not without reluctance, on a future state that proved to be the key. In a matter of two years, the new process led to quadrupled productivity in database, and over two-thirds reduction in cycle time. Now, this way of operating is taken as a given—and a point of pride—in the group.

Three years later, a similar process was implemented in the group responsible for modifying the databases when standard products were customized, or engineered to order, at a customer's request. The database group consistently experienced rework because of incomplete or inaccurate inputs from the engineer-to-order team. And, the engineering group was chronically late getting the new specs to the database team, which then had to rush in addition to performing the frequently required rework. Often, the custom products missed the promised shipment date. Customers were unhappy, and so was everyone working in the process!

This time, lean thinking had spread widely enough that there was little resistance from the engineers and database people to the idea their process could be improved.

In a lean project, the two groups worked together to create a value stream map of the steps in their processes. They immediately realized their steps needed to be interspersed with each other, and that working in batches in department silos was the cause of much of the rework in the database group. After creating a future state process design and value stream map, the project team created a daily update board showing the progression of work through the engineer-to-order and database process, and established agreed dwell times through each step in the process.

In a matter of a month, late releases and deliveries stopped, as though by magic. Both groups now swear by the power of this method of visually controlling their joint process.

Engineering to Order –Mfg and Mkt DB Project Board
9am Daily Standup

Proj #, owner # lines	Order entered	Eng edit	Need to clarify?	Eng design	Mfg database	Mkting database	Effectively applied	Release to mfg	Reason for early, overdue
Dwell time	Date	1 day		1 day	½ day	½ day	½ day	1 day	
T6F31 Rez 2	1/15	1/15 / 1/15		1/16 / 1/15	1/17 / 1/16	(1/18) / 1/17	1/19 / 1/18	1/22 / 1/22	Pricing error found for expedite delivery
T6F68 Pam 3	1/19	1/22 / 1/22		1/23 / 1/22	1/23 / 1/23	1/24 / 1/24	1/24 / 1/24	1/24 / 1/24	Close to previous design
T6L88 Tom 1	1/19	1/23 / 1/22		1/24 / 1/23	1/24 / 1/24	(1/26) / 1/24	1/29 / 1/26	1/30 / 1/30	Expedite price DB rebuild now fixed
T6A96 Phan 1	1/23	1/24 / 1/23		1/25 / 1/24	1/26 / 1/25	1/26 / 1/26	1/27 / 1/27	1/28 / 1/27	
Legend		Out / In	(Late)						Reason overdue: complete when occurs

Figure 6.1   Visual control for progression of work through an office process.

Enterprise Value Streams and Their Political Environment

Successfully implementing lean in office and technical/professional value streams can be more challenging than in the factory. This is not because of greater technical complexity in office processes; Table 6.1 showed how lean tools apply similarly whether in office or factory. (Lean management standards for office processes appear in the Appendix, along with the standards for lean management in manufacturing.) The challenges for lean success in enterprise value streams come from the more complex organizational and political environment encountered in cross-functional office processes.

Think of it this way. In manufacturing, there is almost always one person with responsibility for the plant and its people, processes, and performance. While many functions besides manufacturing are present in factories—production control, supply chain, engineering, maintenance, human resources, quality, finance—everyone understands the plant's goals: ship quality products on time, at the right cost, and do it safely. Some in the plant might report elsewhere in the organization. But when plant performance is at stake, everyone is accountable to the plant manager, whether it looks that way on the organization chart or not.

There is no parallel position in enterprise business processes. Enterprise value streams cross many organizational boundaries, cutting across the vertical "silos" of the functional organizational structure. Products or services get to customers from the efforts of sales, marketing, order management, product development, IT, finance, distributors and a distributor relations group, perhaps engineering and production, and often others. Some of these functions might report to a single higher-level executive, but even so, can you identify a single position with ownership responsibility for the end-to-end process, similar to the responsibility of a plant manager? Almost certainly not.

Business processes almost never appear on the organization chart. Enterprise value streams, another way to refer to business processes, cross many internal boundaries. They rarely have identifiable, accountable ownership or dedicated resources and budgets. Cross-functional business processes typically lack their own measures. Indeed, improving an end-to-end business process often negatively affects the measures of individual departments, which are tuned for optimizing performance on functional measures. For all these reasons, cross-functional improvement projects often come up short. Projects run into internal boundaries and competing priorities among the departments through which enterprise value streams pass, and on which the value stream depends for performance. If a given department's priorities are elsewhere, the value stream project is out of luck.

Organizational Governance for Enterprise Value Streams

Acting to improve an office value stream is an organizationally and politically complex undertaking. Success depends on creating the conditions for the organization to recognize and support a cross-functional approach to improvement projects and business processes. Establishing these conditions does not mean changing organization structures or reporting relationships. At some point in its future an organization might want to take those steps, but they are not a place to begin.

Senior leadership needs to establish a governance process that supports a cross-functional perspective in order for an enterprise value stream improvement activity to survive. The cross-functional perspective is necessary both for initial improvement projects and for ongoing process management after the transition from project mode. Key senior leaders, at the level of CEO and senior VP, can regularly act as a steering and oversight team for lean initiatives. They can require lean projects to have parallel steering groups—the directors or VPs of functions involved in the value stream targeted for improvement—with one person assigned as value stream sponsor. The senior leaders should expect the development of value stream, or business process, measures as one outcome of value stream improvement projects.

Value stream or process measures typically include worker safety (where it applies in the office), quality (first-pass yield or time lost to errors and rework), speed (end-to-end cycle time, sometimes known as lead time), productivity (process time, or actual hands-on time as a percent of cycle time), and externally incurred costs. These measures should show the projected improvement between the current state and proposed future state value stream design, and reflect the effectiveness of the future state implementation.

A particular characteristic of process measures makes them especially effective in sustaining the gains as improvement projects make the transition to the mode of ongoing business process. Process measures are *scalable*. Being scalable means the measures apply to the business process as a whole and to specific responsibilities in each of the process functions. In an end-to-end view, the measures show the velocity, productivity, and freedom from errors and rework at the scale of, for example, the order management process, or month-end closing process, or new product launch process, or post-sales service process. Because the measures can be scaled down, they also apply at the intersections where the business process passes through the participating functions.

To illustrate how safety, quality, speed, and cost can be scaled to apply to functions, here are some examples of process measures applied to the intersection of value streams with functions:

- How quickly available and free from error is the scheduling information the order management representative relies on from master production control?
- How accurate are the material availability and delivery transit times from the inbound and outbound logistics departments and the supply chain department?
- Are the pricing and terms information current as supplied by the contracts and pricing databases?

The measures at the process-function intersections provide objective information about the degree to which functions are meeting their commitments to the performance of key business processes. The senior leader oversight group can rely on these process measures to assess the functional VPs' and directors' accountability for agreed support of business processes in addition to their functional goals. And the measures form an objective basis for horizontal, peer-to-peer accountability among the project- or process-level oversight group.

The most important point is the organization's recognition of the joint performance responsibilities for functions as well as processes. This does not require a change in structure, only that for the purposes of supporting the value stream business process perspective, the organization acts "as if" it were organized by process and has the governance, measurement, and accountability infrastructures to support its critical-for-the-customer enterprise business processes.

Summary

Lean principles and tools are effective in office processes just as in manufacturing. And, just as in lean manufacturing, sustaining enterprise lean applications requires a parallel implementation of lean management. Lean tools apply in office processes just as effectively as in manufacturing, from 5S and workplace organization, work paced by takt time, work cells, in-cycle work separated from out-cycle tasks, defined flow paths, and mixed model production with controlled release through heijunka to level mix and volume. However, until office workers experience the benefits of lean, they can be especially sensitive to the increased accountability that comes with standards for performance and productivity, and with the use of visual controls.

Enterprise value streams usually lack the singular ownership equivalent to that of a plant manager in a factory setting. That, combined with crossing so many more internal organization boundaries, makes leadership alignment an even greater issue, and therefore a greater focus in lean enterprise implementations. Even considering the greater political complexity of enterprise lean, the gains in performance make the added effort absolutely worth it. Improvements in performance from successful enterprise lean initiatives produce at least as much benefit as lean manufacturing initiatives.

LEARNING LEAN MANAGEMENT AND PRODUCTION: SUPPORTING ELEMENTS OF LEAN MANAGEMENT

Chapter 7

Learning Lean Management
The Sensei and Gemba Walks

The principal elements of the lean management system do not seem to be complex or difficult to understand. Yet they represent the shoals on which so many lean initiatives have run aground. Why?

Part of the answer involves discipline, certainly. But, part of that answer involves the process needed to learn how to do lean management and how to be a lean manager. This chapter focuses on one aspect of your own personal lean transformation: learning lean management. (Chapter 8 covers another aspect: leading a lean operation.) This chapter describes becoming apprenticed to a sensei (or lean teacher) and a principal method by which a sensei teaches: the gemba walk.

Your Sensei and "True North" Provide Direction

Lean is tricky, because it is so much more difficult than it seems. Reading about lean, attending workshops on lean, or participating in simulations are no substitute for hands that have experienced implementing lean—and firm hands at that! An effective sensei will be insistent and at times critical to the point of being at least mildly abrasive.

Most of us need a sensei to help us understand how to translate basic lean concepts into actual functioning applications. More than that, your sensei should also instill in his or her students the discipline needed to effectively sustain a lean conversion and have it improve consistently.

Toyota refers to "true north" as its ultimate direction for perfection in lean. It relies on its internal sensei to keep the company on that path, just like early travelers relied on the North Star, Polaris, to keep them headed in the right direction as they traversed unfamiliar territory. In a lean implementation, the sensei plays the role of Polaris. Working with a sensei is not like conventional training. Instead, it more closely resembles an internship or apprenticeship. In these models of teaching and learning, the student learns over time, through experience from applying concepts to actual live situations and carefully observing the consequences under the tutelage of the sensei.

The classic sensei is Socratic in approach, teaching by stretching the student's thinking and perceptions through questions that stimulate the student to consider entirely new possibilities. Students might consider questions such as:

- How can you tell what is normal in this area?
- What would you learn if you measured in smaller intervals of time?
- What is the team leader supposed to be doing in this situation?
- Why should you expect the team leader to know that?
- How could these expectations be made clearer?
- How do you know that the designated person carried out these posted procedures?
- How could someone know who was responsible for this task?
- How could you know these things with more certainty?

Some of the sensei's teaching is likely to be typical classroom instruction, especially early on when introducing the basic concepts of lean or of a particular technique or approach. To be effective, these sessions should be immediately translated to observation and application on the production floor, a destination to which the sensei will often appear impatient to return. Once the conventional training is over, sensei and student begin or resume *gemba* walking to reinforce what has been presented and to extend the lesson through extending the principles to situations encountered where people are doing actual work.

Think of your sensei as a personal trainer, one who sets expectations for you and then teaches, coaches, and prods you to be able to meet them. Can you learn lean production and lean management by yourself through study, application, and self-critique? Certainly you can. Perhaps more pertinent, however, is how long you have and how persuasive you can be with your peers and superiors as you work your way through the learning curve,

CASE STUDY: LEARNING TO SEE PROBLEMS, NOT JUST CORRECT THEM

In one case, I was working with a supervisor on basic 5S discipline in a welding department. Except for the weld tips themselves, nothing in the place had been cleaned since it opened many years earlier. You can imagine its condition: grime and dirt seeming to grow from every surface—horizontal and vertical, top and bottom. After a few weeks of pointing out several particularly dirty areas and talking about the benefits of discipline and order, it became clear that the supervisor was only cleaning up the specific spots we had looked at. I admonished him to "learn to see the dirt yourself!" He did, took initiative to get the entire area cleaned up, and needed no more coaching on this topic.

stumbling occasionally as anyone would with brand new ideas—in most cases, not long enough. This is a place where calling on outside expertise is well worth it, subject to all the caveats of working with external consultants.

In one important way, the sensei should be like any good consultant, recognizing the division of responsibility between client and professional advisor. That is, the sensei or consultant is responsible for teaching, giving advice, stimulating new thinking, and identifying new directions. The client always is responsible for decision making, that is, for whether and how to apply the advice of the teacher. In this relationship, the only decision the sensei makes is whether to continue working with the student, based on how the student follows through on commitments.

Gemba Walking

Gemba is roughly translated from the Japanese as the real place. In this sense, real refers to where the action is happening. To illustrate, Japanese television reporters covering the devastating 1995 earthquake in Kobe, Japan introduced themselves on-camera standing before a site in the quake zone as "reporting live from gemba in Kobe." If your focus were on improving customer service in a call center, gemba would be the call center floor and workstations. For manufacturing, gemba is the production floor. The idea of gemba is simple: go to the place, look at the process, talk with the people.

Gemba walks typically take place on a regularly scheduled basis, usually at one-week intervals. This is enough time to allow the student to digest the lesson and complete assignments the sensei gives, but short enough to maintain a sense of pace. In some cases, the assignment will be to develop an explanation for why something appears as it does and what an alternative might be. As the teaching and learning progress, the gemba walks shift to the sensei suggesting assignments for the student, and then following up on the next walk. In this way, gemba walks become another instance of accountability for bringing actual (what the student has been able to accomplish) in line with expected (the assignment from the sensei).

In these cases, gemba walks become a method for setting and following up on expectations. As the student begins to correctly interpret what the sensei points out, the sensei will make assignments to take action based on what the student has seen. Next, the sensei will expect the student to initiate similar action when encountering the same or similar circumstances in other areas.

Gemba Walking Teaches How to See in New Ways

Gemba walking, to be effective, begins at the top and works its way down the organization as those in higher positions learn enough to teach others. People in hierarchical organizations (which are, after all, most of us) respond to the requests, suggestions, and directives of their superiors. As the superior learns to ask for and teach how to apply the principles of lean management, the subordinate is likely to listen carefully, learn the new expectations, and learn how to comply.

Gemba walking is a practice with a definite tie to the expected versus actual theme in the lean management system. This explains the lean sensei's insistence on starting his or her regimen of gemba walks with either the CEO or the senior operations executive. When the person in the position of ultimate authority in an organization can teach lean principles, expects to see them applied, and is able to evaluate progress on sight, the chances for sustaining a lean initiative are much better than when the initiative starts somewhere in the middle.

The object of gemba walking is to teach the student to see through different eyes what he or she may have been looking at for an entire career. The alternative is for the student simply to follow the directions of the teacher to "do this" and "do that." Some, but usually not much, learning happens this way, and when the sensei departs he or she leaves no lasting transfer of knowledge.

The desired outcome is that the student himself or herself is learning to see where the principles of lean management can be applied. The importance of this is that, in most cases, each application of the principles is an invention derived to fit the unique characteristics of the situation at hand. Few lean applications are literally answers to be found in a book—even this one! As lean management novices become more skilled through gemba walks with their sensei, they gradually develop their own expertise as gemba walkers, teachers, and auditors of lean management. It then becomes their turn to gemba walk with their subordinates, teaching and helping them develop their own mastery of lean production and lean management.

Learning through gemba walking requires patience and tolerance for frustration. It is not fast. One of the main ways of learning is from experience as you work to make the corrections and refinements you find necessary (often prompted by your sensei) as you try new things. There is no good alternative to gemba walks as the method to learn lean management. That is because lean management is a mindset, and mindsets necessarily change and develop over time through personal experience. If that is the bad news, the good news is gemba walks are effective as a learning model, helping you gradually to establish a new, lean way of seeing and thinking. Six months of weekly gemba walks is on the low end of the period necessary to develop a lean approach to managing.

Focusing on process is essential for success in a lean operation. That focus must include the technical elements of lean and the elements of the lean management system. The components of these two aspects of lean—technical production and management systems—are often intertwined with each other. That means effective lean leaders need to be well versed in both sides of lean.

Table 7.1 shows some aspects of lean management that a gemba walk might focus on. Each item is discussed in detail in Chapters 3 through 11. The point here is that a gemba walk can focus on far more than the technical aspects of lean production. When you know what to look for, evidence for the presence or absence of a robust lean management system is everywhere on the production floor. Gemba walking, traditionally focused on the technical side of lean (is inventory being pushed or pulled; is standard work balanced to takt?), is indispensable in learning lean management and especially in maintaining it.

As leaders become proficient in the first several levels of lean, gemba walks are still useful for asking leaders to reflect on what they have done and learned, and for challenging them to go further. This is particularly applicable

Table 7.1 Looking for Lean Management

What You Should See	What People Should Know
Process Focus • Tracking charts show current actual vs. expected status for all processes, in-cycle and out-of-cycle. • Production-tracking charts initialed by supervisors at least twice daily. • Reasons for misses noted on tracking charts.	• How are you doing at hitting your production goals? • How can you tell if out-of-cycle and daily or weekly tasks are getting done as they should? • (Leaders) Is there a regular schedule for gemba walks in this area? What is it? What happens on a typical gemba walk?
Process Improvement • Top 3 to 5 reasons for misses documented and visible at cell/line, department, and value stream information boards. • Summary project plans (A-3s) for improvement posted and current at department and value stream information boards. • Employee suggestion system shows recent suggestions, current action on suggestions, and implemented suggestions with trend chart of numbers submitted and implemented. • A visual daily task assignment and accountability process is in use and current.	• What are the three biggest problems in this area? • How do you know these are the biggest problems? • Is any work being done on these problems? How can you tell? • Is there a regular method for operators to make suggestions for process improvements? What is it? • How can you tell your suggestions are listened to? • (For leaders) What improvement activity is going on in this department? • (Leaders) How do daily task assignments work here? Is there regular follow-up on assignments?
Leader Availability • Team leaders on the floor in their process area virtually all the time and available to operators. • Supervisors on the floor in their process area. • Response system to summon supervisors, team leader, others when needed.	• (Leaders) How many hours/day on average do you spend on the floor? • How do you contact your team leader when you need him or her right away? • How quickly is help available when the process is interrupted by a problem the team leader cannot fix?

Table 7.1 (continued)   **Looking for Lean Management**

What You Should See	What People Should Know
Labor Planning (at team boards) • Rotation path and starting assignments displayed. • Expected attendance chart up to date, displayed. • Qualification matrix up to date, displayed (including qualified out-of-zone operators).	• How can you tell who's supposed to be here on any given day? How can you tell when you have call-ins? • (Leaders) What do you do when there are call-ins? • How do you know how many people you need for a given rate of production? • Do you rotate jobs here? How do you know where you'll be working at the start of any given day? • How can you tell who's qualified to do which jobs in the area?
Standard Work • Operators and leaders have and are following their respective standardized work. • Standard work charts, complete with cycle times for in- and out-cycle work, are posted and clearly visible from operator workstations. • Leaders' standard work is displayed day by day for up to a week.	• Can you show me the standardized work for this station? Do people in this area follow standardized work? Does anyone ever monitor to see it's being followed? • (Leaders) What's your process for monitoring standardized work? How often do you monitor it? • (Leaders) Do you use standard work? Let's look at it for today.
Communication • Daily shift meeting agenda visible on the team info center. • Where applicable, info from other shifts is displayed in cell/line or department info board. • Team leaders', supervisors', value stream daily meetings occur.	• How often does your team meet as a group? Is it a regularly scheduled meeting or just once in a while? • (Leaders) How do you know what topics you'll cover in any given day's start-up meeting? • (Leaders) Do you lead or attend any daily meetings? What are they?

continued

Table 7.1 (continued) Looking for Lean Management

What You Should See	What People Should Know
Workplace Organization • Weekly 5S audit form and action items for the week are current, displayed at team info boards. • Cleaning routines and checklists visible, current. • TPM checklists current at each asset. • Clearly visible indicators of location and quantity for each object in the area. • Signage or identified addresses for tools, WIP and raw materials, reorder points and max quantities, kanban cards. • No clutter, dirt, or debris on floors, shelves, tops of cabinets, under racks and conveyors, etc. • All horizontal surfaces clean. • Cabinets, drawers labeled, contents match labels.	• How do you keep track of housekeeping in this area? Are there standards for housekeeping? • (Of any object) What's this? How can you tell where it's supposed to be? How many of them should be here? • How much material are you supposed to have in this location? How can you tell? • What are the reorder points for (any and all) materials? What's the process for reordering?
Working Buzzer to Buzzer • Work starts and stops on time.	• What times are breaks in this area? Are people usually back on time or are there usually stragglers?

in situations where leaders have led progress to a plateau and either do not know how to push further improvement or have become satisfied with the current state. Here, gemba walks are likely to encounter the bedrock of the batch production mindset. This is the view that for a production manager: "If it ain't broke, don't fix it." This runs counter to the lean principle in which perfection is the goal, and the related tenet that everyone in a lean system has two responsibilities: to run the business and to improve the business.

Being the Sensei: Gemba Walking Your Executives

A consistent question comes up in gatherings of internal lean consultants: how do we engage our executives?

CASE STUDY: HOW GEMBA WALKS CAN REVEAL OPPORTUNITIES FOR IMPROVEMENT

Illustrating this aspect of gemba is a case where a value stream manager had brought his area from chaos to stability and excellent performance. The area missed its daily production targets and pitch rhythm only when materials failed to arrive on time from outside suppliers. The leader was restless; he believed the area could improve further, but did not know what to do. We went on a gemba walk, looking for opportunity.

From the day the plant opened, parts were unloaded from the paint line into kit racks that held components for 10 units. The units could be up to 6 feet long and 4 feet wide, so the racks had to be big enough to hold the components safely. They were big, about 8 feet long by 4 feet high, heavy, and not easily maneuvered. Formerly, they were staged at two-person assembly benches where each unit was built complete from start to finish by the two-person team. Now, they fed an L-shaped assembly line. The painted parts held in the kit racks were hung on the paint line in groups of four units.

I asked the leader if the balance on his assembly process would improve if it were arranged in the classic U shape. "I can't do that; the racks wouldn't fit inside a U," he said, and then quickly realized the implications of cutting down the racks for tightening the footprint of his assembly line, bringing better balance to it, and improving its performance.

Many lean initiatives begin in the middle of an organization. A plant manager or production leader gets interested in lean, begins to experiment with lean applications, and sees dramatic improvement. The experiments expand and eventually attract the attention of executives. Based on these initial successes, the lean pioneers persuade the organization to launch a formal lean initiative, perhaps resourcing a plant or even corporate lean team, a kaizen promotion office, or similar structure.

Executive leadership does not have to do much out of the ordinary in these circumstances. To them, lean is another good results-producing idea from within the organization. The requests for resources are typically rather modest, especially if outside consultants are not involved. And even if they are, it is not unusual to bring in outside help to support a promising initiative when times are good, and especially when the senior levels of the company recognize a need for change.

What is not part of the typical deal, however, is executives committing to, or even recognizing the need to change their own management practices. As lean initiatives expand beyond manufacturing, the challenge of engaging executives grows more difficult, but the principles stay the same: find ways to develop executives' eyes for waste and eyes for flow.

My experience gemba walking in manufacturing was not immediately useful when I was asked to help bring lean to the company's office business processes. On gemba walks in the plants, it was easy to show excess inventory stacked up, or interruptions in production as operators waited for parts or looked for tools and fixtures, and areas that had not been cleaned in, well, in a long time. The differences with areas where lean applications had taken hold were obvious. The enthusiasm voiced by people from the floor who participated in the changes was striking, even inspiring. Gemba walking in manufacturing was a snap compared to office processes.

When you leave the factory floor and enter an office area, very little of the work process is visible. Yet, this was gemba in the office world, and it was here we needed to teach executives with little exposure to manufacturing to see lean and its potential. It was clear to us from the outset that an "eat your spinach" approach was not going to work with these executives. Nobody was holding them accountable for learning lean even though lean applications had transformed the manufacturing facilities. And, they all had important initiatives in their own areas. We needed to build the executives' engagement in lean by helping them learn to see, and then ask for, the benefits of lean applications in their own parts of the business.

Go to the Place, Look at the Process, Talk with the People

Executives typically have limited time and attention to spend on lean. We did not want to spend that time on conventional training, and neither did they. The question was how to make the most of the limited time they would give us. We realized the greatest impact in the office, just as in the factory, comes from going to the place, observing the process, and talking with the people. It makes lean come alive. Just as on the plant floor, the spontaneous testimony of the workers about the impact of lean changes they have been involved in has far more emotional impact and persuasiveness than what the lean team says. And, in the same way, a senior leader's presence in a production area—whether in a factory or office—has significant impact. When an executive comes to watch the process, learn about it in detail from the people, and discuss with them the lean project activities in an area, it adds credibility to the organization's commitment to lean. As executives learn lean and see lean's benefits in improved process execution and customer experience, as well as in improved results, the organization's commitment to lean is strengthened in a virtuous circle.

An effective approach (after a not-so-successful beginning; see the case study "A Process for Gemba Walking Executives") has been to ask for an hour of each senior executive's time for gemba walks. Sixty minutes, even as infrequently as every other month (though a more frequent schedule, up to weekly, is desirable) can make a significant impact when sustained over a year or more. We started the first of these newly designed gemba walks with a *brief* (while walking to the gemba site) overview of lean management as a closed loop system that sustains lean transformations and drives further improvement. We wanted to remind the execs of lean management, and to use it as a conceptual framework for the principles we would focus on in gemba walks. Keep in mind, the issues in progression of work in office processes are far less visible than in the plant, and so are the lean applications. We needed a framework to organize the observations from gemba and link them back to lean as an improvement process.

We structured each gemba walk around one of the lean management standards (modified for use in office processes; see Appendix A and B), repeating the basic standards—visual controls, standard accountability processes, and leader standard work—for several gemba walks. Our thinking was to build foundational understanding of the closed loop nature of lean management. We wanted to help the executives see the value of lean management and learn to ask on their own for its elements to sustain change and drive improvement. The goal was to develop a gemba walk process executives would feel comfortable in while being challenged to learn. We wanted an approach that would quickly build our executive clients' confidence as gemba walkers, and give them the sense of competence in filling this important aspect of their own role in sustaining the lean initiative.

Gemba Walking as a Structured, Repeatable Process

The lean management standards represent staff work. That is, we used a lean management standard as the agenda, structure, and focus for each gemba walk. The standard helped the leader feel prepared; comfortable, confident,

CASE STUDY: A PROCESS FOR GEMBA WALKING EXECUTIVES

After significant and sustained successes with lean applications in manufacturing, the company decided to establish an office lean initiative. This decision was strongly supported by the senior operations VP, who had learned lean by gemba walking with the internal lean team after coming to his manufacturing assignment. He had taken on the role of student for an hour a week while he developed his eyes for flow and eyes for waste. He was an effective champion for lean in manufacturing. As we began bringing lean into the office side of the business, he supported the practice of executive gemba walks from which he had benefited.

Despite his support, the monthly gemba walks with executives responsible for finance, HR, IT, sales, marketing, order management, and product development were running out of steam. We briefed the executives on the lean projects in the areas we took them to see, but the format was not working for them. Even with the early lean office visual controls, there was not that much to see in the work itself. And, despite the success of the lean projects, the executives were not getting that much out of "showing the flag" in the lean project areas and hearing the presentations of the teams involved in the projects. After about a year, we found our executives were cancelling their gemba walks with us at a rate of 50 percent. We needed a different approach!

On reflection, we concluded our gemba walk format put the executives in too passive a role. These are competitive and action-oriented people with very limited time. We decided we needed a gemba walk process that challenged them, engaged them in working to understand what they were seeing, and equipped them with principles, knowledge, and tools they could use themselves. We needed them to learn for themselves how lean management actually works to drive improvement.

Our new approach was to structure the gemba walks in a repeatable, predictable way that included the challenge to compare the actual practices they observed in gemba to written standards for lean management implementation. It turned out that a quick review of the diagnostic questions in the standard on the way to the gemba site was enough preparation for the executives. This approach primed them to ask questions and make observations that provided the basis for rating the area's status on the lean dimension, and comparing their rating with ours. The effects we saw among the executives were: challenges met, measurements completed, and, more subtly, lean lessons learned.

Now, it is not uncommon for an executive to ask on the way to the gemba walk, "What standard are we using today?" The cancelled executive gemba walks have fallen from 50 percent to zero; now when schedules change, the walks get rescheduled. Most importantly, executives who would be lost in a factory environment now expect to see lean applications in their transactional and development processes, and they are increasingly able to ask and even to teach how lean principles might be applied.

and competent. We were already asking our executives to step out of their comfort zones; we did not want them to experience embarrassment. Remember, it is the rare executive who is willing to step completely into the role of student, of novice. Using the standards helped by providing a consistent format with which our executive clients became familiar and comfortable. This enabled them to focus on the gemba "lesson" without the earlier distraction of a different structure or approach every gemba walk.

The diagnostic questions in the standards prepared the executive for what to look for and ask about in gemba to assess specific aspects of the lean production and lean management implementations. Having questions and tips for observations enabled the executives to engage in active learning and draw conclusions experientially, for themselves. We found this to be a much more impactful and effective learning experience than hearing us yammering at them about lean, or receiving yet another presentation.

Taken together, this format helps develop executives' trust that in gemba walks, their most precious commodity, their time, will be organized to add value and advance their ability to lead change and improvement. The observed ratings for each standard provide executives with a measurement tool to compare progress on lean implementation within an area, as well as a way to compare lean status across different areas, divisions, and locations. Once an executive mastered gemba walking the three basic elements of lean management, the lean team was able to expand the focus to other lean management standards. For example, if a lean project area had neglected problem solving in response to repeated process misses, we would introduce the problem solving standard for an executive's next gemba walk, as in the case study "Developing Executives' Eyes for Waste."

CASE STUDY: DEVELOPING EXECUTIVES' EYES FOR WASTE

The order management department had been working at lean improvements for two years, but the department director and managers resisted implementing visual controls. Finally, they created something formatted like an accountability board on which customer service reps posted problems. When they had an order that went on hold for any reason, the reps recorded the problem on a sticky note, put it next to their name on the date the problem occurred, and left it there until it was resolved. The boards were exposing problems; good! However, once the problem situation was resolved and the order released from hold, no action was being taken to understand the underlying causes of the problems or to follow up in any way. When we asked the manager in the area what happened with the accumulated sticky notes, she told us she was saving them and that "eventually they will be compiled." This went on for some time.

As we gemba walked in the area, we asked the order management director about problem solving. He gestured around the floor, saying, "Everyone here is a problem solver!" As we talked with him, we observed that the same kinds of problems occurred over and over. The service reps did a good job of minimizing the impact of problems on customers, but they left the root causes undisturbed.

We brought each of our senior executive lean steering team members to gemba walk the order management visual boards. The executives were by now familiar with visual controls. On these walks, we handed the executives the lean management standard for root cause problem solving. On the gemba walks, the executives acknowledged and reinforced the manager's and director's consistent use of the boards, but also asked what happened with the information from the sticky notes once the immediate problems were cleared up and the orders released from hold.

In a conversation with the VP responsible for the order management area shortly after this series of gemba walks, she told us Pareto charts of problems that had caused orders to go on hold were now being brought to her weekly accountability meeting and assigned for cause analysis and eventual root cause corrective action. The leaders in the order management area had not just gotten the message to do something, they had actually been taught the next steps by the questions they had been asked by the gemba walking executives, all but one of whom was from a different sector of the business.

Summary: Learning Lean Management by Being a Sensei's Apprentice

This chapter concentrated on two aspects of developing and maintaining focus on process. The first involves learning the principles of lean yourself by stepping into the role of student, engaging a lean sensei to teach you the principles and guide you through initial applications. This will happen principally through your gemba walks with the sensei. Before you can teach others, you must develop an initial level of mastery of lean concepts and learn to see where and how to apply them.

Second, you become the teacher through gemba walks with those who report to you, often as you continue to learn from your sensei. Your gemba walking will be most effective if you are in a position of authority in your organization. In this respect, lean is no different than many other things. For any initiative to be successful and lasting, lean included, it must be understood and supported on the organization's own terms. This invariably means lean must flow down through the organization's hierarchy.

Sometimes, a lean advocate somewhere in operations can drive implementation far enough to produce success that gets the attention and then support from the top. Leading from the middle is always a risky proposition. If the boss states agreement with the lean direction you are pursuing, but consistently directs you to act contrary to the principles, well, you know the rest. Lean will not prosper in your setting and will likely join the list of things "...we tried once, but it didn't work here." When executive leadership endorses and embraces undertaking a lean journey, you have a better chance for success. Bear in mind, you may need to take action to engage senior executives in the lean initiative. A structured gemba walk process, even without explicit master-apprentice roles, is an effective approach.

An early test of commitment from the top will be the executive's willingness to enter the role of apprentice to learn from the sensei. Consider the CEO or head of operations who has learned more about lean than plant managers and is able to gemba walk them in their territory. When the executive points out opportunities, teaches the principles, and makes assignments to act on them, it provides an enormous boost to the organization's motivation to begin learning and applying lean principles.

So, at its most effective, gemba walking cascades down through the organization, teaching lean principles and establishing expectations for acting on them.

Lean management is, as much as anything, a way of thinking. A paradox is that this way of thinking arises from new ways of acting, giving credence to the saying: "You can act your way into a new way of thinking faster than you can think your way into a new way of acting." Learning, teaching, documenting, and following up on specific expectations for focus on process are the first steps in implementing lean management and developing a lean mindset.

Chapter 8

Leading a Lean Operation

Leadership is a topic that applies more broadly than lean management, to be sure. It is regularly discussed whenever the subject is organizational change. A lean conversion initiative is properly and usefully thought of as this kind of change, as well as a change in the technical ins and outs of production systems. That is because good engineering does not by itself make for effective change, not by a long shot. Without effective leadership, most large-scale changes in systems do not go well and do not perform up to advertised expectations.

This is emphatically true for lean conversions because, as I have suggested, a lean conversion requires profound changes in thinking and deeply established habits. Without determined leaders and effective leadership, no conversion project is likely to live up to what was hoped for it. For that reason, this chapter touches on nine dimensions of leadership that are needed both for leading an effective lean conversion project, and in subtly but importantly different ways, for leading an ongoing lean operation.

Nine Leadership Behaviors to Learn

Successful leaders are those who behave in particular ways. In other words, success is based on what you do, not on who you are. That is fortunate, because for most of us, it is too late to be born a leader! Behavior can be learned and unlearned. Included here are how you respond to interruptions in production, the way you arrive at conclusions, and what you ask people to pay attention to. Table 8.1 lists and briefly describes these nine

Table 8.1 Dimensions of Lean Leadership

Attribute	For Project Implementation	For Ongoing Operations
Passion for lean	1. Passionate about the potential for lean to make the enterprise more successful and work more fulfilling for all involved.	1. Same as Project Implementation, plus: 2. Willing to make personal changes in one's own work, including using standardized work for his or her own position.
Disciplined adherence to process—accountability	1. Sets expectations, regularly uses a process to track and follow up on actual accomplishment of assigned tasks.	1. Same as Project Implementation, plus: 2. Exhibits intense commitment to focus on explicitly defining processes and disciplined adherence to them.
Project management orientation	1. Prior experience in successfully implemented projects. 2. Uses a defined process to track performance and completion of task assignments. 3. Identifies corrective action where necessary and follows up on it.	1. Able to identify needed changes based on daily process data and assign small-bite daily tasks leading to successful implementation of the changes. 2. Uses explicitly defined visual processes to track and follow up assignments and take appropriate corrective action.
Lean thinking	1. Understands lean concepts. 2. Has had experience applying lean concepts. 3. Talks about and promotes a lean future state. 4. Finds ways to apply and illustrate lean concepts in daily project work processes.	1. Serious about ongoing improvement based on a goal of perfection. 2. Sees with "kaizen eyes." 3. Holds and coaches a root-cause orientation to corrective action. 4. Has learned process improvement/problem solving methods; able to personally lead lean process improvement.

Table 8.1 (continued)   Dimensions of Lean Leadership

Attribute	For Project Implementation	For Ongoing Operations
Ownership	1. Thinks and talks about the area as his or hers to lead, set direction for, change, and improve.	1. Same as Project Implementation, plus: 2. Eager to empower others in the area through structured ways to elicit and implement their ideas. 3. Acknowledges and celebrates improvements made by others at all levels.
Tension between applied and technical	1. Understands the need to sweat the details, as well as to get things done. 2. Willing to listen to technical experts and consider their advice in planning for the implementation.	1. Understands and respects the details behind elements of lean, such as flow, pull, standardized work, etc. 2. Actively supports steps to upgrade performance and expose previously hidden impediments. 3. Takes a "what can we do today" orientation to making change happen steadily, step by step.
Balanced commitment to production and management systems	1. History of effective give and take with people and ideas. 2. Evidence of process focus beyond a "hit the numbers" approach to management. 3. Eager for greater participation by production people as well as others.	1. Personally treats process focus as crucial to the area's success; is able to see waste and opportunity even in leaner processes. 2. Insists on compliance with requirements for visually tracking process performance and execution. 3. Insists on analysis and appropriate, timely action on impediments to normal operation of processes.

continued

Table 8.1 (continued)   Dimensions of Lean Leadership

Attribute	For Project Implementation	For Ongoing Operations
Effective relations with support groups	1. History of getting things done with support from operations support groups such as engineering, quality, production control, safety, finance, HR.	1. Understands roles, responsibilities, and expertise of support groups. 2. Incorporates support groups appropriately in plans for improvement and responses to problems. 3. Makes expectations explicit for support group performance in support of production processes.
Measure process separately from results	1. Breaks the project into small steps with due dates. 2. Frequently assesses and verifies completion status. 3. Acts to resolve problems right away as they come up.	1. Creates measures to frequently document process performance and misses. 2. Establishes regular, frequent review of process misses and trends over time. 3. Teaches and emphasizes cause analysis, root cause solutions, and connections with improved performance.

dimensions of leadership that we have found important in making lean conversion projects and ongoing lean operations successful.

Leading a lean conversion project differs in significant aspects from leading an ongoing lean operation, one that has already been converted or that started as a greenfield. The differences between them are discussed in turn, contrasting what is needed to successfully lead a conversion project with what is needed to successfully lead an ongoing lean operation.

Attribute Number 1: Passion for Lean

It is probably true that passion is something more than mere behavior that you simply can do. It can manifest in many ways, however, in which charisma or force of personality is *not* required. Think of the people some might call "geeks." A geek might be one seriously committed to a pursuit, who talks about it often in terms of possibilities that can make the future look better than the present, draws connections about their subject and the external circumstances facing him or her or the group. That is someone, you could say, who has a passion, whether for long-distance running, religion, politics, or even lean production. Right?

In passion for lean, an important facet involves comparing lean with the alternative. For example, Toyota in 2004 is reported as being seriously concerned about what it describes as a looming challenge from China. It uses that as motivation to improve further and further; this in a company whose market capitalization exceeds that of all its North American competitors combined. Fifty years ago, Toyota was motivated by the threat they perceived from American manufacturers taking over their domestic market.

It is easier to be passionate and to enlist others when you have a case for change based on real external factors that are affecting or likely to affect your enterprise. There is something about a fight for survival or for your place in the market that is more likely to arouse passion than merely a drive for more increased value for the shareholders or bigger bonuses for the executives.

Enthusiasm, intensity about a subject, willingness to engage others on their terms with respect to the threats and possibilities, deep knowledge about the subject, examples from one's own experience—all of these are marks of passion. These are attributes that can be studied, learned, and acquired over time. They grow from believing that there must be a better way for your organization to survive and prosper in a competitive world. That is what my own personal experience has been with lean. I'll bet it has been your experience with lean or other things that have brought you to this point. That is why I contend that lean leaders can be made. I doubt anybody, even Taiichi Ohno, was born "lean." Ohno had to start his journey by studying Henry Ford!

Willingness to Make Personal Change

The best leaders of lean operations I have known are also the ones who have recognized that the methods they insist on others using are also ones they themselves adopt. A principal difference between just leading projects, compared with leading lean operations, is that leaders of ongoing operations have more, and more meaningful, opportunities to take the step of personally adapting themselves to a leaner mode of operating.

I have known advocates of lean who have labeled and taped-off spots on their desks for stapler, phone, and coffee cup, and some who label their inbox tray "WIP" and put a Post-it® on a page near the end of their current pad of paper to signal the reorder point. But perhaps the clearest and most persuasive example of this involves standardized work for leaders (see Chapter 3). Part of this is simply leading by example. Operators will often complain about having to follow standardized work when it is first introduced. When a team leader, supervisor, value stream manager, or plant manager can pull out his or her standardized work for that day and compare notes, it makes a powerful statement. "I use this so I don't forget to cover each of the departmental boards each day, just like standard work in a workstation can prevent assemblers from missing a step that might send a flawed product to one of our customers." That is a lot more persuasive than a statement that in effect says, "Because I have the authority, I'm telling you to follow standardized work." Beyond that, of course, is that a value stream manager who follows his or her standardized work will be far less likely to miss covering each of the departmental boards every day! The same principle—standardized, explicit expectations that help actual performance meet what was expected—is at work in both cases. The passionately committed leader recognizes that and makes the personal change to adopt new, leaner ways.

Attribute Number 2: Disciplined Adherence to Process—Accountability

Setting clear expectations and using a regular process to track completion is crucial for those leading projects to design and implement lean production. Establishing accountability to task assignments and schedules is one of the basics in effective project management. The analogous skill in managing an ongoing lean operation also involves establishing accountability, but in a much more dynamic, live production environment. Planning and defining tasks is still important, but must happen more quickly. These steps are guided by an overriding principle: integrity of processes. A project team has a finite, definable task and at least some time for investigation and analysis. In an ongoing lean operation, the lean leader's focus on his or her processes is what drives much of the accountability.

This process focus is a daily vigilance that begins with what can appear to be an obsession to explicitly define every last process in the leader's area of responsibility. These process definitions typically start with an applicable form of standardized work, for a production line, for example. Hourly or more frequently tracking and recording production versus goal tells whether the standard is being met, and if not, what appeared

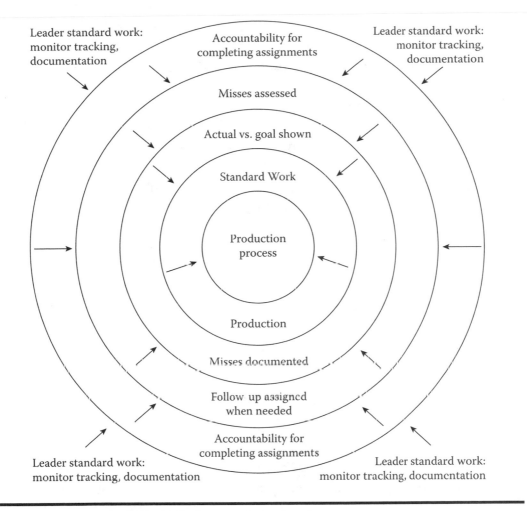

Figure 8.1   Example of multiple layers reinforcing focus on process.

to interfere. That is a process as well. So is a third process, by which follow-up on reasons for missed takt or pitch cycles is regularly assigned in the daily accountability process three-tier meetings. And so is the process to check for completion of assignments on their due dates. That is four levels of definition for a single process. And this does not consider leader standard work as a fifth process to guarantee each of the four steps just listed! See Figure 8.1 for a graphic depiction of this example of a set of reinforcing processes.

In lean management, virtually all processes have initial definitions and documentation. In addition, for each there are secondary processes to verify the initial process was executed, and often further follow up or verification processes. The periodic gemba walk of the plant manager by the operations VP is an example of the secondary verification process. The standard work of the leaders from value stream manager down through team leader and the related procedures extend the verification. The idea is to guarantee, as far as is humanly possible, the integrity of the production process, not simply to set it up and hope it all works as planned.

In many ways, adherence to processes is like the discipline of redundant quality checks in successive workstations in an assembly line. Standardized work in most stations begins with checking a critical aspect of the work elements performed in the previous station. It is the leader's role to establish this climate of discipline in definition and follow-up in which the norm is accountability for faithfully executing the processes.

Attribute Number 3: Project Management Orientation

The necessity for effective project management skills when leading an implementation project hardly needs much comment. Regularly using a well-defined process to follow up for accountability on task assignments is important in a project environment as well as in ongoing operations. The ability to think in terms of work breakdown structures is another project management practice that translates into a daily operating environment. A work breakdown structure is nothing more than the step-by-step sequence of subtasks that, when assigned and completed in sequence, result in completion of a single larger task. Work breakdown analysis is just another way of talking about detailed step-by-step planning.

What is different in an ongoing operation is that the analysis and planning often happens in a stand-up meeting on the floor as the leader is scrutinizing yesterday's performance-tracking charts and other measures of process effectiveness or interruption. The leader, as he or she examines the reasons for missed takt or pitch cycles needs to be able to perform analysis quickly, which might be as simple as using the five whys (a basic method of cause analysis; see the Glossary for a more detailed definition). Next, he or she must be able to identify the initial steps to take, to further understand the cause, put a countermeasure in place, or initiate corrective action. Then, the leader needs to make an assignment generally of not more than a day's duration for a staff member or support group representative to take the appropriate action.

This is very much like performing a work breakdown analysis except that it happens quickly, almost but not quite on the fly, and often with people who have not been exposed to this kind of thinking because they have not been involved in managing projects. That is especially likely to be the case with floor supervisors and team leaders who have come up through the ranks. Over time, a leader using this process to address everyday interruptions, anomalies, and problems in the production environment can teach this step-by-step planful approach to his or her direct reports. For example, if a value stream manager assigned a department supervisor the task of updating standardized work and rebalancing a flow cell when both the tasks and the process were new to the supervisor, the odds of success would be low. Consider this alternative:

- First, the value stream manager introduces the task, then he or she breaks it into constituent parts, such as updating standard work and updating the operator balance chart one position at a time.
- The value stream manager makes the tasks into daily assignments and reviews each one daily as part of the third-tier accountability meeting.
- Next, the leader does the same with the tasks needed to rebalance the cell.
- By the time the work is done, the supervisor has valuable hands-on experience with a basic tool in designing flow processes and has learned, or at least been exposed to, a work breakdown structure to get a complex piece of work done a manageable step at a time.

These project management tools represent valuable skills for an organization to impart to those in junior leadership positions. Value stream managers who have more formal experience in leading and managing projects are in a much better position to do this kind of teaching by example than those who have not.

Managing daily task assignments using visual controls is discussed in detail in the daily accountability three-tier meeting structure and process in Chapter 5. To summarize that process here, the meeting leader writes the task assignment on a Post-it® note. The leader places the note on a names-by-dates matrix in the square that corresponds to the due date for the assigned individual to report on task completion. The names, depending on the level of the meeting, are those of supervisors and support group representatives (tier three), or of team leaders (tier two). Assignments are made, depending on the level of the meeting, by the value stream manager or by the department supervisor. Completed tasks are color coded green, overdue tasks are coded red.

The matrix is part of a value stream or department information center, a visual display and stand-up meeting place located on the floor in the production area. This visual assignment and tracking method highlights accountability for completing daily assignments.

Attribute Number 4: Lean Thinking

Lean thinking in an implementation project is like being a practical dreamer. A project leader needs to balance what we might do in an ideal future state compared to what we can actually accomplish given the scope, schedule, and budget for the project. Lean thinking in an ongoing operation takes a different tack based on an understanding that lean is fundamentally an improvement system. In this respect, lean thinking in the leader of an ongoing lean operation is derived from the goal of attaining perfection in the operating system. This is something of a curse, a sort of "Princess and the Pea" situation where, in the leader's eyes, things are never good enough and improvement is always needed. The leader needs to see where improvement can be made even if he or she cannot say exactly what the improvement should be. That, after all, usually requires the involvement of those with the deepest knowledge of the process in question, those who work in or with it every day. Nevertheless, if the leader has "kaizen eyes," always seeing something that might be improved, the rest of his or her organization will develop the same habits of perception if only to keep a step ahead of the boss! (See the case study "Taking Lean to the Next Level").

Lean Thinking Looks for the Sources of Problems

A lean thinker welcomes (if not joyfully) the appearance of interruptions, anomalies, and problems in his or her processes as opportunities to understand and eliminate sources of variation and disruption. This root cause orientation to corrective action is a powerful engine in driving continuous, lasting improvement. After all, continuous improvement focused on the same set of recurring problems is not exactly what lean thinking is all about! Instead, a lean thinker's version of corrective action is aimed at uprooting the sources of problems so they never appear again. A lean leader's capabilities should include being able to lead process improvement and problem solving activities as an example to the organization and as a teacher and coach for these important tools and ways of thinking.

Attribute Number 5: Ownership

Ownership as an attribute of a lean leader actually has more to do with enabling and celebrating the contributions of others to progress in the area. That is, a lean "owner" definitely is responsible for setting and reinforcing

---

CASE STUDY: TAKING LEAN TO THE NEXT LEVEL

A case illustrating this involves the supervisor described in the section on job-by-job tracking in Chapter 4 ("Make Sure Your Employees Know the Charts Are Not Micromanaging Them"). His fabrication area had come to run smoothly, in part because of the use of job-by-job tracking. Through its use by the operators in the area, the most frequently occurring sources of interruption had been eliminated. The supervisor was not satisfied, and assigned the fabrication team leader the task of Pareto-charting the sources of interruption that remained after the initial clean up had taken place. This was painstaking work, but there were clearly a few things that had moved into the position of most troublesome and the leader was determined to find and eliminate them.

---

direction in the area, just as the leader of a lean conversion does. The lean leader of an ongoing operation sets direction at a high level. He or she then creates conditions and specific structures and processes through which those in the area can participate in making changes that bring the area closer to the overall vision and direction. In this regard, ownership is broadly analo gous to presiding over a democratic process. The principles of lean in this case will be scrupulously observed. The specifics of which changes are made will depend in considerable part on the ideas that come from the staff and from the floor. In other words, the "owner" does not dictate what changes will be made, rather he or she acts to teach and challenge others to develop their own suggestions for how best to move in the established direction.

The examples in the case "Taking Control of Improvements" are the kinds of simple but creative things you can expect when the owner of an area sets the conditions for those who work in it to feel free to make changes for the better.

Attribute Number 6: Tension between Applied and Technical Details

A value stream leader from a traditional production background might be tempted to leave the technical details to the "experts," the engineers or local lean resources. That is, a traditional leader might not take the time to learn and understand machine balance charts and the implications for shrinking machine *changeover* times to reduce inventory quantities in a supermarket. Failure to appreciate the tension between the applied and technical poles in a situation like this can lead to commands simply to "Cut inventory by

25 percent." In a system on the lean journey, this is a sure-fire recipe for widespread stockouts, one I have seen throw a system into weeks of chaos.

These are technical details that lean leaders need to respect and be familiar with. It is true that there is a certain "just do it" mentality in the lean drive to learn from action. It is also true that process integrity and performance can be compromised unnecessarily by a leader's failure to understand how lean principles translate into well-defined capacities, replenishment times, and the like. It is true; lean is not rocket science. It is also true that you cannot cheat physics: cutting inventory without reducing changeovers can easily result in stockouts; taking people out of a line carefully balanced to takt time and asking the rest to "work faster" will likely result in falling short of the day's production requirements or incurring unplanned overtime, not to mention causing resentment and poisoning the reputation of lean.

It is one thing when because of specific conditions a leader deliberately decides to take these kinds of actions with full realization of the likely consequences. It is an entirely different thing when the outcomes surprise a leader who has not learned how lean works from the inside out.

At the same time, lean leaders are most certainly in the business of taking risks. That is the essence of the drive for improvement. Lean improvements usually involve reducing some form of *non-value-adding activity* or resource deployment: reducing times for *setup and changeover*; reducing floor space, inventory, or queue; rebalancing a line to run at takt instead of a fraction of takt; moving people out of a process, linking previously separate processes, or other measures. When they do these things, the leaders deliberately stress the lean system and expose its weaknesses. Armed with this information, they can set out to shore up the weak areas and stabilize the system at a new, higher level of performance. A leader cannot know what will go awry when these cushions are reduced or removed. For that reason, only one of these actions should be taken at a time, in part to isolate the cause of any resulting disruption, and in part to mitigate the risk to the system's ability to deliver for its customers.

CASE STUDY: TAKING CONTROL OF IMPROVEMENTS

There will be plenty of instances where the leader-owner will have to assert the right to interpret what it means to be consistent with the principles. For example, one value stream sent separate schedules to work centers that happened to be lined up in the order of the production process. The value stream manager called this a pull system. He labeled as a supermarket the areas where the WIP and overstock accumulated between work centers. He referred to the expediters who sorted and picked through the stock as *waterspiders*.

This is a clear instance of where a lean owner (in this case, the plant manager), prompted by his lean sensei, asserted his owner's prerogative. He helped the value stream leader better understand the application of lean principles and the difference between a push system (no matter how sophisticated the scheduling algorithm) and a Type B sequenced pull kanban system.

By contrast, you want to see examples where people have taken the teaching and general direction of the owner—for example: "Flow where you can, pull where you can't, and never push!" and create something entirely new that solves a problem or improves a process in a way nobody, certainly not the lean owner, had thought of. When the owner has established the right conditions, there will be many of these instances.

Two further cases illustrate the creativity possible when ownership involves the opportunity to share responsibility for improvement.

One involved a series of small welding cells in a metal fabrication area. It was difficult to tell the status of the cells by looking because nearly opaque weld curtains shielded them. The team leader used dowels to make simple flag poles extending out at a 45° angle from the top of the rods holding the curtains. If the green flag is at the top of the pole, the cell is running, red at the top means trouble, red and green even with each other in the middle means the cell is idle.

In the second case, the TPM facilitator in a machine area devised a simple method for documenting the daily tasks at each machine and at the same time visually indicating the status—completed or not. He took black-and-white and color photos of each task, such as checking a transport belt's tension. He annotated the photos to show the particulars of each task and then glued the black-and-white photos to the side of the machines' control panels. He put the color photos in magnet-backed, rigid plastic picture holders such as you might find on a refrigerator door at home, holding pictures of family or friends. He put the color photos on top of the black and whites under a header label that read: "Daily Tasks." When the operator completed the task, he or she moved the color photo off of the black and white, placing it under a column header label that read "Complete." At the end of the day, the team leader moved the color photos back onto the black and whites and checked off a log sheet indicating the task had been done.

Finally, lean leaders look at every day as an opportunity to move toward better performance. A simple but powerful manifestation of this is the question: "What can we do today?" when considering one or another approach to solving a problem or making an improvement. Analysis and understanding the mechanics of lean are important to be sure, but the lean leader sets the tone for action, even if for small steps. In this mode of leadership, it is often better to act rather than taking another day of analysis and inaction. Weigh the realistic risks (as opposed to doomsday fears) of course, but think of the step as an experiment, an actual rather than theoretical analysis, testing the proposition being considered. Lean is in many ways an everyday version of experiential learning, sometimes confirming what you anticipated, sometimes surprising you, and sometimes doing both simultaneously. Experience is really the only way to learn what lean really is; your actions provide the classroom in which the lessons are given.

Attribute Number 7: Balance between Production and Management Systems

Leaders in a lean conversion project typically and appropriately focus most of their attention on the design details of the physical production system, and rightly so. It is up to the leader of an ongoing lean operation to establish the lean management system that sustains and extends the gains from the *technical lean implementation*. Of course, if the lean project leader also happens to be the leader who will run the area once the implementation is complete (a practice I definitely recommend), he or she will benefit from thinking about elements of the management system during the project phase.

In too many cases, the technical details continue to rivet the focus of the leader even after implementation of the technical design. This is a frequent cause of failure of the implementation to deliver on its promises, a cause far more common than technical miscalculation. The leader must not consider the job "done" when implementation of the technical design is complete. Instead, an effective lean operations leader continues to look for and invariably see waste and thus opportunity in even the newly implemented processes. When the leader engages in constructive critique of his or her own work and focuses on opportunities for improvement, he or she sets a tone for the orientation to continuous improvement to take root and spread.

As important, the lean operations leader brings an intense focus on process, specifically treating process focus as a crucial element in the lean area's success. This focus includes personally following up on requirements for maintaining visual process controls for performance and execution:

■ Are hour-by-hour or pitch-tracking charts being completed in a timely manner or in batch mode at the end of the day?

■ Can team leaders and supervisors speak knowledgeably about the flow interrupters or other process disruptions recorded on the charts?

■ Are the reasons for misses clear and specific enough to act as a basis for moving to the next steps?

■ Are controls in place for *noncyclical processes* such as weekly 5S audits, operator-based maintenance tasks, periodic scheduled maintenance activities?

■ Are controls in place between processes, particularly the "re" processes: rework, reorder, refinish?

The visual controls and focus on process and reasons for abnormal operation will yield a trove of data on how a lean area is working and the instances when it fails. Maintaining the visuals and tracking tools is work for many people. When they see their work taken seriously, used as the basis for analysis and problem solving, and when problems get fixed and interruptions are eliminated, it makes all the effort of the new routine worthwhile. So, the data must be analyzed, ideally involving to whatever degree feasible the people who generated and recorded the data. The analysis needs to entail using the smallest tool for the job (many problems do not require a designed experiment, for example, where a carefully conducted Five Whys? will do). Most important, the analysis needs to result in action. Indeed, the maxim from Kurt Lewin: "No action without data; no data without action!" applies here.

This is a lot for a lean leader to keep up with. When the leader recognizes that his or her job is to act as the guarantor of the integrity of the processes in his or her area, it becomes clear that this is the new work for a lean leader. There is no delegating the task of personally establishing the importance of process focus in a newly established lean operation. Over a period of years this kind of follow up can become less frequent, but it never goes away.

Attribute Number 8: Effective Relations with Support Groups

A lean operation is a finely balanced system. All of its component parts must operate effectively for the whole to succeed. Manufacturing is an important part in the equation, but not the only part. For example, here are some other considerations:

- What does it matter if manufacturing has reduced the time it takes to change over from making one model to the next if the equipment involved breaks down on a random, frequent basis?
- What benefit is there from a well-balanced, smoothly flowing assembly operation if the purchased parts are constantly out of stock?
- How significant will be the impact on morale from a well-run suggestion system if the safety of those in the area is not given the highest priority?
- What will be the benefit of a system for frequent *rotation* among workstations if HR policies have not been changed to reflect this requirement?
- What is the point in establishing visual pull systems if accounting still insists on recording transactions every time inventory is moved?

Clearly, support groups—production control, engineering, maintenance, human resources, quality, safety, accounting—need to be part of the picture in a well-functioning lean operation. The lean leader needs to think of them as resources, not as convenient repositories of blame for the system's shortcomings. They need to be incorporated into the daily life of the area, involved in problem solving and improvement plans and activities. A diversity of perspectives and resources is needed for a finely tuned lean system to run smoothly and to recover from interruptions. Support groups can bring much of both to a lean operation.

Not only should these contributions by support groups be welcomed by the lean manufacturing leader, he or she should be able to expect them. After all, it is a fair question to ask, what better way for support groups to deploy their resources than in support of the lean production process? For this reason, most support groups are expected at the daily value stream meetings, and expected to carry out tasks assigned to them by the lean leader in response to problems reflected in the performance-tracking charts or opportunities for improvement.

Manufacturing and the support groups in a lean operation need each other too much and too intensely to be able to afford the finger pointing and isolationism that were possible in a batch-and-queue world. Typically, it behooves manufacturing to take the first steps, inviting the support groups into the lean circle. It is not unusual for manufacturing to be asked to follow up with training in lean tools and techniques for the support groups, since it is also not unusual for manufacturing to have started off on the lean journey alone.

Attribute Number 9: Don't Confuse Measures of Process with Measures of Results

Leading a lean conversion project is in many ways an exercise in holding team members accountable for producing the results as documented and anticipated in the project plan. Good project management practices include frequently verifying that intermediate step-by-step tasks have been completed. When small steps run behind schedule, the project manager has the information to intervene in the early stages of a developing problem. The goal is to head off problems when they are still small, preventing them from growing large enough to threaten overall project schedule and budget performance.

In the world of project management, close monitoring of day-to-day, step-by-step progress is the equivalent of lean's emphasis on frequent focus on process. Understand your problems as quickly as possible so you can act to eliminate their causes and the threat to expected production. Those new to lean are often shocked at the emphasis on bringing problems to light, compared to the common conventional practice of covering problems and burying the explanation. Lean thinkers, as Shingo observed, regard interruptions and breakdowns as nuggets to be mined for clues to the best next places to focus on improvement. Put another way: take care of your process, and your process will take care of you and produce the results you expect.

CASE STUDY: RESULTS-ONLY FOCUS CORRUPTS PROCESS MEASURES

In a visit to a plant said to be far along the lean and lean management journey, I was surprised to see "pitch attainment" on the agenda for its twice-daily production meetings. I was more surprised to learn the goal for this measure was 95 percent for each of the plant's four value streams. Pitch for each value stream was set at 30 minutes; that is, the actual versus expected number of units produced was measured every 30 minutes. For an eight-hour shift, 95 percent meant 15 of 16 pitches meeting expected production.

Going into this plant, my understanding of pitch measurement was straightforward. Start with a production-tracking chart based on takt time or another measure for expected pace of production. Using the tracking chart, monitor production and record the health of the process by documenting each instance of problems such as flow interruptions, process misses, and system breakdowns. Then, through a standard accountability process, assign tasks first to understand the root cause of the problems, and then to eliminate them. (In this plant, the only production visual controls were in assembly areas, itself a puzzlingly incomplete implementation of visuals.)

So, the expected target of 95-percent pitch, and the label "pitch attainment" seemed odd to me. I gemba walked later that day with an engineer from the plant lean team. I was interested in the visual controls the plant was using, so we looked closely at value stream information boards, then moved on to the production-tracking chart in the assembly area of one of the value streams.

This was a mixed model value stream producing two kinds of units, freestanding and wall-mounted. Takt time and pitch were the same for each type of unit: 60-second takt and 30-minute pitch, for 30 units every 30 minutes. Assembly alternated every 30 minutes between freestanding and wall-mounted units. The production tracking chart had a row for each pitch, for example from 7:00 to 7:30 am, and columns for expected number of units, actual number produced, variation from expected, cumulative production, cumulative variation, and reasons for misses. If actual number of units fell short of expected, the actual number produced was highlighted in red. When actual met expected, the number was highlighted in green.

The tracking chart was pretty standard, but what was recorded on it stopped the engineer and me in our tracks. After actual production of 30 units in each pitch the first four pitches of the day, the rest of the pitches alternated between 30 and 28 units completed. Yet, the actual of 28, short of expected production by two units, was highlighted in green with nothing written in the "reasons for miss" column on the chart. As the engineer and I stood in front of the chart scratching our heads, the assembly team leader came up, introduced himself, and politely asked if we had any questions.

We told him we could not understand why pitches that were short two units still showed green with no recorded reasons for misses.

Here is what he told us: "We've been short parts for wall-mounted, but the whole team's here today and the line's been running good, right at takt. If we'd of had the parts, we would've run 'em at takt, so I colored those pitches green."

It took me a few days to understand fully what the engineer and I had seen and heard. I had learned the manufacturing VP who recently became responsible for this business unit was a classic results-oriented manager. His leadership style was described as direct, blunt, and demanding. He set the goals. The plants submitted their plans. He approved them, but only after reducing proposed budgets and upping projected results. Then it was up to the plants to perform. At first, when walking through the plants occasionally, this executive saw red entries on production tracking charts. This plant had been using the same kind of tracking for several years. Red meant missed pitches in assembly or, in upstream areas, problems with equipment material or yield. Red meant problems. Problems threatened results. Problems, therefore, were not good. Problems attracted attention—and heat—from the VP. When all measures were green, he shifted his attention to someone else's plant.

In the case of measures showing red, the ensuing conversation between the executive and the plant manager might well have gone something like this: "You gave me your plan, I provided the resources we agreed on; do you need my help meeting your goals?" There was only one acceptable answer to this question: "No, sir!"

I knew the plant manager and his staff well enough to trust that nobody had been told to cheat on their performance measures. Yet, I also knew in the chain-of-command organizations in which most of us work, it is important to deliver what the boss asks. In this case, the boss was asking for green pitches 95 percent of the time. Altogether, the message was clear enough down to the level of team leader. Fudge, "tweak," or put your own interpretation on the measures if you must, but make them hit the target. This turns out to be a common experience, one you may have heard about or seen.

Kermit the Frog of the Muppets famously said, "It's good to be green!" (not referring to ecological values). Perhaps more to the point, in this VP's organization, it was good not to be red.

The VP had come late to lean; in fact, he had not come to lean at all. By any criterion, his thinking remained thoroughly conventional. He had moved from a division where his success had come from focusing intensely on cost and results. The plants he now led had been into lean and process focus for eight years, and had progressed, in part, by paying attention to problems and their causes. Now, the plants were being driven to be green, rather than to find and eliminate root causes of production interruptions, such as parts shortages.

Lean designs are finely tuned and delicately balanced, in part to show quickly where abnormalities interrupt production or cause defects. Focusing on process, a principal outcome of lean management, can easily be subverted by the "more is better" thinking characteristic of a conventional results orientation, as in: if some green pitches are good, more green is better, and all green is perfection. When a conventional-thinking leader sees red on a tracking chart, he or she may figuratively be "seeing red." That is, "If our lean conversion is a success, why am I seeing red pitches? Green is our goal, so green is what I want to see!" You can practically hear the words, right?

Measuring percent pitch *attainment*, the result of this thinking, corrupts pitch-by-pitch performance as a measure of process health. Calling it pitch attainment causes this classic process measure to morph into yet another end of day tally of results. Habits die hard; left unchecked, the "results" habit drags process measures into yet another backward-looking measure. Your process has almost certainly not attained perfection, but compromised measurement suggests it has. With that, conventional results-oriented attention shifts to the next crisis. In doing so, the conventional leader turns away from the search for improvement, away from what is truly at the heart of lean.

A Measure of Process or Result?

Many subtle distinctions separate lean thinking from a conventional batch and queue approach. One of them involves measuring process versus measuring results. It can be tricky. How can you tell when a process measure is no longer being used to reflect the health of the process? What marks a process measure that has been corrupted by the habits of results thinking—even if inadvertently?

One cue is batch size. Here, batch refers to the length of time reflected by the measure, for example, an hour, a day, or a week. The lean adage: "Smaller quantities more frequently!" reminds us to be wary of large batches and applies to measures just as surely as to inventory. Effective process measurements occur relatively frequently, with relatively brief intervals between observations. The decision you make about how often to take measurements answers the question: "How long do I want to wait to know whether my process is operating normally?" The lean thinker's answer is "Not very long!" (though see "Frequency of Observation," below).

Measurement that frequently records performance is designed to catch process misses, interruptions, abnormalities, or more generally, to discover problems quickly and close to their source. (Think of process measures as analogous with medical screening exams; how long between checkups do you want to wait to learn if your new baby or grandchild has a health problem? The earlier you catch a problem, the sooner treatment can begin and the better the chances for resolving the problem. The difference, of course, is that medical conditions generally develop more slowly than problems in a production process, so for adults, an annual physical can be frequent enough.) Frequently checking how a production process is operating exposes problems and allows you to contain them. Frequent measurement also keeps you close in time to the appearance of problems, which puts you in a better position for problem solving when you return to the issue.

By comparison, when considering daily pitch attainment percentage, the time period in question is usually a shift, which batches the pitch-by-pitch results. This is the same effect as reporting an average for the shift rather than showing an hour-by-hour or pitch-by-pitch performance profile. In other words, this kind of reporting, even though *based on* frequent measurement, has the effect of lumping the data points together, smoothing over problems and making it more difficult to see them clearly. As with any other example of batching, process problems are hidden in the batch. The problems could be bad parts, inaccurate specifications, incorrectly processed orders, or pitch cycles with process misses. The problems are concealed by the batch, rather than highlighted as Shigeo Shingo would advise.

This kind of averaging or summary percentage reporting measures results. "What was our pitch attainment today?" is equivalent to asking: "What was our productivity today?" The point is not that measuring results is bad; not at all. Results are important, but I am sure your organization already has enough measures of results. By aggregating process data across periods, you lose the benefit of process measurement, which is its sensitivity to identifying process problems.

Lean is all about process improvement. Its benefits in safety, quality, speed, and cost are byproducts of striving to find and eliminate waste. Constantly seeking improvement is the bedrock of lean and lean thinking. Looking for, finding, and eliminating problems are key elements in lean. Shingo's advice was to seek out problems even where none are visible, and then work to eliminate their causes. Why? To drive improvement. Process measures reflect this lean point of view when you use them to expose problems.

So, if it looks like a process measure but you are not using it to highlight problems, you are missing the point. You already have summary measures of safety, quality, speed, and cost to measure the results of your process at the end of the day. Use them for that purpose. Meanwhile, preserve the focus on specific pitch-by-pitch process misses. Treat these problems as opportunities to improve and make a point of acting on them. Keep a list, a rogues gallery, of the problems discovered and tally the problems permanently eliminated. This kind of scoreboard reflects an emphasis on process, a focus on improvement, and using process measures appropriately, to drive improvement.

If you sense a "Don't bring me problems!" mentality surrounding what you originally intended as measures of process health, that should be a clue to a morphing or already-corrupted measure now being used as one more gauge of results. As a lean thinker, it is your role to reinforce the value in finding and focusing on problems as guideposts to potential improvements, and to rehabilitate the way your organization uses measures to drive improvement on a continuous basis.

Frequency of Observation

Batch size, expressed as the time interval between taking process measurements, is one way to assess whether your measures are process- or results-focused. Use your judgment when setting the interval for measurement frequency. In a mature lean high volume, repetitive manufacturing operation, pitch intervals might be as brief as five or ten minutes, usually determined by pack-out container quantities.

Circumstances are different with lower volume, high cycle time production. It might take several hours, a day, or more to produce a unit when the work is production of technical design specifications or drawings, for example. In a case like this, you might be well served by a measurement pitch of once or twice a day. In production with very long cycle times, for example refurbishing and upgrading complex electronic gear, the complete job might be measured in weeks. In cases like these, do you want to wait days, or even weeks to know work is progressing normally? Probably not. Instead, consider breaking these long jobs into shorter intervals—sets of tasks of a few hours' duration. By pacing work this way, you will be much closer to its actual progression and more likely to spot and preserve information about problems, all the better to eliminate them and improve your process. Workers might protest being micromanaged, but as with the case study in Chapter 4 ("Make Sure Your Employees Know the Charts Are Not Micromanaging Them"). the point is to focus on the process—not the worker—to expose and eliminate the kinds of problems that interrupt and frustrate those doing the work.

Lean Leaders Recognize Imperfection

When someone in authority is asking for green, there are many ways to satisfy the leader. This is not necessarily cheating. People rationalize adjusting measures, tweaking the way performance is tracked, just as the assembly team leader did. The sad result is that problems get covered, hidden from the leader who cannot see the potential value in red measures. The health of the process and mining those nuggets for process improvement becomes a lower priority. Worst of all, improvement slows or stops altogether. People in the area see it, of course, and with that see lean as just another flavor of the month.

The reverse of all these conditions is also true. Leaders who have learned to be lean thinkers ask for results, certainly. Results matter, but not above all. Lean-thinking leaders also ask how: "How many problems we have found, what have we learned about their causes, have we eliminated the causes, and how can we be sure they have not returned?"

Lean-thinking leaders know their processes are not perfect, and so look for ways to stress a process that is green *too much* of the time. One rule of thumb is: when measures are green more than 75 percent of the time, lower the water. Shortening lead times, linking processes, cross-training people, decreasing inventory, increasing changeovers—all these stress the system. These are examples of the lean adage to "lower the water to expose the rocks." Then, go after the rocks, those causes of red measures that are exposed by the stress. Lean-thinking leaders know how to mine the rocks for the nuggets they contain, and to convert them to improvement. Eliminate the rocks and the system stabilizes at a new, higher level of performance. That is one route to "reaching the next level."

So, respect the integrity and intent of your lean measures as indicators of the health of your process. You already have plenty of ways to measure results. Do not compromise your measures of process; pay attention to them and they will help you drive improvement.

Summary: Consistent Leadership Is the Crucial Ingredient in Lean Operations

Changing from batch production to lean is difficult because the two are so different. Lean management calls for responses that are opposite those that have been learned and reinforced over a career in batch and queue operations. No change is easy, but swapping one habit for its contradictory opposite is particularly challenging. Because of that, leadership and leaders' persistence and consistency over time is essential for successfully transforming from batch to lean.

George Koenigsaecker, among others, has noted that leadership is always in short supply, which may account for the disappointing track record of attempted lean conversions. A slightly different slant on Koenigsaecker's idea is from Rensis Likert, who noted, "Nothing changes until leader behavior changes." That is the point of this chapter; what leaders learn to do is the crucial ingredient in a successful lean conversion.

Specifically, a leader's behavior is more important than his or her personality—being inspiring, charismatic, or emotionally impactful. I have seen forceful, charismatic, inspiring leaders utterly fail to understand what was needed to sustain lean conversion efforts. I have seen leaders with a good conceptual understanding of the need for lean management utterly fail to execute the basics, such as teaching subordinates and holding them accountable for applying what they had learned. The leaders of successful lean transformations, in my experience, were relentless in teaching and expecting to see live, on-the-floor examples of lean management in large and small examples everywhere. You would call them dogged in their persistence; you would call few of them charismatic. Significantly, none of them knew anything about lean when they started; first and continuing, they were students.

Success in a lean conversion ends up depending on those who lead the organization. They must teach, inspect for, reinforce, and hold all accountable for management practices consistent with the principles of lean. As leaders improve their lean management skills, their newly lean operations stabilize and begin paying off in better and better performance.

Nobody is born knowing these principles and how to implement them. Everyone has to learn them through practice, trial and error, and coaching. You can learn them, too. That is one of the main points of this book. With exposure to a few straightforward principles and some examples of how they can be applied, you can learn to lead and implement lean management and by doing so see your lean conversion live up to its potential.

Chapter 9

Solving Problems and Improving Processes—Rapidly

The lean management system consists of more than its four principal elements. A root cause orientation to problem solving, a rapid response system, and a progressive approach to process improvement are among the elements that round out the system. This chapter covers each of these topics. (Chapter 10 covers people-related elements.)

A Root Cause Orientation to Problem Solving

Any manufacturing process will experience problems that interrupt or threaten production. That is as true of lean systems as of any other. A key distinction between lean and batch-and-queue systems lies in how they deal with these inevitable problems.

The typical response in batch and queue is to work around the problem, often in creative, sometimes unconventional ways. The focus, of course, is on doing what it takes to meet the schedule. In a lean environment, the typical response is to ask why the problem occurred and what caused it.

This reveals one of the least obvious aspects of the lean production and management systems: Lean is an improvement system. Implementing a lean production system does not solve problems. Instead, lean exposes problems, so you can see them, eliminate their causes, and improve.

You have probably heard the metaphor about implementing lean: you are "lowering the water to expose the rocks." That is, as you implement lean production, you reduce the extra resources—both formal and informal—that were in place to protect the batch-and-queue system from long-unaddressed problems. These "just-in-case" resources are the "water" that lean implementations "lower." The idea in lean is to systematically expose the problems that have always been present, but covered over, hidden by the extra resources, like the water behind a dam covers what used to be dry land. Once exposed, the problems can be analyzed for cause, and then eliminated.

As you lower the water, the problems show themselves. Some are listed below:

- Setups take hours and hours. Batch solution: Keep extra inventory on hand to cover the changeover time.
- A work center produces defects seemingly at random a quarter of the time. Batch solution: Keep extra inventory on hand to draw on in case we hit a run of bad parts.
- A piece of equipment goes down like a yo-yo, but does not come back nearly that fast. Batch solution: Keep other equipment on hand that in a pinch can be set up to produce the needed parts, even if the process is not quite the same.
- A rash of special orders comes in that only Lai Yue knows how to process, but it overloads her. Batch solution: Call the customers and push out lead times. Tell Lai Yue she has to work Saturday and Sunday.
- A supplier just cannot seem to deliver the full order, at least not on time. Batch solution: Again, cover this unreliability with extra inventory to draw on, just in case.
- Well, that's just George (or Jane): He (or she) is like that some days. Batch solution: Just work some OT or add someone else to the line to take up the slack.

Lean exposes these problems, some of which you knew you had, but had given up ever resolving. As a perverse kind of bonus, lean also exposes problems you had no idea were lurking, waiting for the chance to bite you. Yes, that really is the sound of opportunity knocking; it just sounds like you gritting your teeth!

Workarounds Are Anti-Improvement

Once problems present themselves in the form of flow interrupters in a variety of disguises (process quality, equipment reliability, supplier performance, support group responsiveness, operator skill deficits, leadership commitment, and on and on), you have two choices.

The first is tried and true: Go back to the stashed extras you were supposed to have gotten rid of with the lean implementation, but had not quite gotten around to. Pull them into the process. Do a workaround and meet the schedule. The schedule is the object, right? Tomorrow maybe things will work out better.

The second alternative is to do what you must to patch up the process. After all, you have customer commitments to meet. But as you do, take careful note of what seems to have gone wrong. Document it in the management system tools you are beginning to use. Come back to the problem as soon as you can, and begin asking simple questions such as: Why? What was the cause of this interruption? Drill down to the root cause. Identify the top three interrupters for the week or month. Begin to work on either preventing recurrences or setting alarms to alert you that an episode of a known problem is about to happen. Keep working progressively down the list of known interrupters as you discover and eliminate root causes.

A New Way of Thinking

This sounds simple, but it takes a new way of thinking from the perspective of most who grew up in a batch environment. Consider this contrast: In batch-and-queue systems, leaders are expected to quickly work around problems to meet the schedule. When the workaround is successfully in place, the problem is considered solved; tomorrow is another day. By comparison, lean leaders are expected to perform cause analysis and put a root cause solution into effect (see the case study "New Leaders Uncover the Cause of Old Problems").

Should Perfection Be a Goal?

This example is not a dramatic one, but it illustrates an important point noted in Chapter 8: Lean thinking involves being serious about pursuing improvement with the goal of eventually reaching perfection in process and execution. Before the change in this illustration, one of the team leaders was usually available to come off his or her job to perform the rework, even though that meant skipping other duties (that potentially could have included monitoring standardized work in the upholstery process). The problems were virtually never severe enough to cause a miss in daily schedule completion. In the previous batch-and-queue environment, one that still existed in other parts of the plant, working some overtime to achieve daily schedule completion was routine and perfectly acceptable.

Several things made the difference in turning the lean corner in the upholstery operation, which by the way, went on to many more incremental improvements that taken together have transformed the appearance, performance, and productivity of the area. One factor was faithfully maintained documentation at final assembly. When attention shifted from schedule completion to process quality and yield, the initial data were available right away for Pareto analysis to reveal upholstery as the leading source of interruption.

CASE STUDY: NEW LEADERS UNCOVER THE CAUSE OF OLD PROBLEMS

A case illustrating this difference in thinking comes from an area building a hot new product. The product included upholstered components that were subassembled in a process for sewing and upholstery linked to the final assembly line and supplying it in sequence one unit at a time. The assembly-line team leader was scrupulous about maintaining documentation of flow interrupters that caused his takt-paced line to miss its goals for hourly performance, even though his records hardly ever sparked action.

A common flow interruption at final assembly was wrinkled upholstery. When that occurred, the unit had to be shunted to the repair area, disassembled, the upholstered subassembly returned to the feeder process, taken apart and reworked, and the unit reassembled. This process caused considerable delay; the result was missed output goals at final assembly. Initially when these problems occurred, they were simply reworked, often by the team leader in either final assembly or the upholstery area. The workarounds caused some overtime, but because it was not tracked separately from the regularly scheduled overtime used to meet strong customer demand, it was not examined.

A retirement and two reassignments brought new leaders to the area. They paid more attention to their resident lean sensei than had their predecessors. The previous leaders had seemed more interested in maintaining their numbers for cost and schedule completion than in bringing the area to a new level of lean operation.

As the new leaders in the area progressed in their lean thinking, they started to analyze the hourly tracking charts from final assembly and the log sheets from the final assembly "hospital," or repair area. The new value stream manager and her two supervisors found upholstery to be the single leading cause, both for units going into the repair area and for the final assembly line missing its hourly goals. Further investigation (including a more specific definition of what was meant by "bad upholstery") identified wrinkles and puckers as the most frequent causes for rejects.

The upholstery supervisor followed up. He found standardized work in the upholstery area called out the correct process, but without much in the way of specific detail. He also found that the upholstery process was rarely monitored for anything other than volume of output.

Further investigation showed that the main causes of rejected, wrinkled upholstery were either not enough fasteners used to attach the fabric to the substrate, uneven spacing of the fasteners, incorrect sequence of fastener application, or all three. In addition, wrinkling varied between two types of upholstery fabric, requiring a different number and spacing of fasteners for the two different classes of material.

The supervisor and team leader in the upholstery area, having reached an understanding of the leading causes of rejected subassemblies, built a life-sized display of the correct number and spacing of fasteners for the two different materials, retrained the operators, and monitored performance against the newly clarified standard. The wrinkled upholstery problems virtually disappeared from final assembly.

In the meantime, a downturn in orders had occurred so that overtime was no longer routine. Now, extra hours were directly traceable to production problems. With the change in the upholstery process, the decline in need for unplanned overtime could be observed as a result of this improvement.

A second factor, and the most important, was a gradual change in the mindset of leadership in the area, prompted by ongoing coaching by the plant's resident lean sensei. As thinking shifted from schedule completion to process quality and yield, the leaders began to ask why they had continuing upholstery rejects. They took a systematic approach to discovering the causes of the problems, and to eliminating them so the problems did not recur. Once they focused on improvement, rather than living with a long-standing but manageable problem, they were able to make a permanent fix, a permanent process improvement. The supervisor in this area has come to see perfection as a goal, though he does not talk about it in these terms. Rather, he talks about the need to make further improvement. A clue to the larger goal of perfection, however distant and even indefinable, is that he sees no end to the possible improvements.

Structured Problem Solving Process

It is one thing to set perfection as a goal; it is another thing to put in place the tools that allow you to make progress toward the goal. A structured problem-solving process is an important step on this journey. If you have not been exposed to one, find yourself a six- (or seven- or eight-) step problem solving process and learn how to use it. You may want to get some people trained in problem solving. Or, you may simply want to start asking for the steps one at a time as circumstances dictate, coaching your leaders on how to carry out each step. Depending on the number of people you need to reach, it might be enough to deliver the training on a just-in-time basis as the need for the next step comes up and a teachable moment presents itself with one of your team members. Conventional training closely linked to application can work, too. The basic steps are the same regardless of the brand of process you use and how you train people in it:

Step 1: Identify and define the problem
Step 2: Quarantine the problem and take other immediate remedial actions
Step 3: Involve the appropriate, knowledgeable people
Step 4: Conduct root cause analysis
Step 5: Identify root cause solutions, assess them, and test the preferred alternative
Step 6: Implement the root cause solution
Step 7: Monitor and revise the solution as indicated by performance data

At first, this might be no more demanding than asking people to apply the five whys when problems arise. More sophisticated approaches can come later.

Taking people through the steps, one at a time, with each step closely followed by application, is often the most effective way to introduce these ideas.

Who Makes Improvements?

The orientation to cause analysis and pressing for perfection one step at a time will quickly produce opportunities for improvement that outstrip the capacity of technical professional support groups. In a conventional batch environment, this would be just another instance of the typical bottleneck in getting engineering, or quality, or production control, or whomever to work on a request for a process improvement made by a production floor leader. That is because in a conventional batch production operation, improvements are "left to the experts."

In this conventional scenario, a technical project team moves into and then out of a production area, leaving in its wake what are intended to be permanent fixes. Sometimes these "fixes" only work on paper, in which case they are quickly undone. However, sometimes project teams' fixes work quite well. But, because it works, it gets no further attention. The process remains static, often for many years, without further improvement. No further changes are made. That may be because the leader's mindset ("It ain't broke!") blinds him or her to further opportunities. Or, leaders may not know how to lead improvement efforts themselves with mostly their own resources. The likely waiting time for a response by a technical project team is often so long that it is not worth initiating the request.

Short-, Medium-, and Longer-Term Improvements

In a lean environment, the expectation is that everyone has two responsibilities. The first is to run the business on a day-to-day basis. The second is to improve the business, or contribute to improving it, continuously. We have already seen one example of this dual responsibility in the daily accountability process and its task assignment board. Improvement efforts in lean management usually fall into one of three categories (with movement between categories as experience dictates) determined by scope, scale, and duration of the improvement task. Table 9.1 lists these categories.

Simple problems or straightforward improvements can be assigned and managed in the daily accountability process three-tier meetings. For example, a team leader might be assigned to make a shadow board for tools

Table 9.1 Options for Improvement Activities

Duration of Tasks	Typical Focus	How Managed
1–5 days	Fix an immediate problem, implement a simple improvement, simple cause analysis	Daily task assignment board; follow up at three-tier meetings
6–30 days	Problem solving process for more complex cause analysis, solution, or recommendation	Via one-page (A-3) visual project plan reviewed at weekly project review session
30–90 days	Longer-term or more complex problems or opportunities	Via one-page (A-3) visual project plan reviewed at weekly project review session

Note that while these categories do not explicitly include acting on employee suggestions for improvement, any such suggestion can be easily fitted into one of these three. Chapter 10 covers employee improvement suggestion systems in detail.

currently kept in drawers and often missing when needed. With the shadow board in place, the team leader might be assigned to update team leader standard work to verify tools have been returned to their indicated places at the end of each shift.

Recommending Future Improvements

Another outcome of an initial investigation from a daily task assignment is to recommend a project for the list of future kaizen improvement events in an area. For example, investigation of the cause of an intermittent backup on an assembly line identified interruptions in a packing operation caused by poorly organized parts and materials that often resulted in the operator having to leave the workstation to search out the proper materials. In this situation, two kaizens in succession have attacked organization, material resupply, and parts presentation in the pack area. The kaizens were one week in duration, held about six weeks apart. The second event refined the work of the first based on the intervening experience.

Managing Improvement Activities

You may, at first, find it confusing to determine the relationship among short-, medium-, and longer-term improvements. The best advice is to start and sort things out as you go. Experience says you will figure out a method that makes sense for you and those who are involved in it. Do not hesitate to consider these arrangements as experiments on the way to establishing a stable process. Here are a few guidelines to use in sorting out your process:

- Manage each improvement with a single person
- Manage improvements visually in only one location
- Manage each improvement with only one schedule
- Hold review sessions at least once a week
- Avoid projects that extend more than 90 days; form serial subprojects as needed
- Avoid making lists (black holes) of projects; manage the queue visually
- Group activities of like duration with like management (e.g. daily board, weekly A-3s)

CASE STUDY: LONG-TERM SYSTEMATIC CAUSE ANALYSIS OF AN ASSEMBLY LINE PROBLEM

Some matters are less clear; for example, if laminate tops are being scrapped because of units moving intermittently on the bed of a shaping machine, is it the machine, the material, the method, the operator, or Mother Nature? In this case, it was not at all clear; each potential cause had to be ruled out by a problem solving team that was formed to investigate after several fixes had been attempted, only to see the problem recur. (It turned out to be Mother Nature in the form of seasonally varying humidity, to be brought under control by erecting a humidity-controlled holding area for the substrate material.) This kind of project required systematic cause analysis involving several people, including technical specialists, operators, team leaders, and the supervisor. The team reached its conclusion in the 30-day period and made its recommendation.

This is an example of a problem solving project readily managed on a generic visual project form. Toyota refers to this form as an A-3 after the technical name of the tabloid-sized (11"x17") paper on which it is printed (see Figures 9.1a and 9.1b). The summary-level Gantt chart on the A-3 project plan makes it easy to color code completion of milestones (green in the week due for on time, red until the week

---

completed for overdue milestones), so it lends itself well to visual management of expected versus actual.

In this example, the recommendation of the problem solving team turned into a project to design, specify, procure, install, and test the humidity-controlled holding area. This is one example of a project of between 30 and 90 days' duration, also readily manageable in a weekly project review in front of a board displaying the A-3 project plans and green or red status of that week's milestones. Some of the project tasks might have shown up on a daily task accountability board. An example might be for the supervisor to review a mock-up of the holding area with the out-cycle operators who would be involved in retrieving the loads of substrate.

Improvement Resources and Skills

One of the roles of a site lean leader is to teach floor leaders how to recognize opportunities for improvement, and then how to act on them with their own resources. A frequent approach is for the site lean leader to teach and coach supervisors and team leaders to lead kaizen events. These are tightly focused, time limited (usually no more than a week, often less), small-scale intensive improvement projects.

Kaizens are specifically designed to make incremental changes, and there may be a series of kaizen improvement events that focus repeatedly on a single small area. The results are cumulative, gradually making step after step in improving flow of production, easing the physical tasks of the operators, reducing setup times and inventory, improving quality, making equipment more reliable, and so on. An additional important feature of kaizen events is their make up. The composition of the kaizen team, usually seven or fewer participants plus a leader, is mostly production people from various areas in the facility. It is a very powerful method for members of the production workforce to learn the principles of lean.

Technical professionals will often provide consultation and support to kaizen teams along with the site lean leader, but most of the work is done in the teams themselves, which is one of the reasons kaizens are such powerful vehicles for training. Concept meets application in a kaizen team, and the application is direct, hands-on experience.

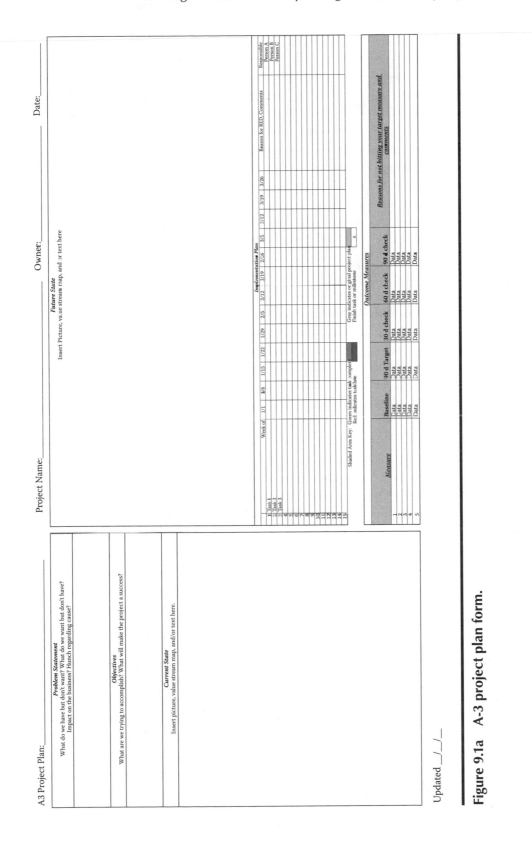

Figure 9.1a A-3 project plan form.

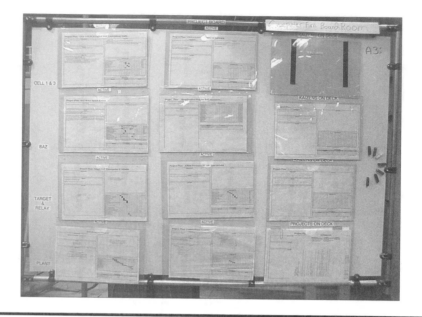

Figure 9.1b A-3 project plans of a project plan board. Rows one through three on this project board are for each value stream in this plant. Row four is for plant projects. Active projects are in columns one and two, on-deck projects and kaizen plans in column three. Plans are reviewed weekly. Weekly milestone due dates are noted in gray. Milestones are coded green when completed, red until completed. A note in the blank spot, upper right, says two on-deck kaizen plans required.

CASE STUDY: WORKING WITHOUT A RESPONSE SYSTEM (NUMBER 1)

The first case occurred, not coincidentally, in the plant where the supervisor "stored" the production-tracking forms on the floor under his desk. The lean conversion involved switching from a build-complete process at a number of stand-alone two-person workbenches to a single progressive build assembly line. In the bench-build process, a number of subassemblies were produced in batches upstream from assembly, picked into kits based on a schedule, and pushed up to the benches. The progressive build line incorporated a number of these subassembly areas in an integrated takt-paced flow production process. Signals went out to subassembly production from the single schedule point in the flow process.

It was extremely rare for production to stop in the bench-build scenario. There was always the option of working ahead based on the schedule. And, if one bench experienced problems, it was likely the others could keep on producing while the problem load was pushed aside and the next one brought in. In the flow process, when there was an interruption, 13 people stood around waiting for the problem to be identified and fixed. Two temperamental pieces of automated equipment were built into the flow process. They failed repeatedly. Worse, the failures were intermittent.

To the credit of the project team designing the new flow process, they recognized the need to establish a quick response process and told the support groups they would need their support in a different and more timely way than in the past. Maintenance, engineering, and materials management agreed, and for the first several weeks when the "911" calls went out, the response was timely. A host of flow interruptions quickly emerged as the new process began operation. There were frequent material shortages outright, and material supply errors resulting in mix-ups in the sequence of parts to the various stations on the progressive assembly line. There were problems with alignment of parts in assembly that used to be muscled through at the benches. Now, these problems caused repeated disruptions in flow at the 36 second takt time. The automated equipment also failed intermittently, causing further interruptions.

It was a pretty typical startup for a lean conversion. The system was doing what it was supposed to do, exposing flow interruptions. Unfortunately, there was no accountability process in place. The increasingly frustrated value stream manager reported the maintenance, fit-up, and equipment problems in daily plant staff meetings, the way it had always been done. The response was to put the problems on a list of functional projects, also the way it had always been done. The response system also quickly regressed to operating the way it always had.

The plant manager at the time had left the lean conversion to his project team. The new layout looked good from the aisle and when everything was right, it ran beautifully. But as soon as the project team, with its support group specialists, disbanded a few weeks after the start of production, there were no extra resources on hand to resolve problems that repeatedly surfaced. The plant manager expected nothing different in the way his support groups responded. And he had no inclination to change the reporting relationships of the support groups. The management system had not changed in the rest of the plant, and the converted area continued to struggle until the product line was moved out of the plant.

A Rapid Response System

You have team leaders on the floor paying close attention to the way the process is operating. The new lean approach is great when it works, but quickly comes to a halt when things go wrong. Ouch! When that happens, you need a response—fast. There are several ways to summon help quickly. The range includes simple call lists (be sure a phone is close at hand), specially designated pagers (often red in color) carried by designated support group representatives who are "on call," escalation systems based on number of missed cycles, automated escalation systems, and so on.

Do not be lulled by these arrangements; a rapid response system is not about the cool technology you use to summon assistance.

The necessity of changing the connection between support groups and production areas is an often-overlooked aspect of lean production. For lean to be sustained without yielding to the temptation to go back to buffers of time, labor, and material, quick response is needed when interruptions arise, as they definitely will. What comes to the surface is simply this: The most important activity in a production facility is production. The tasks and projects that engineering, programming, skilled trades, quality, supply chain, and scheduling work on are not unimportant. They are just not as important as what happens on the production floor when one of these specialists is needed to, as the name indicates, support manufacturing.

CASE STUDY: WORKING WITHOUT A
RESPONSE SYSTEM (NUMBER 2)

The second case involved the same plant as the first, and two of the people who had served on the project team for the first project. One of them had been the co-leader responsible for the lean technical design alongside the person who had become the value stream manager. In the new project, this former co-leader wore both hats: project team leader and value stream manager. Two other factors came into play. Instead of converting an existing batch-built process to a lean one, this project involved a high profile new product. And there was a different plant manager. The organization structure and reporting relationships of the support groups remained exactly the same as before.

This time, the value stream manager implemented a complete lean management system along with the physical implementation. Because it was a new product, the plant manager's boss was more engaged in the project, and so was the plant manager. The company had had several years of experience in lean conversions since the first case. More people had been exposed to the tight interdependency within a lean production process, as well as between the production area and its support groups. The plant manager agreed to be part of the response system, the last one on the call list when production was stopped. According to the response system, he was to be called when production was interrupted for half an hour.

An element in the response system was a log sheet kept right by the line-side telephone from which the "911" calls were placed. The log recorded actual versus expected response times in the escalating network of calls, and reasons for misses when they experienced delayed responses to calls for help. These "reasons for misses" were reviewed no later than the next day.

There were few misses on the occasions when "911" calls went out. The supervisor virtually always responded within the expected three minutes. The plant manager always responded when his number was called, even if the response had to be by phone. He expected a timely, in-person response from the support group members assigned on a given day to wear the response system red pager.

This time, the response system worked. Leaders were aligned and the management system was in place to record, review, and act when actual did not meet expected throughout the process. No change in structure was needed, but for the system to work as it did the many other changes noted above were required.

This is often a new idea. In the previous batch-and-queue operating environment, there were buffers of hours or even days between operations. When one element of the process experienced problems, it was naturally isolated from the others by the inventory waiting between each process— the "queue" in batch and queue. In this world, it was important to respond to problems on the floor, but rarely was there a sense of urgency to the response. Support groups had goals and projects that they focused on. The phone calls (or emails) could usually wait, and usually did. But no more.

Some would immediately conclude that a different organization structure is required, that is, a value stream organization in which support group members report directly to the value stream manager. Depending on the disposition of higher-level leaders, this can become a political struggle that absorbs time and energy and does not always yield the hoped-for outcome. An alternative is to focus on the production process and the accountability process that helps to sustain it.

It is typically easier to gain commitment for measured, timely response to a call for support than it is to get the organization chart changed. The former is like apple pie and motherhood: Who could argue with agreeing to a rule-governed quick response to a stoppage in production? On the other hand, a proposal to change reporting relationships can easily be perceived, and often rightly so, as an assault on a fellow manager's power base. You have enough things in your newly converted lean process to worry about already without picking that kind of fight. The cases presented describe two scenarios: one where the plant manager and support groups were not enrolled in a response system in advance, and one where they were.

Support Groups Must Keep Pace with Production

These examples illustrate the often unanticipated implications for the organization that follow from the newly lean production area. For lean management to work effectively, the support groups have to be prepared to respond at a pace determined by the takt pace of production—at a minimum, that means support groups realigning priorities and leadership expecting accountability for the new priorities. Organization structure is not much of an issue when site managers understand the implications of lean and are willing to hold their staffs accountable for supporting a new, lean direction.

Organizations need functional groups to maintain ready technical expertise and skills. Nothing in lean management suggests disbanding the central functional organizations. In the longer run, it does make sense to dedicate support group staffers to lean value streams on a long-term rotational basis. As the process changes that radiate out from lean conversions become clear, the switch to dedicated value stream organizations should be a less emotional issue than at the outset.

Summary: Finding the Root Cause of Problems Is Key

Lean is an improvement system in which several apparently contradictory elements are joined. First, the system is designed to expose problems, occasionally bringing production to a complete halt until the problem is resolved. Second, the orientation to root cause problem solving seems to suggest dramatic, large-scale projects to eliminate problems. Yet a primary method for eliminating causes of problems is to make repeated incremental improvements, clarifying problems and recommending solutions that can often be implemented in a week by a kaizen team. One of the keys to effective process improvement is developing a clear understanding of the cause of the problem, using the tools and logic of systematic problem solving processes.

Separating improvement activities into short-, medium-, and longer-term is a way to give appropriate emphasis and attention to each kind of improvement.

Not all problems can be resolved right away. Some require emergency or short-term countermeasures that allow production to continue while the cause of the problem is diagnosed. Because lean production systems are so tightly interdependent, when a problem occurs in production, a quick response is essential. For these reasons, a response system is an important part of any lean system. The most challenging aspect of putting such a system in place is realigning the priorities and perhaps the measures of support groups. Otherwise, the response system exists in name and hardware only.

Chapter 10

People—Predictable Interruption; Source of Ideas

People and their ideas for improvement are close to the heart of lean production. They can also seem to be close enough to the neck to cause a pain there. Perhaps that is because of lean leaders' experience when they go to start production only to find one or more people have "called in" as unplanned absences. With production finely balanced to the rhythm of takt time, missing a person or two is a big deal. Without just the right number of people, flow does not flow, pull can deteriorate into stockouts, and the takt beat is uneven and sporadic.

People issues may not seem to lend themselves to the process-focused comparison of actual and expected. In actual application, the lean management approach works well with matters of attendance, rotation and staffing, performance issues, and employee involvement in process improvement suggestion systems. This chapter shows how. Learning lean is a hands-on proposition. Effective lean training calls for something different from the typical classroom approach. The training group in human resources (HR) can help develop coaching-based training if they understand the need. HR policy issues also come into play when talking about people issues in a lean conversion. Matters such as job grades and classifications, pay systems, start and break times, job rotation, and layoff policies are likely to need attention in support of a lean environment.

Whom Do I Expect Today? The Attendance Matrix

The first people-related issue is the most frequent one to arise: Who is here for work today? We know people will be absent, we just do not know who and when. Typical arrangements for handling absenteeism include carrying extra people—as many as 8 to 10 percent seasonally—to call on when people unexpectedly call in to say they will not be at work today. So, there are extra people in the plant. Just try finding them when you come up short! Often it is a time-consuming scramble that ends in frustration for all involved. I cannot get the person I need or have been promised; the person I do get did not want to come and is not trained in the work I need to have done. There is a striking lack of process in many places, just like this scenario. The first question a lean sensei will ask is: What is the process here? In the case of attendance, there is none. Is an absence process possible?

Many attendance tracking processes are limited to the number not expected at work. That is, we use calendars for the coming year to write in those workers we expected to be off on vacation, in large part, so we do not grant too much vacation in any single week to handle seasonally expected demand. So, the vacation log tells me who will not be available.

A different approach is to use an attendance matrix (all the people on the team, by every day of the month, a page per month for the year) filled in to tell me those whom I can expect to be at work tomorrow. Entries in the matrix identify:

- Those with planned vacation for the day (usually coded yellow for that person's row for the days of planned vacation);
- Those loaned out to another area or otherwise assigned (for example, to a project) and thus, unavailable for work for a period of time (coded blue);
- Those on medical or other leave (coded green).

I should be able to count on everybody else showing up, ready to go. When people call in, they get coded red for the day. If they are late, they are coded half red (see Figure 10.1).

Do people dislike being coded red? Sure they do! Do we count on everyone we have planned on to show up in order to have a productive day? Sure we do! Should people be accountable for their presence when the team plans on it? You bet! Toyota is said to hold startup meetings at the beginning of the shift in large part to tell who has reported for work so plans can be

Figure 10.1 Attendance matrix.

Note: Absence status is shown by color codes. In this black and white example, hatching and shading represent the colors. One color scheme defines yellow for vacation, red for unplanned absence (call-in) or late, green for medical, blue for project or loaned out.

adjusted as needed. At their assembly plant in Kentucky, employees with perfect attendance for the year are eligible to participate in a raffle where cars are the grand prizes. Showing up is important in a lean workplace! Think of the savings associated with not having to deal with as much absenteeism as you do today. Of course, unforeseen things will happen to cause even reliable people to have an unplanned absence on occasion. Still, showing up when planned is important in a lean environment—for everyone.

Who Starts Where Today? The Labor and Rotation Plan

Job rotation through a home rotation pattern is a common feature in the lean workplace. Rotation helps prevent ergonomic injury from repetitive motion. It results in a cross-trained workforce with the flexibility to move to any of several jobs as needed. And, it means that many people are looking at each job, making a more fertile field for producing suggestions to improve the job for ease, safety, quality, or efficiency.

Rotation also requires more work for the team leader, who has to establish quickly who starts where at the beginning of work. Relying on memory is one way. But can the team leader reliably recall who started where yesterday, or where everyone ended? Probably he or she cannot. What about asking people where they started or finished the day, or the same questions, but for people who are off today? That does not seem like a good plan either. An alternative is a simple set of visual controls that go along with the expected attendance matrix and a qualification matrix. Taken together, these form a suite of tools for labor planning.

Completing the Labor Planning Suite

A labor and rotation plan is a map that identifies the workstations and assignments in a work area—production workstations, team leaders, waterspiders, etc. In most cases, an abstract schematic that identifies only the workstations or the names of other assignments works best. A label (magnetic is helpful here) for each team member's name goes on the map at the location where that person starts. A rotation schedule (clockwise, zigzag, or a matrix of names and workstations) completes the picture. The attendance matrix shows who is expected to be available for the next shift. It only takes a few minutes at the end of the day to set up the next day's labor plan, moving the nametags from where they were yesterday. This way, people can quickly find their starting assignment at the shift start-up meeting (see Figures 10.2a and 10.2b).

Who Is Qualified for Which Jobs?

Training records usually reside in a file cabinet somewhere, either in a supervisor's drawer (not great) or in the training department (worse). When someone calls in as an unplanned absence and production is set to begin, you need to know *right now* who you can call on to fill in, even if only briefly to get production going. A qualification matrix (see Figure 10.3) tells you who is qualified at what level for which jobs. It includes information for all the people on your team as well as some from outside it. For example, if others have been interested enough in your area to become qualified in it, or have moved on from your area to another, they would appear on the matrix with the level of qualification they had achieved.

With this information, you are not simply asking for a warm body to fill in, hoping they can learn the work, keep up, produce good quality, and avoid injury. Instead, you can go to your three-tier meeting, at which labor balance is high on the agenda, and make a specific request for Giacomo and Eva, who you know are qualified to fill the openings you suddenly find yourself facing.

These four tools—the expected attendance matrix, labor plan, rotation map, and qualification matrix—make up the labor-planning suite. They provide, at a glance, information about availability, daily starting position, and qualification. Like other visual controls, the labor-planning suite raises the level of accountability, especially the case for attendance with the attendance matrix. The suite also makes patterns visible that may not have been seen as clearly, such as positions where too few people are qualified, the extent of cross-trained people from other departments, or patterns of attendance that had gone unseen.

How Can I Encourage Participation? The Idea System

Setting up conventional employee suggestion programs is quite straightforward. Making them work is another story. Traditional suggestion systems require considerable overhead: engineers costing-out proposed improvements; managers sifting, sorting, and culling; administrative people recording

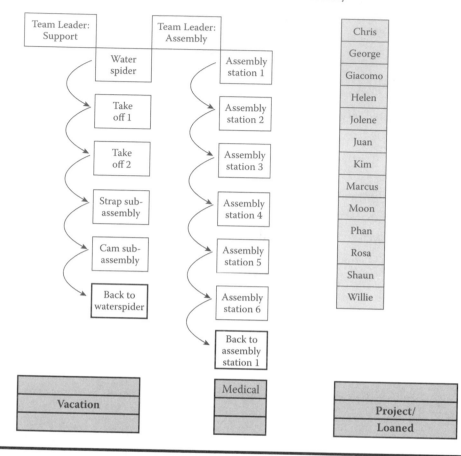

Labor and Rotation Plan: Sled Assembly

Figure 10.2a   Labor and rotation plan.

and routing information; and often several months later, the employee being thanked for a suggestion that "...we just can't commit resources to at this time." Not very motivating!

When lean is truly an improvement system, it produces a steady stream of employee-generated suggestions for improvement. The question is how to get the stream started and then, how to keep the ideas flowing? Before an improvement idea system can work, the organization has to want it to work and has to believe employees actually have ideas to contribute and a desire to do so.

And, as I suggested in Chapter 5, the organization must have developed the capability for tapping leaders' latent potential for making bite-sized as well as larger improvements while they also attend to their daily run-the-business tasks. The vacation paradox plays an important role in sustaining process improvement suggestion systems, in the following way.

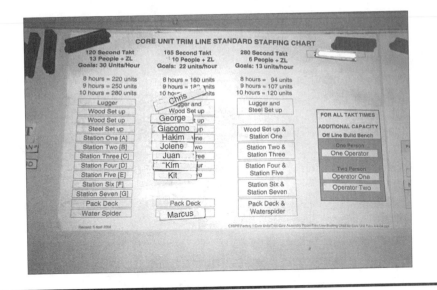

Figure 10.2b Example of a labor planning board.

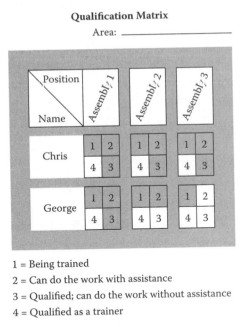

1 = Being trained

2 = Can do the work with assistance

3 = Qualified; can do the work without assistance

4 = Qualified as a trainer

Figure 10.3 Sample skills matrix entries.

In a takt-paced lean production environment, virtually no time is available in a routine production day for operators to work on improvement activities outside of structured improvement events such as kaizens or problem-solving teams. Most of their day is consumed by their standardized work; break time is about all that is left. So, operators are going to have no time to work on implementing improvements they have suggested. And, the benefit from suggestion systems does not come from the suggestions, it comes from implemented improvements. The question becomes "Where do the resources come from to work on implementing employees' suggestions for improvement as an improvement suggestion system is getting underway, and once it is established?"

Who Will Work on Suggested Improvements?

The answer is found in the long-term effect of the vacation paradox. Supervisors and team leaders learn through experience with daily task assignments that they really do have time most days to work on improvement, especially in a stabilizing lean environment. This previously unavailable capacity becomes part of the new "way we do things around here." As it does, this makes it possible for team leaders, supervisors, and support group representatives to allocate the time for working on improvement ideas, including those that come from operators through the improvement suggestion system. That is the key that unlocks the gate to sustainable participation in the suggestion process. Consider the case study "What Happens When Ideas Are Neglected."

A Visual Improvement Suggestion Process

As with much else in a lean operation, there is power in making the improvement idea process visual. The usual reasons apply: when actual versus expected is visible and followed up, accountability for commitments and performance increases. Posting suggestions for all to see can encourage more suggestions as well as stimulate ideas that build on each other. A visually controlled suggestion process can convert the concept of "listening" to something you can see. This is a powerful attribute, especially in the context of lean conversion projects where the target is changing long-entrenched ways of doing things. Failure to listen to employees' ideas is often among those old ways. Coming from that kind of history, one might think operators actually have been "checking their brains at the door," and either do not have any ideas worth listening to, or are uninterested in improvement.

In my experience, nothing could be farther from the truth. For one thing, the opportunity to be heard is powerfully motivating for people. That is true even when the only outcome is having been listened to. Further, in most cases operators have not stopped having ideas. They have only given up

CASE STUDY: WHAT HAPPENS WHEN IDEAS ARE NEGLECTED

First is the composite portrait that is typical of well-intended lean implementation projects. When suggestion programs are introduced, especially in the course of a lean transformation process, many operators will submit ideas. Partly this is a function of the attention the area is getting from the project team working on the lean implementation. The team will often solicit operators' input on design and feedback on its initial operation. Suddenly, lots of ideas are flowing, because ideas are being listened to and acted on—by the extra resources in the area from the project team.

Then the team begins to pull out and eventually disbands and moves on. They indeed have been able to act on many of the ideas from the area's operators who, as a result, typically continue to submit them. The ideas not directly related to the project are often left on a to-do list. And, new ideas continue to come in as people gain experience with the new process. The poor supervisor is left with a pile of suggestions to go along with an entirely new production system to debug and learn how to run. Figuring out the newly redesigned area is where the supervisor puts his or her attention, generally leaving the pile of ideas untouched. The pace of work on ideas slows dramatically and typically stops altogether. At the same time the stream of ideas is drying up and stopping.

This is usually a frustrating mystery to the leaders in the area, who often genuinely want the help and support of operators to make the area successful. The leaders have seen the quality of the suggestions and the lift people experience from seeing them implemented. And now, nothing! But much else is pressing, and soon the leaders' attention has understandably shifted to things about which they know how to do something.

Applying the vacation paradox to implementing suggestions

The second illustration involves a case of waiting for the vacation paradox to take hold, and then applying it to an improvement suggestion process. This was an example of dramatic change and improvement from the first blush of a lean transformation in an assembly area. Management was rightly pleased with the change, but the value stream manager knew much remained to be accomplished. She began using a version of the three-tier meeting process plus regular routine audits and gemba walks to generate task assignments to the supervisor, team leader, and support group representatives who worked with the area.

Just as you would like to see, the area did not rest on the accomplishments of the project team. Instead, it kept improving, driven by the ongoing process of assessments from the production-tracking data, conversion into short-term assignments, and follow-up for daily accountability. This process went on for several months, becoming a routine. The value stream manager then initiated a suggestion system for process improvements. One of its features was that it was a visual system, described below. Second, and most important, was that it involved the supervisor and team leader sorting the suggestions and taking responsibility for getting them implemented in a few days or at most a week, in just the same way they had become used to taking responsibility for acting on daily improvement task assignments.

The value stream manager recognized that implementing some of the suggestions was beyond the scope of the team leader or even the supervisor. So, she separated the "idea board" into two segments. The upper half displayed the ideas and status of submissions from the team members that were being worked on or were in queue for the supervisor or team leader. The lower half of the display held team members' suggestions that the value stream's support groups were working on. The value stream manager held a portion of the stream's support group capacity in reserve for assignment to work on employees' worthy suggestions that were beyond the scope of local line management to complete. She held a weekly meeting with her value stream support group representatives, the area supervisor, and the team leaders to evaluate the week's ideas. At this meeting, they agreed on ideas to be assigned to support group members. Those idea cards were then moved to the to-do column in the lower half of the board with the assigned person's name noted on the card.

The result was a continuing steady flow of suggestions from operators reinforced by a steady stream of suggestions, often modest, for making improvements in the process, which continued to improve. Not all the improvement was attributable to employee suggestions. Nevertheless, the team has remained open to change, in large part because they have the regular experience of being listened to when they make suggestions for change.

on the futility of making suggestions. Indeed, in the project scenario above, when project teams ask for suggestions and feedback, they are typically inundated with ideas. The problem becomes the organization's inability to respond to them. At that point, ideas stop coming, and quickly.

Making Listening Visible

So, how can a visual control make listening visible and accountable and give operators a sense of ownership and pride in improvement?

Use a format that encourages brief, readily displayed ideas. That is, require suggestions in writing on cards or Post-its®. This way, they are brief, easily displayed, and quickly moved. (For those who cannot write in English, dictating the idea to one who writes it down is perfectly acceptable.)

Keep your spreadsheet application in its holster; do not make lists of ideas! Remember the fingerprint factor. Keep and manage the ideas in the original form—the idea card. People have more sense of ownership when suggestions retain their fingerprints, their own handwriting and signature. Computer-generated lists are a form of alienation, especially for those who do not work in this medium every day. If it is in the computer, the idea has become "yours." If it is in my handwriting, it stays "mine."

Create a visual representation of the way ideas move through the improvement process:

- First, ideas are submitted.
- Second, they are screened and either advanced to a queue or rejected.
- Third, they become actively worked on.
- Fourth, implementation is complete.

Such a process can look like Figures 10.4a and 10.4b. In them, you can see column headings for Ideas, To Do, Doing, and Done. As the cards move across the board and the tally of implemented suggestions climbs, it is difficult for holdout curmudgeons to maintain that, "Management never listens to us." Take them to the board, show the movement of cards, and point out the number implemented—each still in the handwriting of the person who made the suggestion—and suggest this way of being heard is open to them as well.

The process is uncomplicated:

Step 1: Employees write idea cards (or Post-its®) and post them in the Ideas column.

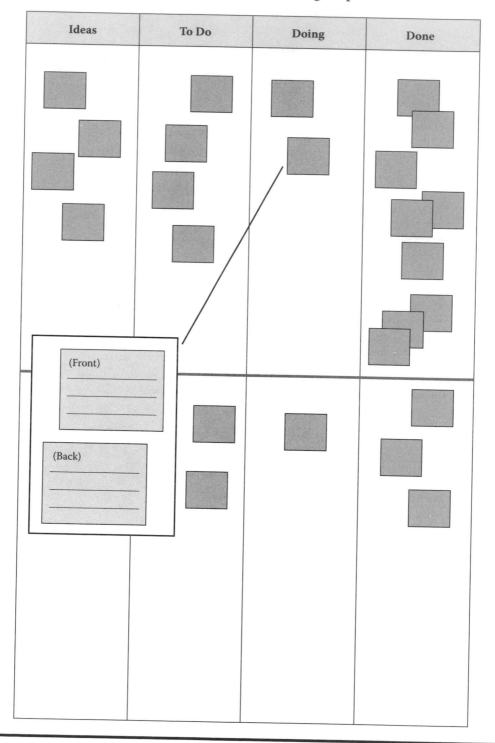

Figure 10.4a   Suggestion system idea board.

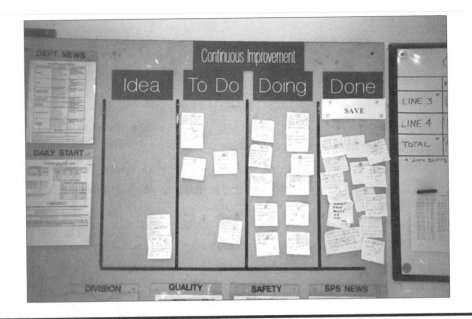

Figure 10.4b   Improvement suggestion idea board.

Step 2: Once a week or more often, the supervisor and team leader review newly submitted ideas to advance them to the To Do column or reject them. They note the reason for rejection on the back of the card, and talk with the author about the reason for rejection. In practice, few ideas are rejected. Reasons for rejection are typically scope (things for other departments to do), relevance to the business, or conflict with lean principles.

Step 3: At least once a week, the value stream manager, supervisor, team leader, and value stream support group representatives review the new submissions. They identify ideas that are beyond the resources or ability of the supervisor and team leader. Those ideas get moved to the support group segment of the board (below the dividing line in Figure 10.4) and assigned to a specific individual.

Step 4: The supervisor and team leader move ideas from the To Do to the Doing column and assign them for implementation, noting the assignment on the card. The assignments are usually to the supervisor or team leader. The number of active suggestions is based on the capacity to get them done within a week. As work progresses or is completed, brief notes on the back of the card document plans and actions.

Step 5: As an idea is implemented, move the card to the Done column and update the tally of implemented ideas.

Step 6: The team leader covers the status of the suggestion process once a week in a daily tier-one start up meeting, congratulating those whose ideas are Done, or implemented, and reviewing ideas that have moved to the Doing column.

Step 7: Some organizations use team rewards for reaching designated levels of implemented suggestions, such as pizza upon reaching one implemented suggestion per team member (or the equivalent number). Others find the motivational impact of people being able to influence their environment and being recognized for it is enough to keep the process healthy.

The improvement suggestion system is explicitly connected to the three-tier meeting process. The same expected versus actual accountability review applies to employee suggestions as with any other improvement assignment. Ideas assigned to team leaders show up on the department-level (tier two) task assignment board. Those assigned to support group representatives show up on the value stream-level task assignment board.

Lean Training for Line Leaders

A person's rank in an organization does not have much bearing on how they learn to be a lean thinker and implementer. There is some benefit in learning from a book, class, or presentation, but people in any position really learn lean by hands-on involvement and one-to-one coaching.

This is inconvenient! It implies that mass classroom training on lean principles, though efficient, does not get the job done. Unfortunately, we cannot expect lean training classes alone to transform first line supervisors and team leaders into lean thinkers.

It is not unusual for initial lean training in an organization to come from outside, from a lean consultant or sensei, as noted in Chapter 7. The sensei may do some limited classroom training but mainly the sensei spends one-on-one time with executives, plant managers, and perhaps with second level production leaders, selected engineers, and specialists. One-on-one coaching from a sensei can be very effective, but it goes slowly and is costly. (Indeed, this is a constraint Toyota has experienced; its growth has outpaced its sensei resources.) As a result, the sensei's exposure to the rest of the organization is limited, and, even with the original select group, typically does not continue beyond a year.

The key point is that hands-on experience and coaching is the way people learn lean. This raises important questions: How can organizations bring personal coaching to the large number of team leaders and supervisors? And what are alternatives to the expensive external sensei?

Where Conventional Training Fits In

Conventional training does play a role in improving lean knowledge and applications. My preference is for lean training to be delivered by lean implementers. After all, "sensei" translates as teacher, or one who has gone before. The training delivery of an experienced lean hand might not be polished compared to a professional trainer. But deficits in style are usually more than overcome by the authenticity that comes from personal experience, especially from within the organization. Many consulting firms and universities offer weeklong or longer lean training programs. If you have no access to internal resources, these can be a starting point. But keep in mind this lean advice: smaller quantities more frequently, delivered to the point of use. Where you can, provide lean training when and where it is needed on the tool, skill, or principle to be used. Where possible, avoid training that batches all the tools and principles together; in other words, avoid over-production in training just as elsewhere.

Where you can, understand the need for a specific lean tool or concept, and then focus training on it. Consider needs like these: the ability to do root cause problem solving to eliminate a flow interrupter; knowing how to use a machine balance chart to calculate kanban quantities; or learning to make observations in order to balance work so it flows among people in a work group. This is a more effective approach than referring people to tab 11 in the binder they brought home from their weeklong training session. When using this modular approach to training, you can increase its effectiveness by immediately assigning students to apply in their work areas what they have learned in class. Then, follow up by assessing the application and giving feedback on what was done well and what could be improved. The close linkage of concept and real world application can be powerful.

Sometimes, that "ah-ha!" experience is enough for an individual to firmly cement the understanding and how-to skill … but not very often.

When the sensei works with a student, he or she tailors the approach to the individual. What part of a concept have you mastered? What needs more work? If you can see the need for an application in situation A, can you recognize the concept's application in situation B, in a different

CASE STUDY: TRAINING BY THE BOOK, OR BY THE FLOOR?

A new manufacturing VP thought more lean training was the answer to improving performance, and requested help from the corporate training group. A year later, corporate training delivered a curriculum that filled a three-inch binder. The contents were organized in modules, each covering a separate topic such as value stream mapping, plan for every part, kanban pull systems, leading team start-up meetings, and standardized work. The modules were lengthy, each at least half a day in class, and included classroom tests and assessment forms to rate applications on the floor.

Some plants ignored the material; others struggled to deliver it. In the company's most advanced lean plant, the plant manager and lean leader knew they needed a better way to develop the lean skills of team leaders and supervisors. They decided to use what they could from the binder.

Phase 1: Training. With help from their plant trainer, they revised and shortened each module to no more than two classroom hours. The plant manager told the plant's support group leaders, team leaders, and supervisors that to remain in those positions he expected them to complete all the (revised) modules and pass each test. The plant devised a flexible sign up schedule for classes, and also put the modules online. A few team leaders chose not to complete the series and returned to production jobs. The plant staff and the rest of the team leaders and supervisors completed the modules and passed the tests. So far, so good.

Phase 2: Assessing on the job. Several months after the training was completed, the plant manager and lean leader recognized the lean training had been only partially successful. Some of the "graduates" were effectively able to use the skills and tools in their daily work while others were not. Again, the plant modified the material in the training binder to fit their need. This time, they reworked the assessment into a development plan, expanding a generic numeric scale to descriptive comments on each module's practices, noted in three categories: below expectations, meets expectations, exceeds expectations. Blank development plans in hand, they met individually with a small pilot group of team leaders in their own areas to assess the practices covered in the training. The pilot revealed different gaps in performance from a variety of causes. Some leaders understood a concept but not how to apply it. In other cases, a given module did not directly apply in a particular work area, such as flow design in a lot-by-lot fabrication area. Some lacked the computer skills to create or update forms or tracking charts, or needed coaching in leading meetings, or in interpersonal skills.

Phase 3: A team of coaches. The assessments and development gaps uncovered a need for tailored follow-up. The plant decided to experiment with one-on-one coaching using its own resources. They assembled a coaching team of individuals with the skills needed to address the development plans. One of the coaches had deep technical lean expertise, one was good at spreadsheet programs, another coached interpersonal skills and how to prepare for and lead stand-up meetings. An individual team leader might have 20- to 30-minute coaching sessions from one, two, or three coaches a week, on the floor in his or her work area.

Phase 4: Expanding development. The pilot leaders were reassessed after four to eight weeks of coaching. All had closed the gaps identified in their development plans. Based on this success, the plant extended the approach to all the team leaders, again a small number at a time to match the capacity of their coaching team. During this process, it became clear that some supervisors had development needs similar to those of the team leaders who reported to them, so the plant began including developmental assessments and coaching for supervisors as well, particularly on the skills to be more effective coaches for their team leaders.

The outcome. Overall, most of those who passed the training module tests were able to close the gaps identified in their individual development plans, but some did not. The plant manager, reflecting on the process and improved lean skills among plant leaders, calls the approach of training-assessment-development plan-coaching a critical factor in the plant's continued lean progress and improved operating results.

part of the operation, or in an altogether different part of the enterprise? A repeated algorithm behind the sensei's approach to teaching and learning is "knowledge, practice, feedback." The sensei should work with you, as long as you show motivation and progress, until you can see, for example, how the concept of load leveling or production smoothing (heijunka) applies in an engineering or marketing department just as it does in a physical production value stream. In fact, taking office and technical/professional people to a manufacturing setting can be helpful. Seeing in a physical, three-dimensional operation an otherwise abstract concept can help make the connection between concept and its potential applications.*

Lean knowledge comes from practice in seeing and in doing. Knowledge, whether from training or another source, is only the beginning. Knowledge along with practice and feedback (an application of plan-do-check-act) leads to knowing *what* the concept is, *why* it is important, *how* it works, recognizing *where* it can apply, and being able to *implement* or *teach* it in disparate and apparently unrelated circumstances. Conventional training, regardless of approach, can open the door to the lean journey, but coaching is needed to see the path and progress along it.

What If Production People Don't Buy into Lean?

Problems with buy-in are almost always problems with leadership. These often include at least some of the following: a poorly articulated or weak case for change, not bothering to respect people's legitimate questions, failure to set clear expectations at all levels, weak or inconsistent follow-up on newly announced accountabilities and processes.

Even when none of these problems is present, some people on the production floor are just ornery. They bring a variety of personal and personality problems to work that lead them to refuse to accept the team leader's authority. That is especially a problem when you have just established team leader positions. A few people are likely to test the system in ways that can be difficult or impossible for a supervisor to observe or document.

Providing team leaders with a measure of formal authority is an effective way to respond to these initial challenges, as well as those that arise from time to time. This stops short of including team leaders in the process of administering formal discipline. That should be left to supervision. Instead, it involves authorizing team leaders to make documented observations of problem behaviors that the supervisor can act on as a basis for disciplinary action.

That is not the same as the team leader administering formal discipline, and the documented observations do not always lead, and do not require, the supervisor to take disciplinary action. Further, each instance that results

---

* A word of caution: Manufacturing plants can be overwhelming to those with no plant experience and who are at the very beginning of learning lean. If your background is all manufacturing and your students' is all office, let the students develop familiarity with a lean concept before showing its application in the plant.

in a team leader's documented observation should be part of a conversation between the team leader and the employee in question. The authority comes from the fact that the team leader's notes are a sufficient basis, by themselves, for supervisors to take such disciplinary action as they see fit, without needing to have observed the behavior themselves. The effect on the responsiveness to team leaders' requests and suggestions is positive and dramatic.

Several conditions must be present for this process to be effective:

- First, supervisors and team leaders need to understand what constitutes enough to trigger documenting a problem.
- Second, the supervisor must follow up on the team leader's action, if only with a conversation with the employee acknowledging the incident. Otherwise, employees will have no more reason to pay attention to the team leader's requests than before.
- Third, the process has to be simple and easy to use.

One example of this is supplying team leaders with a pocket-sized pad of preprinted notes. The notes list categories for behavior that needs improvement on the front side. On the back, to acknowledge and reinforce helpful behavior, the categories list positive contributions (see Table 10.1). When the team leader observes behavior worth noting, he or she talks with the employee, shows him or her the note, then signs it and gives it to the supervisor. The supervisor responds within a shift, either talking with the team leader to better calibrate standards and/or talking with the employee.

Of course, it is important to be sure in advance that team leaders have the interpersonal skills to handle these kinds of interactions potentially

Table 10.1 Typical Items on Team Leader Notes

Thanks for	Please Work to Improve
Volunteering	Starting/stopping work on time
A positive attitude	Keeping up with standardized work
Offering a suggestion	Handling kanbans properly
Preventing a problem	Meeting requirements for quality
Extra effort	Following 5S standards/procedures
Other:	Other:
Team Leader comments	Team Leader comments

involving conflict. It is important for supervisors and team leaders to reach a mutual understanding as to what kind of behavior warrants what kind of response, and timeliness of follow-up.

Responding to Low Performers

As work becomes balanced and flow depends on everyone in the system meeting expected outcomes, low performers show up like they are under spotlights. These low performance situations can be troubling for leaders to deal with, but keep in mind that everyone in the shop is watching what you do. Does everyone have to keep up or are we willing to sacrifice performance for one or two? There is a direct five-point checklist to review in determining what to focus on when working to turn around problems in individual performance.

- Are the tools and equipment the person is using calibrated and working properly?
- Are parts and materials they are using within specifications?
- Has the person been trained?
- Have expectations for performance been made clear?
- Has there been regular feedback on performance?

If you rule out these benign explanations for a person's inability to do the work in a newly lean area, your options begin to get limited. As you go through these considerations, it can be helpful to keep a distinction in mind. There are those who "can't" do the work, perhaps unable to keep up in a takt-paced setting. Then there are those who "won't" do the work, for many reasons. Your organization may have a place for people who "can't" meet expectations in production environments. Whether or not such a haven is available, you almost certainly have a progressive discipline system. You may be used to using discipline only in cases of objectionable conduct, especially in a production workforce. More likely you use the discipline system for performance problems among the salaried workforce. You will need to seriously consider using your progressive discipline system for performance in the factory as well.

In these instances, the use of progressive formal discipline is an unambiguous sign to the employee that the performance problem is a real one that might eventually cost them their employment. When the alternative becomes unavoidable, some from the "won't" group suddenly become able to do the work everyone else does. In other cases, formal discipline is an increasingly clear signal for the person to find another position to move to where they can meet expectations, if such a position exists.

This is not a happy situation to encounter, but it is an implication of moving to a tightly defined, closely linked production process. If these cases are not managed, many in the operation will find the commitment to lean production open to question. It will be that much more difficult to develop disciplined adherence to standards if the standards do not apply universally.

Human Resources Policy Issues in Lean Management

Lean management will almost inevitably involve changes to your organization's human resource policies. Any change is best accompanied by a restatement of the business case for the change to lean production and an explicit connection between the case for change and the specific change at hand. Table 10.2 summarizes some of the policy areas that may be involved, their connection to lean production, and some potential obstacles to overcome in making the change.

The changes in policies may be dramatic and far reaching, such as changing hourly pay systems from piecework to a flat rate. They may involve changing the policy that governs job elimination related to process improvement activity and subsequent exposure to layoff. They may involve the kinds of changes in authority and application of the discipline system outlined above. Some changes are more mundane, like changing break or start times, though any and all of these changes are capable of sparking emotional reactions. Having a firm grasp of why you are making the change and anticipating the questions and reactions you are likely to face are important preparation for working through these potentially contentious issues.* Keep in mind that the best reaction often has nothing to do with stating the logic behind the change. Giving people the opportunity to make their displeasure heard is often the most effective thing you can do, especially since you are unlikely to be able to satisfy the desire to turn back the clock to the way things were before.

Your HR group is more likely to respond to your requests for support if they know something about the rationale for converting to lean production.

---

* See David W. Mann, 2000, "Why supervisors resist change and what you can do about it," *Journal of Quality and Participation* 23 (May/June): 20–23, for a description of a method for preparing leaders for these kinds of encounters.

Table 10.2 Potential Policy Issues in a Lean Conversion

Policy Area	Link to Lean Production	Potential Obstacles
Rotation	Rotation mitigates risk of repetitive stress injuries in work elements repeated at a takt pace; it results in a multiskilled workforce with many able to step in when needed; and it provides many eyes on each job, which increases the chances to see and suggest improvements.	Rotation must apply to all or it may be unenforceable. When initiated, not all may be able to succeed at each job in the rotation pattern. Will that disqualify those who cannot meet quality and takt requirements? What options will they have?
Layoff	Even though lean will result in elimination of some work, nobody will lose employment as a result of process improvement. Lean should make us more competitive, preserving jobs in the long run. Layoffs might be needed if business conditions change.	Are you willing to temporarily absorb employees made surplus by lean improvements? If not, forget about employees' cooperation and involvement in improvement.
Classifications and grades	Lean works best with a flexible, multiskilled workforce. Specialized knowledge is now contained in standardized work; previously complex jobs have been redesigned to support flow or to make them easier, like quicker setups. Existence of many grades and classifications no longer warranted because of the changes in the jobs.	Many are proud of the grade or classification they have achieved and will see consolidation as a loss. Are you willing to work your way through this with your people? Can you reach agreement with your union, if applicable, balancing other changes with this one?
Pay	Lean works best with a flexible, multiskilled workforce. Because work has been restructured into smaller elements, and we have begun rotation and consolidated grades and classifications, the pay system needed to change to catch up with changes on the production floor.	Reducing distinctions in pay may end up reducing the pay of some employees. Are you willing to work your way through this with people, perhaps by phasing in the change?

Table 10.2 (continued)   Potential Policy Issues in a Lean Conversion

Policy Area	Link to Lean Production	Potential Obstacles
Common or synchronized start times	Lean reduces buffers of inventory between processes. To maintain leaner, lower levels of inventory, production needs to begin and end at specific times so we make what we need when we need it.	Start times can be surprisingly emotional. Are you willing to work your way through this with people? Can you phase in this change to give people time to adjust personal or family arrangements?
Common or synchronized break times	We need to make what we need when we need it. Synchronizing breaks in continuous process areas may be required for that. With balanced, takt-paced work, when one person leaves, everything stops. That means when one breaks, all break.	Some have been able to manage their own schedules, including longer or extra breaks. You will have to be willing to enforce break times more than you may have in the past, often an unpleasant duty.

HR is likely to be interested in how lean is changing the shop floor, people's jobs, and access to information, and their opportunities to participate in changes that affect them. Involve HR as much as you can, as early as you can—changing policies can take quite a bit of time in many organizations.

Take HR executives to the floor and show them what the new ways look like in comparison to the old. Share with them the case for change. Introduce them to the statistics on ergonomic benefits from the new job designs and from rotation. Show them the visual proof of your methods for involving employees, for listening and responding to their suggestions. Enroll them on your team; they'll come to help out eventually if not right away.

Summary: Resolving People Issues to Support Lean Production and Lean Management

Predictability in the daily availability of people and a structured approach for responding to unplanned absences would be desirable in any production environment. It is especially important in a lean production environment paced by takt time. Lean management provides a suite of labor planning tools that makes attendance more visual, thus raising the level of public accountability for coming to work. Lean management's labor planning tools bring stability at least to the process of responding to unplanned absences.

An effective employee improvement suggestion system can be deceptively demanding if those in leadership positions are not prepared to respond to what is, in effect, new work being delegated to them in the form of improvement suggestions. The vacation paradox builds new capacity for acting on suggestions. Until that capacity is in place, it is best to hold off implementing an idea system. Actual versus expected and visual control applies in managing the suggestion system just as it does in most of lean management. Employees appreciate being able to see the progress of their ideas, and leaders benefit from the increased trust in lean that comes from the visual evidence of having listened to and acted on ideas from the shop floor.

Training is often part of HR's responsibilities. Lean training is most effective when the training group partners with operating units first to understand lean and the role of coaching in lean learning. With this foundation, the training group can help develop the materials and approaches the operating units need to develop lean skills and thinking throughout their workforce.

A lean implementation can raise questions about a number of HR policies. Lean requires much more precision in execution than a batch-and-queue system, so issues that interfere with disciplined adherence to lean processes must be addressed quickly. Equipping team leaders to make authoritative observations of problem behaviors is one step. Preparing to apply progressive discipline to "can't" and "won't" performers is another. Beyond that, a series of policy changes may be called for, ranging from pay and consolidation of grades and classifications to required performance in job rotation, alterations in layoff policy, and changes in break and start times.

It is a good idea to involve the HR organization early and thoroughly in lean. With a context in which to view the requested changes to support lean production and lean management, HR is much more likely to understand and work to accommodate your requests.

Chapter 11

Sustain What You Implement

The purpose of lean management is to sustain a lean production system. Without a lean management system, lean production implementations often falter, sometimes fail, and virtually never deliver up to their long-run promises. So, what sustains the lean management system?

In a word, it's you.

As a leader in your lean production environment, you are the force that can motivate and sustain lean management in your unit. That applies no matter what your position, whether you are responsible for a team or department, a value stream or plant, a business unit, or the organization as a whole.

Expectations for processes and the ability to compare actual versus expected is the thread that connects the elements in lean management. The person at the top of the unit, however defined, is in the position to set expectations and, most importantly, to follow up on them. Defining expectations and holding people accountable to them is the key to a successful lean implementation. The higher in the organization this extends, the better the chances for success.

Making accountability easier to see and execute is the objective that underlies lean management's ways of thinking, its tools and approaches. But, do not confuse tools and techniques with the indispensable ingredient: you as the chief accountability officer. Without you, no tools, no processes, no books can make your lean implementation a healthy, growing, improving proposition. This chapter shows how leaders must sustain the lean management system.

You Already Have a Management System!

Why is accountability such a big deal, such an important factor in sustaining lean systems? The reason is written in your organization's history: You already have a management system. Actually, you as an individual might be developing a new one, but almost everyone working in a newly converted lean operation still has the old one pretty firmly in place. Because of this, even with all the discipline and accountability you can muster, you should expect to see backsliding in just about every aspect of lean you implement. Do not expect to like it, but be prepared for it.

Why does this happen if you have carefully implemented lean management along with lean production? Recall Smokey the Bear and the difference between breaking and extinguishing habits. You should not expect the new ways to stick just because people have adhered to them for a day or week. The old ways will reassert themselves in people who are very good, even you! Remember, nothing worth doing stays done forever without diligence, discipline, and hard work. The case "Don't Solve Production Problems by Heroics" illustrates these points. This cautionary tale only serves to illustrate that nothing worth doing stays done by itself. As much as lean management is about anything, it is about this.

What Should *You* Do?

Stick to what you have just implemented. You have installed the engine, drive train, and controls of the lean management system. Do not leave it in the garage, waiting for things to get difficult before learning how to "drive" your new management system. Proficiency in lean management is like many other things; you get better with practice. It shows when you have to perform under pressure.

Consider the steps you have taken: You have defined expectations for performance and implemented tools to compare expected versus actual execution. These expectations are defined in day-to-day, operational terms in leader standard work. An important element in this standard work is to regularly reinforce visual controls. The visuals reflect adherence to or variation from processes and expectations. Then, the daily three-tier meetings and the cycle of assessment, assignment, and accountability will lead to temporary countermeasures while causes of variation are found and eliminated.

Rely on Leader Standard Work

The steps you need to take should be documented in your own standardized work. Follow it as you would follow a recipe for success. Require and reinforce others to follow their standard work as well. Reinforcement comes by briefly reviewing each subordinate's completed standard work document every day. Respond in a timely and appropriate way to requests they have noted on their standard work forms. Respond as well to the other things you see on the forms. Is there a pattern of missing a particular element or elements? Does what you observe in the production area square with what you see in notes made on the standard work documents? When you treat your subordinates' completed daily standard work forms as living documents that prompt action, you powerfully reinforce standard work as "the way we do things around here—now." This is especially true when problems beset your area.

Keep in mind the team leader who said her standard work allowed her to turn down requests to do others' jobs that would have distracted her from her duties. Also recall the supervisor who was able to steer his way out of chaos by returning to his standard work. With it, he regained control with much less time, effort, and frustration than in the few days following his vacation. Leader standard work is the lean management tool of highest leverage. Look to it to sustain your lean management and production implementations.

Maintain the Visual Controls

Where you have implemented visual controls, follow up to be sure they are being maintained. Verifying that visuals are current and the information on them is accurate and clear should be one of the key items on your standard work.

When problems arise in areas without visuals, quickly develop a tracking process and analysis appropriate to the problem. That is, when a reason for missed pitch is vague to the point where you have to ask the person who wrote it "What does this mean?", you have the opportunity to discuss the characteristics of well-written problem statements. Remember the axiom: no action without data (even if action and data are concurrent), no data without action! When reasons for misses are absent from the tracking forms or not clear enough to form the basis for taking the next step, treat these occurrences as teachable moments. You will have to explain several times how the data from visuals lead to assessment, assignment, and accountability for putting countermeasures in place and eliminating root causes. As people begin to see longstanding problems resolved, based on what appeared on their visual controls, most eventually will make the connection.

Without the information from well-executed visual controls, you will be driving your lean management system in the dark without either map or headlights. You can get somewhere that way, but you will have the occasional crash and when you arrive, you will have no idea how to get there again.

Visuals give you the information you need to choose the direction to apply your resources for root cause improvement. With visuals, you can dig out of problems; without them, you are likely simply to keep on digging the same holes over and over again.

CASE STUDY: DON'T SOLVE
PRODUCTION PROBLEMS BY HEROICS

A new product was replacing an older one on a 90-day schedule, so volume estimates for the new product were accurate. The leadership team for the product startup had considerable experience designing and operating two lean conversions, but only briefly. The processes they designed for this product incorporated much of what they had learned. They implemented a mixed model, one-piece-flow assembly cell. A dedicated fabrication area replenished what assembly consumed, based on visual pull signals from fabrication's supermarket. As the preparation and debugging period ended, they seemed ready to take on the production volume from the outgoing product that was being replaced by their cosmetically identical, but internally superior, new model. Even so, as production shifted from the old to the new product with a sharp increase in daily production, all manner of material supply problems broke loose. These problems had been lurking, but now were flushed out of hiding by the product cutover and sudden fivefold increase in volume that came with it.

The assembly supervisor was a veteran of two previous lean conversions and had seen the kinds of glitches that come with a new operation. In this case, the glitches seemed to have gotten the better of him. On the occasion in question, about a month after the cutover, shortage of a particular purchased part threatened to shut down his assembly operation. This was on the heels of many frustrating days of start-and-stop operation caused by other shortages. The supervisor decided to keep assembly running, opting to hold the unfinished units in a finished goods staging area until the missing parts could be supplied and installed.

He was found the next day in the staging area down on his knees installing the missing parts himself. He explained he had continued to build units the day before "just to get the order to the customer faster." When pressed, he had to admit his old-style "heroic" response had in fact created more delay. Standard operating procedure in the response system (that he had been involved in developing), when encountering a stockout, called for stopping the assembly operation and its 25 or so people and calling materials management. Depending on the situation, the assemblers were either to stand and wait, or work on "job-jar" items until a resolution was reached.

The needed parts had been in the building at the time, on the receiving dock. It is quite likely the materials manager, who would have been summoned by the response system, would have been able to locate and deliver the parts to the line after an annoying but relatively short delay. Production could have resumed and the units would have been on their way to the customer a day earlier at the cost of a half hour of overtime.

Bear in mind, this case involved a supervisor with a history of commitment to lean. He understood and practiced the principles well and was considered a good lean supervisor. Yet, when the wind blew hard enough, the embers of the old habits—"keep it running; we'll fix 'em later"—flamed back to life. He did not need scolding, but he did need to be reminded that working around the "rocks" exposed in the system does not pave a path to success in lean.

Further, a look at the production-tracking chart in his area showed no entries documenting problems with material availability or delivery. The supervisor and his team leaders were too busy fashioning workarounds to tend their own process and document reasons for missed pitches. Without these data, the supervisor and value stream manager were unable to show what were their biggest problems. The result was more energy put into expediting, firefighting, and finger pointing.

Without data to systematically identify frequency and duration of interruptions, nobody, neither support groups nor floor leaders, could create a picture of what was happening and act to identify and address causes. All anyone could do was react to the last incident. The result was to replace stockouts with expedited overstock. The area was soon swamped with unneeded material. All of this occurred in a value stream that regularly held three-tier meetings led by a value stream manager with experience using them effectively! But here, in the absence of data, the daily assignments were mainly for expediting.

After a few weeks of this kind of chaos, the value stream leader realized that one of the team leaders in the assembly cell had to "stay home" in the cell. This team leader's mission, no matter what, was to faithfully complete the entries on the performance-tracking chart each pitch, actual units produced versus expected and the reasons for misses. With this information, the value stream leadership team was able to Pareto chart interruptions and take systematic action to uncover and then resolve the causes. Within a few weeks, the clutter in the area diminished and production began to stabilize.

Conduct Gemba Walks Regularly

If you have had the benefit of gemba walks with a sensei, remember that others may not have had the same opportunities to learn and apply; had their efforts reviewed and critiqued; and had the chance to apply again. The mantle of sensei now is on your shoulders, even if you continue to work with your own sensei, and even if you do not consider yourself an expert.

The learning model for lean management especially, just as for lean production, is the master-apprentice relationship. When you gemba walk others, you accomplish several things. You give others the opportunity for tailored, one-on-one learning. You demonstrate the importance of going to the place, looking at the process, talking with the people as a key in assessing process performance. And, in a structured, scheduled way you reserve time to observe people and processes, draw inferences about steps you need to take, and refresh your ground-level view of how the process is operating to bring to your tier of the daily accountability process.

When you are in the production area, be alert for even small incidents that signify old thinking or habits. As a teacher, use what you see on the production floor to refresh and enliven basic lean principles; it makes it easier for people to make their own connections between lean concepts and what it means to apply them.

You should expect to teach many lessons repeatedly, even with your best people. Recall the supervisor kneeling in the shipping area completing the assembly work he had shortchanged the day before. Have patience with people, but only so much. Try using the rule of three before considering next steps with individuals who seem slow either in understanding your lessons or in taking them to heart. That is, give people three chances (which might be on successive weeks' gemba walks on a given point, for example) before beginning to discuss performance.

As you give feedback, be most firm with those in the positions of most authority. When you convert to lean, everyone's knowledge of what it means and how it works starts at zero. Just because some are in positions of greater responsibility does not mean they automatically know more about lean production and lean management than their subordinates. Indeed, unless they have invested their own time in hands-on implementation activity, they may know less about lean management than those below them.

This is not about who is "on board" with the new program, nor about executives being quick studies. This is about learning to think differently by having been involved in acting differently. The leaders in your organization represent your greatest leverage. If anything, you should be most demanding of their speed in progressing on the lean learning curve, which will mean requiring them to go to gemba and, once there, to become directly involved.

Finally, prepare yourself to be reminded on occasion by others of your own need to more faithfully follow the principles.

Keep Yourself Honest

I often hire a guide the first time I go fishing in a new area. I find it helpful to benefit from one with knowledge and experience when in new territory. Expert, experienced consultation is an essential ingredient in the mix as you pursue your lean conversion. Usually, you will find your sensei in the ranks of outside consultants.

Using a consultant in lean is like fishing in another way, too. Folk wisdom holds that if you give me a fish I can feed myself for a day. But, if you teach me to fish I can feed myself for a lifetime. In other words, sustaining lean production and, especially, sustaining lean management, largely has to be a do-it-yourself proposition. Yes, you can call in your sensei periodically to assess your status, but in most cases you will find that he or she is telling you things you already know, but have somehow overlooked, allowed to slide, or missed in some way. Is there an alternative to paying for a periodic scolding by your sensei (who in any case soon will likely make the suggestion to cease these visits)?

Even if you relied heavily on a consultant to design your lean production system—a practice I do not recommend—it is a practical impossibility to rely on a consultant to sustain your new system. The same holds true

Table 11.1 What Consultants Can and Cannot Do For You

Rely on your sensei to:	Rely on yourself to:
Teach lean principles, techniques, how to see the difference between batch and lean	Implement the new lean system and lean management
Offer advice, critique, suggestions, prods	Make decisions regarding how to proceed
Stretch and challenge your thinking	Make decisions regarding how to proceed
Provide "ah-ha!" insights	Create and maintain disciplined adherence to the system
Stimulate you to take action	Continuously compare actual to expected
Review and critique your lean management practices	Work directly with your subordinates regarding executing their expectations and extending the system in there areas

regarding lean implementation project teams. You may have needed a team for some of the more technical and analytic aspects of technical design and implementation, but you cannot rely on them to run your area for you.

Consultants, internal or external, can talk with your leaders about expected versus actual outcomes until they are blue in the face, all to no avail. Unless the boss makes it clear by his or her behavior that something new is expected, subordinates will continue to conduct business pretty much as usual. The nature of discipline in organizations is that it is always a domestic product, never an import! (See Table 11.1.)

Assess Your Lean Management System

It is a good idea periodically to assess the overall status of your lean management implementation. This is an idea derived from the lean principle of pursuit of perfection. An assessment using the measurement provided here or another one should do three things for you.

First, the dimensions and questions themselves should help to clarify what you are working toward, for yourself and for the rest of your organization. In this respect, they are standards, and are better referred to in that way. They are not to be attended to only when assessments roll around. They represent steps toward lean goals, things to keep in mind routinely. Because the assessment dimensions represent the standards you are striving to achieve, the questions should be known to all—in advance of an assessment and on a regular basis. It is common in lean organizations to feel that the more you achieve, the more lies ahead to be done. You will most likely come to refine and redefine your understanding of what it means to achieve a standard, raising the level of expected performance as you go. This will reflect your growing understanding that lean is an improvement system.

Second, an assessment should tell you where you stand relative to your standards and relative to your earlier status. It gives you a data point with which to evaluate the effectiveness of the work you have been doing to improve since the last measurement. This is not exactly profound, but without a standard of comparison it is easy to believe that all is going pretty well, people understand what they are being asked to do and why, and we are making progress. Good: Now prove it.

Third, the results of an assessment will help you identify where you need to focus efforts to improve. It may also lead you to conclude that you or your organization need another dose of targeted help from the outside, perhaps from peers in a noncompeting industry, from a professional association, or from a teacher. Either way, the results should help clarify a next set of goals for shoring up a category where results have not been up to par with others, or for choosing one or a few areas to focus on for improvement in the next assessment.

Details of the Lean Management System Assessment

The lean management standards cover process and behavior, and apply with slight variations in office (administrative, technical, and professional) settings, as well as in manufacturing settings. There are nine manufacturing dimensions and eight office dimensions (visuals for production support is omitted from the office standards). The standards define five levels of system status. This section lists the categories and levels in the standards. Both sets of standards are in the Appendix and are downloadable at www.dmannlean.com and http://www.crcpress.com/product/isbn/9781439811412. A downloadable version of the radar chart assessment report (see Figure 11.1 for an example) in spreadsheet format is also available at both websites noted above.

Dimension	Actual	Maximum
Leader Standard Work	3	5
Visual Controls-Process	4	5
Visual Controls-Support	1.3	5
Standard Accountability	4	5
Value Stream Maps	2.7	5
Process Definition	2.3	5
Process Discipline	2.3	5
Process Improvement	2.7	5
Problem Solve	3	5

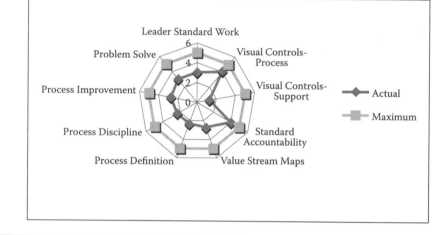

Figure 11.1   Score profile radar chart for lean management assessment.

Lean management standards dimensions:

1. Leader standard work
2. Visual controls—production
3. Visual controls—production support *(manufacturing only)*
4. Daily accountability process
5. Value stream mapping
6. Process definition
7. Disciplined adherence to process
8. Process improvement
9. Root cause problem solving

Levels in the lean management standards:

Level 1: Pre-implementation
Level 2: Beginning implementation
Level 3: First recognizable state
Level 4: System stabilizing
Level 5: Sustainable system

Conducting an Assessment

The lean management assessment should be conducted on the floor by looking and asking. Make direct observations (e.g., "Are the visuals current? Are the reasons for misses clear enough for taking the next step?"). Talk with people (e.g., "Do you have a regular way to make suggestions for improvement? Please tell me about it. In your opinion, how well does it work? Have you ever made a suggestion? How about the people you work with?")

Prepare a format that lists the criteria by level for each category to guide and record observations (or download the format based on the one in the Appendix). That way, documentation supporting a rating is right there with the criteria. Table 11.2 provides an example of such a format. Appendix A includes a complete lean management assessment for manufacturing settings and one for office settings. Figure 11.1 shows the radar chart format for displaying assessment ratings.

When Should You Assess?

Do it now. It does not matter how far along you are in your lean journey. If you are just starting, an assessment will help you share expectations with others, and it will give you a baseline to judge how far you will have come.

Of course, you have activities going on right now that will show improved results if you hold off on the next assessment so you can see the progress. That should always be true! Instead, establish a schedule and stay with it. Measuring yourself every quarter is enough of an interval to expect to see progress—a long enough period of time in which to achieve improvement. It may also be a short enough interval to make it seem rushed, at least initially. An assessment is not a takt-paced activity, but assessments on a regular schedule embody the ideas of time and pace that are so important in lean.

A related point is to keep the assessment process simple and free of bureaucracy. If you will be conducting an assessment every 90 days, then that is all the more reason you will want the process to be straightforward, rather than a burdensome time-eater. And, you will want the results in a timely fashion so you can get started on the next set of improvements. After all, your next assessment is coming up in 90 days!

Who Should Assess?

You have several options. All of them should reflect the "open book" nature of the assessment tool and process. That is, if the assessment categories and

Table 11.2 Example of an Assessment Observation and Rating Form

Lean Management Standards: Manufacturing Leader Standard Work	Date and Location

Diagnostic Questions:

1. Do leaders have standard work? Do they follow it? Do you carry it with you as a routine? Do you have it with you now?

2. Is leader standard work regularly reviewed for updating? Has it been updated recently; when was the last time?

3. Are standard work documents used as working documents, as a diary of the day? Are the leader standard work documents reviewed daily by leaders' supervisors? Weekly with the subordinate?

4. Is there a regular place where completed standard work documents are stored? Is it visual? Is a leader standard work form available for all to see?

5. Has leader standard work been used in this area in transitions between leaders?

Progress			*Notes*
1	Pre-implementation	No leader standard work is in evidence.	
		Some leaders have heard of the idea of leader standard work.	
		Most leaders see standard work as applicable to production work only.	
2	Beginning implementation	Leader standard work exists for a few isolated positions.	
		Where it exists, leader standard work is carried some of the time and filled out irregularly.	
3	First recognizable state	Leader standard work has not been revised. Most leaders talk about it as a compliance, check the box exercise.	
		Standard work is in place for all leaders in the value stream, team leads through value stream manager. The standard work for all leaders has been revised once.	
		Most leaders carry their standard work with them, follow it, and use it as a working daily document.	
		Most leaders understand the benefits of standard work and can give examples of how it has helped them.	

Table 11.2 (continued)   Example of an Assessment Observation and Rating Form

Progress			Notes
4	System stabilizing	All leaders carry and follow leader standard work and use it as a working daily record.	
		All superiors regularly review subordinates' standard work documents daily.	
		All leaders can identify how standard work benefits them. Standard work is regularly reviewed and revised.	
5	Sustainable system	Standard work is regularly reviewed daily by the next level as a monitoring and communication vehicle. It is reviewed weekly jointly by subordinate and supervisor for patterns, revisions.	
		Completed standard work documents are visually maintained by day of week for each leader. A blank copy of leader standard work is posted in the area.	
		All transitions between leaders include review and walkthrough of leader standard work. All new leaders follow standard work from day one in the job.	

Few < 25%; Some < 50%; Most > 75%; All = 100%.

questions describe your standards for lean management, would you not want them to be widely understood and practiced? One way to do that is just like the method you might use to calibrate with a subordinate on other assessments, such as a weekly 5S audit.

In the case of a 5S audit, you begin by reviewing the audit items with the subordinate (or group of subordinates). Then, each takes an audit form and conducts the audit jointly. Compare ratings for each observation. Discuss points where you see things differently to come to a common understanding of what a particular item means and how it should be scored. The following week, conduct the audits separately and then compare results. Discuss points of difference, go together to look at the specific area where your ratings differed, and come to agreement on how to score the item in question. Continue a second or third week until you are reasonably well calibrated. In this way, you have imparted your version of expected and how it compares with the commonly observed actuals.

You can use the same approach with the lean management assessment. Work your way down through your organization, starting with the people who report to you directly. As practice, before you go "live," assess an area jointly with your direct reports or with your supervisor, comparing notes as you go. Then assess another area individually. Compare findings. Consider starting with a single assessment category applied across an individual's or staff's area of responsibility to get a good sample of observations to compare. When you are calibrated on that category, go to the next. This can easily be part of your regularly scheduled gemba walks.

As you complete the calibration process with this first level of your organization, ask them to continue the process with those who report directly to them. You might want to add an item to your standard work to spot-check calibration as the process spreads more widely, just as your standardized work calls for spot-checking execution of other items in your subordinates' standard work.

You will have to consider the size of your organization as you commence a regular program of assessment. Each unit down to the team leaders should assess their status every 90 days. Maintain a profile (such as a bar chart or "radar" chart—see Figure 11.1) of category scores on display where you post your improvement plans for the period.

Wherever practical, a unit's assessment score profile should be based on the assessment by the leader of the next level in the organization—the unit leader's boss. At a certain scale, this will become impractical on a 90-day schedule. In those cases, consider a mixed model of assessors. Higher-level managers (plant managers, operations directors, VPs) should participate in complete assessments of subunits on a regular schedule to maintain a common understanding of standards of assessment top to bottom throughout the organization. Regular assessments for large subunits, such as large value streams, can be conducted by a team with rotating membership drawn from the leaders of other units, along with a core made up of members of the organization's lean team. These conditions will make it more important that assessment questions are reflected in the regular "inspection" items in the gemba walk protocols for leaders whose scope of responsibilities is large.

Interpreting the Assessment

It is more meaningful to look at assessment scores as a profile of the scores rather than as a single average value. That is because low performance on one dimension can have effects that spread through the others and eventually seriously compromise the way the lean management system performs. An average could easily conceal this finding. And averages provide no guidance on where to concentrate improvement efforts. Figure 11.1, a radar screen profile format, is an example of a directly interpretable profile format. Where it is meaningful to compare one unit with another or a single unit's performance over time, the total of category scores (with a possible range of 5 to 40) and a "consistency index" of the point spread between the lowest and highest category scores serves as the best measure for overall comparisons. Again, an unaddressed low score in one category will eventually be reflected in low scores in others as well. Here, the consistency index will draw attention to gaps in performance.

Keep Asking These Questions!

Lean starts with physical changes. Until the "facts on the ground" or on the production floor are different, there is not much to be gained from implementing lean management. But, as you begin making physical changes, do not implement them by themselves. Just as changes in the management system do not stand well by themselves, neither do technical changes. Every technical change requires support by the management system to maintain its integrity over time. If that is not a law of nature, it is darn close to it! Every time an element of lean production is implemented, also implement the elements of the management system needed to sustain it: expected versus actual visually controlled and added to the appropriate leader standard work.

   As a check, each time a technical or physical element of lean is put in place, including each time a change is made for improvement, ask these questions:

1. What lean management practices must accompany this element or change to sustain it as it was intended or to test its effectiveness?
2. How will these lean management practices be sustained?
3. How will you verify and monitor normal operation of the technical process?

A sensei trained in the Toyota approach to lean production asks three questions about just about everything:

1. What is the process?
2. How can you tell it is working?
3. What are you doing to improve it (if it is working)?

Table 11.3 Some Answers to Lean Management's Questions

Element of Lean Production System	Element of Lean Management System
Pull system supermarket	Supermarket daily/weekly audit process; current findings and trend posted
	Visual controls for "to be ordered," "ordered and due," and "overdue" deliveries
Kanban replenishment system	Comparison of actual replenishment cycle time versus standard set up plus run time for each order; reasons for misses noted
Flow line balanced to takt time	Hourly or more frequent production/pitch tracking versus goal and reasons for missed takts noted
	Daily value stream performance and task follow-up accountability meeting
Team leaders	Team leader standard work, supervisor and value stream manager standard work
Waterspider line-side supply	Timed standardized route; comparison of actual route cycle time versus standard time for each cycle; reasons for misses noted; routes regularly audited
Lean implementation activity of any kind	Daily and/or weekly gemba walks with a lean teacher making and following up on assignments for improvement

The additional questions I am suggesting may be implicit in these Toyota questions. No matter, ask them explicitly! Table 11.3 illustrates how some of these questions can be put into effect.

A Lean Culture Is a Beautiful Thing

Perhaps the best way to tell you are in an operation with a lean culture is to make a return visit to it. You should not have to be away long, only a few weeks. When you return, you should see things have changed. The changes do not have to be big; in fact, they can be pretty small in scale. Nevertheless, you should be able to hear people talk about the changes with a mixture of satisfaction and critique—like the do-it-yourselfer who talks with pride, yet points out the flaws in the beautiful piece of work he or she has just accomplished with his or her own hands. You should expect to hear something like this: "It is different than it was before. Here is how and why those differences are improvements. This is what remains to be done and what we are working on right now. Come back in a week and we will really have something to show you!"

The vision for the future can bud in the present when people become used to thinking about making things even better than they are today. In this way especially, a lean culture is a beautiful thing!

Summary: Maintaining Lean Management

Nothing sustains itself, certainly not lean production or lean management. So, act to sustain what you have done by following the processes you have implemented:

1. Use your standard work to establish or stick with a routine for monitoring your processes and the standard work of others. Remember, standard gives you the most leverage in lean management.
2. Check the status of visual controls as part of your routine. Insist that those responsible keep them current with accurate and complete entries where reasons are called for. Teach people, over again where necessary, why visual controls are important, where they fit in lean management, and how they drive action for improvement.
3. Follow up on what you expect in your daily three-tier accountability meetings. Assign tasks to stabilize, diagnose, and improve your area. Follow up on assignments and use visual accountability tools, for example, assignments posted on due dates and coded green for complete, red for overdue. Do not shrink from green/red color coding.
4. Schedule and stick with regular gemba walks with each subordinate. Stick faithfully to the schedule. Get a feel through asking questions what he or she knows well and what areas need strengthening. Give homework tasks to develop understanding and follow up assignments the next week. Take notes on your gemba walks; expect your students to do likewise. Remember the first purpose of gemba walking is to teach.
5. Everywhere, ask, "What is the process here?" How could someone tell? Is it working? How is it sustained?" Where necessary, note task assignments and gemba walk topics based on the quality of answers.

6. Establish an assessment schedule and a plan to phase it in. Share the detailed assessment categories widely. Post results where they can be seen. Expect to see evidence of improvement activities, such as A-3s, daily task assignments, and other process improvement work to address low-performing categories.

7. Realize you will never be done and take steps to avoid burnout for yourself and others. Organize a regular process for sharing internal best practices so you and your team can recognize the successes you have achieved, even as you gird for work on further improvement.

If you have not started, choose one item from this summary list and begin with it. Practice it, add another, practice both, add a third. With every step, you will find yourself further along your own lean journey.

Finally, remember what sustains the lean management system, and ultimately, the lean culture that grows from it. It is you and the example you set by your disciplined adherence to the system you have put in place.

Appendix A

**Lean Management Standards: Manufacturing
Leader Standard Work**

Date and Location

Diagnostic Questions:

1. Do leaders have standard work? Do they follow it? Do you carry it with you as a routine? Do you have it with you now?

2. Is leader standard work regularly reviewed for updating? Has it been updated recently; when was the last time?

3. Are standard work documents used as working documents, as a diary of the day? Are the leader standard work documents reviewed daily by leaders' supervisors? Weekly with the subordinate?

4. Is there a regular place where completed standard work documents are stored? Is it visual? Is a leader standard work form available for all to see?

5. Has leader standard work been used in this area in transitions between leaders?

Progress			Notes
1	Pre-implementation	No leader standard work is in evidence.	
		Some leaders have heard of the idea of leader standard work.	
		Most leaders see standard work as applicable to production jobs only.	
2	Beginning implementation	Leader standard work exists for a few isolated positions.	
		Where it exists, leader standard work is carried some of the time and filled out irregularly.	
3	First recognizable state	Leader standard work has not been revised. Most leaders talk about it as a compliance, check the box exercise.	
		Standard work is in place for all leaders in the value stream, team leads through value stream manager. The standard work for all leaders has been revised once.	
		Most leaders carry their standard work with them, follow it, and use it as a working daily document.	
		Most leaders understand the benefits of standard work and can give examples of how it has helped them.	

Progress			Notes
4	System stabilizing	All leaders carry and follow leader standard work and use it as a working daily record.	
		All superiors regularly review subordinates' standard work documents daily.	
		All leaders can identify how standard work benefits them. Standard work is regularly reviewed and revised.	
5	Sustainable system	Standard work is regularly reviewed daily by the next level as a monitoring and communication vehicle. It is reviewed weekly jointly by subordinate and supervisor for patterns, revisions.	
		Completed standard work documents are visually maintained by day of week for each leader. A blank copy of leader standard work is posted in the area.	
		All transitions between leaders include review and walkthrough of leaders' standard work. All new leaders follow standard work from day one in the job.	

Few < 25%; Some < 50%; Most > 75%; All = 100%.

Lean Management Standards: Manufacturing Visual Controls—Production   **Date and Location**

Diagnostic Questions:

1. Are visual controls in evidence for production processes in flow *and* pull areas? Are they current?

2. Are reasons for misses or flow interrupters described clearly and specifically enough to decide what next steps to take?

3. Are visuals regularly reviewed and used to drive improvement? How? Are improvements stimulated by visuals limited to crisis situations, or are there many, often small, improvements driven by visuals?

4. Are visuals in regular use for out-cycle tasks like waterspider routes, operator-based maintenance tasks, etc.?

5. Are visuals revised and changed as conditions change and issues either emerge or are resolved? Example?

6. Are visuals regularly signed off/initialed by leaders in the area?

7. Are visuals self-documented with "who does what here when" information at or on the visual controls themselves?

Progress			Notes
1	Pre-implementation	There are no visual controls in evidence.	
2	Beginning implementation	Production tracking charts are posted in flow area only.	
		Production tracking charts complete for few days or intervals of observation. They are often filled in irregularly with a focus on production numbers only. Reasons for misses are absent or too vague for action.	
		There is no or only irregular daily review of production visuals; response to information on the visuals is either absent or irregular. Visuals are a check the box activity.	

Progress			Notes
3	First recognizable state	Production tracking charts in flow areas are filled out regularly.	
		Most reasons for misses are specific and actionable.	
		Visuals are reviewed daily, and most of the time drive specific action assignments on an identified major interrupter or problem.	
4	System stabilizing	All reasons for misses are clear and actionable.	
		Visuals are reviewed daily, and regularly lead to specific action assignments on small as well as large flow interrupters and other problems.	
		Tracking charts are in use at pacemaker, in flow and in pull areas. Visuals are added and discontinued as needs change.	
5	Sustainable system	Visuals are in regular use for out-cycle tasks throughout the value stream.	
		All production charts are initialed several times daily by department and value stream leaders, and occasionally by plant managers and executives.	
		Visuals are regularly analyzed to identify most frequent interrupters or problems, which then drive problem solving and improvement implementation.	

Few < 25%; Some < 50%; Most > 75%; All = 100%.

Lean Management Standards: Manufacturing
Visual Controls—Nonproduction   **Date and Location**

Diagnostic Questions:

1. Are visuals in evidence for nonproduction processes such as labor planning, 5S, etc.? Are they current?

2. Can leaders explain how actual versus expected performance can be visually controlled in nonproduction tasks?

3. Is review of nonproduction visuals included in the appropriate leaders' standard work?

4. Are improvements stimulated by visuals limited to crises or are there many improvements, small as well as large?

5. Are visuals regularly reviewed and used to drive improvement? How? Example?

6. What visuals are used to display and monitor TPM schedule and performance, SPC charts, daily calibration, quality checks, etc.?

Progress			Notes
1	Pre-implementation	No visuals exist.	
		Monitoring and reports of production support activities, if any, are on IT systems, in rarely referred to books, or in local, informal, undocumented systems.	
2	Beginning implementation	Some leaders understand it is possible and the reasons for applying expected-versus-actual visual tracking for nonproduction processes.	
		Initial visual controls are posted for a few processes, but completion and review of them is irregular.	
3	First recognizable state	Many visuals are in evidence, most are current.	
		Most visuals are monitored and reviewed regularly as defined in leader standard work.	
		Reviews of the visuals drive action on some major issues.	

Progress			Notes
4	System stabilizing	Charts and tracking processes are in place for all recurring production support activities.	
		Reviews regularly lead to actions on small as well as large issues.	
		TPM tasks, schedules, and assignments visually displayed using heijunka methods, and TPM performance is visually displayed either at the machine, at the TPM heijunka, or both.	
5	Sustainable system	There is immediate (one-day follow up) on lapses in maintaining production support visuals.	
		Tracking data from production support visuals are regularly analyzed for trends to identify opportunities for improvement.	
		All problems identified in production support visuals are followed up for root cause solutions.	

Few < 25%; Some < 50%; Most > 75%; All − 100%.

Lean Management Standards: Manufacturing
Daily Accountability Process   **Date and Location**

Diagnostic Questions:

1. Do regular meetings focus on the status of processes as well as on results? How often?

2. Do start up meetings have clear purpose and agenda beyond today's production requirements/issues? Examples?

3. Do regular meetings result in task assignments to improve processes, and follow up past assignments currently due?

4. How are improvement assignments managed: visually, or by spreadsheet or list?

5. Do visual control charts result in task assignments to address interruptions?

6. How many leaders are familiar with basic project management techniques such as job breakdowns, and use them regularly? Examples?

7. How well integrated are support groups in value stream improvement activities? Examples?

Progress			Notes
1	Pre-implementation	Daily plant, value stream meetings focus only on traditional production/shortage issues.	
2	Beginning implementation	Team start-up meetings are held sporadically at the floor, department, and value stream levels.	
		Team start-up meetings often lack a clear purpose. Meeting agendas mostly focus on the production numbers, schedules, and hours.	
		Team, department, value stream meetings regularly held but few tasks assigned or followed up at department, value stream meetings. Attendance inconsistent. Many task assignments incomplete, many moved from original due date.	

Progress			Notes
3	First recognizable state	Most team, department, value stream meetings regularly held. Most use task assignments; follow up occurs at department and value stream meetings. Attendance is consistent. Most assignments are completed, most stay on the original date.	
		Task assignments are mostly made in response to major disruptions. The work breakdown approach is used in making some task assignments.	
		Many leaders consistently use the green/red color coding convention.	
4	System stabilizing	Meeting agendas are regularly followed, attendance is faithful.	
		Review of prior day's visuals results in assignments on small as well as large items (some of which are converted to A-3 projects). Task assignments from many sources, not just visuals.	
		Green/red coding is a regular practice. Task notes stay on original due dates Many completed tasks reflected in positive trends in value stream's measures.	
5	Sustainable system	Accountability is routine; boards and green/red coding are used effectively for long and short term assignments.	
		All supervisors grasp, regularly use basic project management tools in determining task assignments.	
		Appropriate support groups routinely participate in value stream accountability meetings and are integrated into value stream improvement activities.	

Few < 25%; Some < 50%; Most > 75%; All = 100%.

**Lean Management Standards: Manufacturing
Value Stream Maps**   **Date and Location**

Diagnostic Questions:

1. Are there documented plans for improvement visible in each area—at least each department?

2. Are current process improvement activities visual in each area?

3. Are value stream maps used to identify and track process improvements?

4. Are value stream maps available for current and future state?

5. Do future state maps show planned kaizens, completion status of kaizens, and specific targets for improvement in measures of process performance?

6. Who prepares value stream maps for the area? How many of the area's leaders are proficient value stream mappers?

Progress			Notes
1	Pre-implementation	Value stream maps are not in use, or were used once but are out of date. They are not part of the area's approach to improvement.	
		Few people if any in the area are proficient at value stream mapping.	
2	Beginning implementation	Value stream maps can be seen posted in the area, may once have been used as an improvement planning tool, but they are out of date.	
		Some technical specialists (engineers, lean leads) know how to map value streams. Most line manufacturing leaders do not.	
		Value stream maps, when present, show the current state only. Or, if future state maps are present, they are out of date.	

Progress			Notes
3	First recognizable state	Most areas have visible plans for improvement; many of these shown as current and future state value stream maps with kaizen bursts showing planned improvements and reflected on A-3s.	
		Some of the future state maps show planned improvement in specific value stream process measures (such as lead time, %value-added time, yield, productivity, uptime, change-over times).	
		In areas with current value stream maps, supervisors and superintendents are proficient value stream mappers and drew their own maps.	
4	System stabilizing	All value streams display current state and 90-day future state maps showing improvement goals (measures) and activities (kaizens).	
		All supervisors in the value stream are proficient value stream mappers, draw their own maps, use mapping to systematically understand opportunities large and small.	
		Completion status of kaizens Is shown on the value stream maps, linked to A-3 boards, and reflected in status of progress against 90-day goals.	
5	Sustainable system	Value stream maps are used regularly in the area's communications. Front line leaders teach value stream mapping.	
		All zone leaders are proficient value stream mappers. All departments and teams use posted value stream maps to show their improvement plans	
		Each area's performance (down to the team) is reflected in the current state measures summary on its value stream map (e.g., lead time, %VA time, yield, productivity, uptime, change-over).	

Few < 25%; Some < 50%; Most > 75%; All = 100%.

**Lean Management Standards: Manufacturing
Process Definition**   **Date and Location**

Diagnostic Questions:

1. Are there documented definitions for all production and production support processes? Where is the documentation located?
2. Is the documentation current; does it match actual practice?
3. Is standard work available for production tasks? For how many levels of takt time? Is it posted?
4. Are operator balance charts available, for each takt, and posted in the areas they reflect?
5. Are definitions available, and posted, for tasks in the management process (e.g., who fills in charts, standard meeting agendas, etc.)?
6. Are job breakdown sheets used for process documentation? For training? Who maintains them? Are they current? Examples?

Progress			*Notes*
1	Pre-implementation	Process documentation is either in books or in IT systems.	
		Most process documentation is out of date and does not match actual practice.	
2	Beginning implementation	There is evidence of discussions in progress to replace obsolete definitions with lean visuals for process controls, process tracking, work instructions, training documents.	
		Operator balance charts are present in a few flow areas, though few if any are current, and few if any represent multiple takts.	
		Standard work is posted in flow work stations for one takt time.	
3	First recognizable state	Assembly processes are defined by standard work charts.	
		Standard work charts are for one level of takt in areas that operate at multiple takt times.	
		Most other processes are documented; or visual documentation is present in most.	

Progress			Notes
4	System stabilizing	Areas that produce at multiple takts have operator balance charts and standardized work for each level of takt.	
		Definitions are in place for all production and management processes.	
		Process definitions are kept at the point of use or application and are up to date with actual practice.	
5	Sustainable system	Expected performance for all processes has been defined, documented.	
		Actual practice matches process documentation.	

Few < 25%; Some < 50%; Most > 75%; All = 100%.

Lean Management Standards: Manufacturing Process Discipline   **Date and Location**

Diagnostic Questions:

1. Are defined processes regularly followed (e.g., 5S, punctuality, noncyclical audits, PPE, etc.)?

2. Do crisis situations result in short cutting processes (e.g., production tracking, rotation, kanban triggers, etc.)?

3. Are manufacturing process audits carried out? Are support process audits carried out? By the leaders in the area or by outsiders?

4. When audits or tracking turn up noncompliance or misses, are problem-solving tools used?

5. To what degree does process focus lead to process improvement activity? Is there observable visual evidence?

6. How regularly do leaders conduct gemba walks to teach as well as to inspect? How many leaders do so?

Progress			Notes
1	Pre-implementation	Leaders' attention is mostly on expectations for results.	
		Lack of consistent discipline is evident in production scheduling, 5S, punctuality, material control, and most other processes.	
2	Beginning implementation	Processes followed when things run smoothly, but abandoned when problems arise.	
		A few leaders can speak to the lean rationale for process discipline and sticking with it.	
3	First recognizable state	Most leaders focus on obvious processes, e.g., standardized work, production tracking, and pitch attainment.	
		A few leaders focus on other processes such as TPM, 5S, pull systems, punctuality, labor planning.	
		Most areas are doing a good, clear, specific job of recording why interruptions or misses occurred.	

Progress			Notes
4	System stabilizing	Process focus includes noncyclical areas such as standard work in production control, waterspiders' reasons for missing pitch, visuals for scheduled maintenance as well as operator maintenance.	
		Routine audits on health of pull systems, actual versus expected change-over times, water spider routes, and other processes.	
		Most leaders using process-tracking data to identify and act on improvement activities.	
5	Sustainable system	There are regular and frequent reviews of all production and related processes, including routine audits to maintain processes (i.e., 5S, pull systems, TPM, labor planning).	
		All process misses beyond production tracking produce task assignments for improvement.	
		Paretos of "top three" misses across all processes drive Improvements.	

Few < 25%; Some < 50%; Most > 75%; All = 100%.

**Lean Management Standards: Manufacturing
Process Improvement**   **Date and Location**

Diagnostic Questions:

1. Who usually gets involved in process improvement: technical types, leaders, IT, other support groups, suppliers, workers, etc?

2. Who would most leaders say are the people most responsible for process improvement?

3. How are assignments made for process improvement tasks? Are the assignments and their status visually maintained?

4. How typical is it for improvement assignments to end up with actual improvements having been made?

5. Are kaizens a regular part of the improvement process in the area? For what kind of things? Who participates; who leads them?

6. Does improvement work focus mostly on big, technically led projects or are small improvements also pursued?

7. Is there a regular way for employees to suggest improvements? What percentage of employees make suggestions? How many are implemented (few, some, most, all)?

Progress			*Notes*
1	Pre-implementation	Improvements are made by formal project teams, or in response to catastrophic failures.	
		IT, Finance, HR, other support groups lead improvement projects	
2	Beginning implementation	Project teams make small improvements based on feedback during initial debugging	
		Most leaders see improvement as responsibility of technical groups like IT, finance, HR.	
		Suggestion systems may be introduced but are not sustained.	

Progress			Notes
3	First recognizable state	Most leaders see process improvement as an area for their involvement. Some line leaders are actively involved in supporting improvement activities in their areas.	
		Most value stream managers and some other leaders are using daily accountability boards to drive improvements with green/red coding. Some tasks are completed on time, result in improvement. Some use A-3 boards for larger-scale improvement projects.	
		Most leaders have participated in kaizens, a few have led kaizens. Few or none are qualified to facilitate kaizens.	
4	System stabilizing	Most leaders clearly see process improvement within their responsibility and can give examples of their involvement. All leaders have participated in kaizens; most now regularly lead kaizens.	
		Most leaders are effectively using daily task assignment boards, weekly A-3 reviews as demonstrated by audits of the process, the boards, and the completed tasks.	
		Some leaders experimenting with employee process improvement suggestion systems.	
5	Sustainable system	Task assignments from regular stand up meetings regularly result in small and large improvements.	
		Visual employee suggestion systems are established, sustained with steady input of ideas, output of implemented improvements. Improvement plans and targets visibly displayed at value stream, department info centers.	
		Many leaders qualified kaizen facilitators. Plants have lean resource teams to support local improvement activities and train employees in lean through rotational assignments for interested individuals who meet qualifications.	

Few < 25%; Some < 50%; Most > 75%; All = 100%.

Lean Management Standards: Manufacturing
Root Cause Problem Solving   **Date and Location**

Diagnostic Questions:

1. How often are workarounds used instead of investigating and resolving underlying causes of problems?

2. How often do leaders rely on data and analysis to attack a problem versus gut feel, intuition, or impression?

3. To what degree do leaders expect changes will expose previously unseen problems that cannot be specifically anticipated, but proceed anyway?

4. How frequently do leaders ask why something happened versus just asking what will we do to get back on track?

5. How frequently are leaders involved in leading problem solving efforts?

6. How well understood and widely used are problem-solving tools such as 5-whys, 8-step problem solving? Do leaders teach problem solving?

7. How frequently do leaders raise expectations for process performance in order to uncover the next level of process interruption or problem?

Progress			Notes
1	Pre-implementation	Problem solving only focused on workarounds, not on finding what caused problems.	
		Where cause analysis problem solving is used, it is in formal technical project teams.	
		Leaders can't describe a problem solving process, or if they can, rarely if ever follow it.	
2	Beginning implementation	Leaders have begun using visuals to collect problem data but place little emphasis on pursuing cause analysis.	
		The most common response to problems is still to workaround and cover the cause with buffers of inventory, hours, etc.	
		Evidence of one or a few attempts at systematic problem solving.	

Progress			Notes
3	First recognizable state	Leaders beginning to ask why and pursue root causes for major problems.	
		Workarounds are recognized as such; evidence of problem solving methods used to understand and attack need for workarounds.	
		Uncovering production interrupters still viewed as troubling surprises.	
4	System stabilizing	Many leaders now asking why and pursuing root causes for problems small and large and beginning to use some form of structured problem solving, at least the 5 Whys.	
		Leaders expect to surface rocks with process changes and to resolve them at a root cause level.	
		Many leaders are seeking to improve their processes.	
5	Sustainable system	Leaders regularly expect cause analysis and pursuit of root causes for problems large and small.	
		Routine, systematic use of problem solving tools to seek root cause solutions.	
		Process designs and measurements tightened up to uncover next level of problem: stated ultimate goal is to have perfect processes.	

Few < 25%; Some < 50%; Most > 75%; All = 100%.

Appendix B

Lean Management Standards: Office
Leader Standard Work   **Date and Location**

Diagnostic Questions:

1. Do leaders have standard work? Do they follow it? Do they routinely have it with them?

2. Is leader standard work regularly reviewed for updating based on new issues and changes?

3. Are standard work documents used as working documents to record notes and observations?

4. Are standard work documents reviewed at least weekly with leaders' supervisors?

5. Is there a defined place where completed standard work documents are stored? Is it used?

6. Has leader standard work been used in this area to facilitate transitions between leaders?

Progress			*Notes*
1	Pre-implementation	No leader standard work is in evidence.	
		Some leaders have heard of the idea of leader standard work.	
		Most leaders see standard work as applicable to repetitive production work only.	
2	Beginning implementation	Leader standard work exists for a few isolated positions.	
		Where it exists, leader standard work is carried some of the time and filled out irregularly.	
		Leader standard work has not been revised. Most leaders talk about it as a compliance, check the box exercise.	

Progress			Notes
3	First recognizable state	Standard work is in place for all leaders in department or value stream, team lead through value stream sponsor. The standard work for all leaders has been revised once.	
		Most leaders carry their standard work with them, follow it, and use it as a working daily document.	
		Most leaders understand the benefits of standard work and can give examples that illustrate how it has helped them in their work.	
4	System stabilizing	All leaders carry and follow leader standard work and use it as a working daily record.	
		All superiors regularly review subordinates' standard work documents at least weekly.	
		All leaders can identify how standard work benefits them and the process. Standard work is regularly reviewed and revised.	
5	Sustainable system	Standard work is reviewed at least weekly by the next level as a monitoring and communication method. Subordinates regularly review it with superiors to uncover patterns and consider revisions.	
		A standard process is followed for turning in, storing, and reviewing completed standard work documents for each leader.	
		All transitions between leaders include review and walkthrough of leader standard work. All new leaders follow standard work from day one in the job.	

Few < 25%; Some < 50%; Most > 75%; All = 100%.

**Lean Management Standards: Office
Visual Process Controls**   **Date and Location**

Diagnostic Questions:

1. Are visual controls in evidence for balancing workloads to show pace and progression of work? For exception management?

2. Are reasons for misses or flow interrupters described clearly and specifically enough to decide next steps to take?

3. Are visuals regularly reviewed and used to drive improvement? Are the improvements stimulated by visuals limited to crisis situations, or are the many often small improvements driven by visuals?

4. Are visuals regularly used for support tasks, e.g., material replenishment, rotation of tasks, planned absences, skill versatility?

5. Are visuals revised and changed as conditions change and issues either emerge or are resolved?

6. Are visuals regularly signed off/initialed by leaders in the area?

7. Are visuals documented with "who does what here when" information at or on the visual controls themselves?

Progress			Notes
1	Pre-implementation	There are no visual controls in evidence.	
2	Beginning implementation	Production or exception visuals are used only to show the status of work; who's doing what, and to balance workloads.	
		Tracking charts for value adding and support processes complete for few days or intervals of observation; often filled in irregularly, focus only on production numbers. Reasons for misses absent or too vague for action.	
		There is no or only irregular daily review of process or production exception visuals. Response to information on the visuals is either absent or irregular. Visuals are a check the box activity.	

Progress			Notes
3	First recognizable state	Some support processes and systems have visual tracking for completion or reliability. Production or process tracking charts, where they exist, are current.	
		Most reasons for misses are specific, complete and actionable with little additional information.	
		Visuals are reviewed daily or on a regular schedule, often drive specific action assignments on identified major interrupters or problems.	
4	System stabilizing	Tracking charts in use for each flow path, value stream, handoff, production area. Tracking charts used balance loads and reflect expected vs. actual pace or progression of work. Visuals added, discontinued as needs change.	
		All reasons for misses/exceptions specific, complete, actionable with little added information.	
		Visuals are reviewed daily, regularly leading to specific assignments on small and large interrupters and other problems.	
5	Sustainable system	Visuals are in regular use for support tasks and systems throughout the value stream.	
		All process and production-tracking charts are initialed at least daily by department and value stream leaders and occasionally by executives gemba walking in the area.	
		Visuals are regularly analyzed to identify most frequent interrupters or problems, which then drive root cause problem solving and implementation.	

Few < 25%; Some < 50%; Most > 75%; All = 100%.

**Lean Management Standards: Office
Standard Accountability Processes**   **Date and Location**

Diagnostic Questions:

1. Do regularly scheduled meetings focus on the status of processes as well as on results? How often?

2. Do start up or stand up meetings have clear purpose and agenda beyond today's production requirements?

3. Do regular meetings result in task assignments to improve processes, and follow up on overdue assignments?

4. How are improvement assignments and projects managed; visually, by spreadsheet or list, or not at all?

5. Do visual control charts result in task assignments, problem solving, or project assignments to address interruptions?

6. How many leaders are familiar with and able to apply basic project management techniques like work breakdown structures?

7. How well integrated are support, customer, or supplier groups in value stream improvement activities?

Progress			Notes
1	Pre-implementation	There are no regularly scheduled meetings to make or follow up on task assignments or projects for improvement or remediation.	
		Daily department and value stream meetings focus only on traditional production and volume issues.	
2	Beginning implementation	Start up or stand up meetings are held sporadically at the team, department, and value stream levels.	
		Start up or stand up meetings often lack a clear purpose, meeting agendas mostly focus on the day's production goals and schedules.	
		Team, department, and value stream meetings regularly held but little use of task assignments or follow-up. Attendance is inconsistent. Many dates slip, no or inconsistent use of visual issue, assignment, or project tracking.	

Progress			Notes
3	First recognizable state	Team, department, value stream meetings regularly held using task assignments. Follow-up occurs at department and value stream meetings. Attendance is consistent. Most task assignments are completed; most stay on the original due date.	
		Tasks mostly assigned in response to major disruptions. Some leaders use implicit work breakdown approach in assigning some tasks.	
		Many leaders consistently use the green/red color coding convention to indicate completed on time or overdue status of assignments.	
4	System stabilizing	Meeting agendas are regularly followed; attendance is faithful.	
		Review of prior day's visuals results in assignments on small and large items (some become A-3 projects). Tasks assigned from many sources, including employee suggestions, gemba walks, not just production and process tracking. Most leaders are familiar with and use project management logic for task assignments.	
		Green/red coding is a regular practice. Accountability tasks stay on original due dates. Many completed tasks reflected in positive trend in value stream measures.	
5	Sustainable system	Accountability is routine in tasks and projects. Boards and green/red coding used effectively for long- and short-term assignments.	
		All leaders grasp, regularly use basic project management tools to determine task assignments, dependencies, and durations.	
		Supplier and customer groups routinely participate in value stream accountability, A-3 review meetings, are integrated into value stream improvement activities.	

Few < 25%; Some < 50%; Most > 75%; All = 100%.

**Lean Management Standards: Office
Value Stream Mapping**   **Date and Location**

Diagnostic Questions:

1. Are there documented plans for improvements in each area in the value stream, or at least in each department?

2. Are process improvements posted and visual in each area?

3. Are value stream maps used to identify and track process improvements?

4. Are value stream maps displayed for current and future states?

5. Do future state maps show planned kaizens, completion status of kaizens, and specific targets for improvements in process measures?

6. Who prepares the value stream maps for the area? How many of the area's leaders are proficient value stream mappers?

Progress			Notes
1	Pre-implementation	Value stream maps are not in use, or were used once but are out of date. They are not part of the area's approach to improvement.	
		Few people in the area are proficient at value stream mapping.	
2	Beginning implementation	Value stream maps can be seen posted in the area, and may once have been used as an improvement planning tool but are now out of date.	
		A few technical specialists in the area know how to map value streams. Most of the leaders do not.	
		Value stream maps, when present, show the current state only. Or, if future state maps are present, they are out of date.	

Progress			Notes
3	First recognizable state	Most areas have plans for improvement; posted, with many of these shown as value stream maps of current and future states with kaizen bursts indicating planned improvements also reflected on A-3s.	
		Some future state maps show planned improvement in specific process measures such as cycle time, % C+A, process time as % of cycle time.	
		In areas with current value stream maps, some team leaders are proficient mappers and draw their own maps.	
4	System stabilizing	All value streams display current state and 90-day future state maps showing improvement goals for process measures and kaizens to achieve the goals.	
		Team leaders in the value stream are proficient mappers and draw their own maps. Mapping is a tool used systematically to understand opportunities large and small.	
		Completion of kaizens is shown on the value stream maps, linked to A-3 displays, and reflected in status of progress against 90-day goals.	
5	Sustainable system	Value stream maps are regularly used in the area's communication process. Front line leaders teach value stream mapping.	
		All leaders (managers, directors, VPs) are proficient mappers and interpreters. All departments and team areas use posted value stream maps to show their improvement goals.	
		Each area's process performance (down to the work team) is reflected in the current state process measures summary on its value stream map (e.g., lead time, process time as % of cycle time, % C+A, productivity, etc.).	

Few < 25%;, Some < 50%; Most > 75%; All = 100%.

Lean Management Standards: Office
Process Definition   **Date and Location**

Diagnostic Questions:

1. Are there documented definitions for all production and support processes? Where is the documentation located?

2. Does the documentation match actual practice?

3. Are production tasks and processes documented in Job Instruction Training format with Job Breakdown Sheets and standardized work or procedures?

4. Are standardized procedures documented, available for recurring tasks and situations? Is this information readily accessible?

5. Are definitions available and accessible for management process tasks, e.g., who fills in charts, standard agendas, etc.?

6. Is documentation updated as processes change? Is this an assigned and executed responsibility? By whom?

Progress			Notes
1	Pre-implementation	Process documentation is either in books or in IT systems.	
		Most process documentation is out of date and does not match actual practice.	
2	Beginning implementation	There is evidence of discussions in progress to replace obsolete definitions with Job Instruction Training and Job Breakdown Sheet documentation, visual process progression tracking, and/or production controls.	
		Standardized procedures are documented and available for some tasks and situations.	
		Work balancing/leveling and volume-dependent staffing procedures are available in a few areas or for a few tasks.	

Progress			Notes
3	First recognizable state	Standardized procedures are documented and available for most high volume/everyday jobs.	
		Job Breakdown Sheets are in use to document work instructions and training procedures for most high volume/everyday jobs.	
		Standardized procedures and aids (checklists, templates, etc.) are available for high volume/everyday tasks.	
4	System stabilizing	Areas that produce at variable volumes/rates of demand have defined, documented roles, procedures, Job Breakdown Sheet training for variable staffing levels.	
		Definitions and Job Breakdown Sheets are in place for all production and management processes. Responsibility for maintaining documentation is defined.	
		Process definitions are kept at or are accessible at the point of use or application, and are up to date with current actual practice.	
5	Sustainable system	Expected performance for all processes has been defined and documented, often in Job Instruction Training forms and formats.	
		Actual practice matches process documentation.	
		Maintaining process definitions and documentation is a clearly defined, assigned, and consistently executed responsibility.	

Few < 25%; Some < 50%; Most > 75%; All = 100%.

Lean Management Standards: Office Process Discipline

Date and Location

Diagnostic Questions:

1. Are defined processes regularly followed, e.g., 5S, standardized procedures, checklists/templates, regular meetings, etc.?

2. Do crisis situations result in shortcutting processes, e.g., process tracking, standardized procedures, etc.?

3. Are work processes tracked for compliance with standardized procedures and practices? By people and leaders in the area or by outsiders?

4. When audits or tracking turn up noncompliance or misses, are problem solving tools used to understand the causes?

5. To what degree does focus on the defined processes lead to process improvement activity? Is there observable evidence?

6. How regularly do leaders conduct gemba walks to teach as well as to inspect? How many leaders do so?

Progress			*Notes*
1	Pre-implementation	Leaders' attention is mostly on expectations for results and consistency of practice, and discipline to defined processes is generally lacking.	
2	Beginning implementation	Processes are followed when things run smoothly, and are abandoned when problems arise.	
		A few leaders can speak to the lean rationale for process discipline and sticking with it.	
3	First recognizable state	Most leaders focus on obvious processes, e.g., standardized procedures for recurring tasks, production and process tracking, measures of pace.	
		A few leaders focus on other processes such as work balancing, cross training, controlled release of work.	
		Most areas are doing a good, clear, specific job of recording when interruptions or misses occur.	

Progress			Notes
4	System stabilizing	Process focus includes customer and supplier areas and support activities such as system downtime, materials and supplies, cross training.	
		Routine audits take place to assess cross training, work balancing, proficiency with tools and practices, accessibility and up to date status of documentation for standardized processes and procedures.	
		Most leaders are using process tracking data to identify and act on improvement opportunities.	
5	Sustainable system	Regularly scheduled and performed reviews of production and related processes result in appropriate, periodic revisions and updates of standards.	
		All process misses beyond production and process tracking are considered for task assignments for cause analysis and/or improvement.	
		Pareto analysis of most frequent and/or serious misses across all processes drives short-term improvement assignments and longer cycle (A-3) improvement projects when warranted.	

Few < 25%; Some < 50%; Most > 75%; All = 100%.

Lean Management Standards: Office Process Improvement

Date and Location

Diagnostic Questions:

1. Who usually gets involved in process improvement in this area? Specialists, leaders, IT, area employees, etc?

2. Do leaders teach problem solving?

3. Is there an organized, structured approach to problem solving? Examples, visible evidence for it?

4. Who would leaders say are the people with responsibility for process improvement?

5. How are assignments made for process improvement tasks? Are the assignments and their status visually maintained?

6. How typical is it for improvement assignments to end up with actual improvements having been made?

7. Are kaizens a regular part of the improvement process here? Who gets involved? Who leads the kaizens?

8. Does improvement work focus mostly on big, technically led projects or are small improvements also pursued?

9. Is there a regular way for employees to suggest improvements? What percentage of employees make suggestions? How many are implemented (few, some, most, all)?

	Progress		Notes
1	Pre-implementation	Improvements are made by formal project teams, or in response to major failures.	
		IT, Finance, HR, other support groups lead improvement projects.	
2	Beginning implementation	Project implementation teams make small improvements based on feedback during initial debugging.	
		Most leaders see improvement as responsibility of technical groups such as IT, finance, HR.	
		First attempts made to introduce systematic problem solving and related leader training. Suggestion systems may be introduced but are not sustained.	

Progress			Notes
3	First recognizable state	Most leaders see process improvement as an area for their involvement. Some leaders actively support improvement activities in their areas. Some leaders teach problem solving. Evidence of structured problem solving.	
		Most leaders in area use accountability task boards to drive improvements with green/red coding. Some tasks completed on time, result in improvement. Some A-3 plan formats in use for larger improvements, some use of future state VSMs to display current improvement plans.	
		Most leaders have participated in kaizens, a few have led kaizens. Few or none are qualified to facilitate kaizens.	
4	System stabilizing	Most leaders see process improvement as their responsibility, can give examples of their involvement. All leaders have participated in kaizens; most now regularly lead kaizens. All leaders teach problem solving.	
		Some leaders are experimenting with employee suggestion systems for process improvement. Systematic problem solving is in use by most and evident in the area.	
		Most leaders effectively use task assignment boards, weekly A-3 reviews with visible evidence of boards, reviews, improvements. Most use future state value stream maps to display planned improvements and goals.	
5	Sustainable system	Task assignments from regular stand up meetings regularly result in small and large improvements.	
		Employee suggestion systems established, sustained with steady input of ideas, output of implemented improvements. Improvement plans, targets visibly displayed in the area. Problem solving activity and thinking in evidence among all in the area.	
		Many leaders qualified kaizen facilitators. Departments have kaizen/lean resources to support local improvement activities, train employees in lean through rotating assignments for those interested and who meet selection criteria.	

Few < 25%; Some < 50%; Most > 75%; All = 100%.

**Lean Management Standards: Office
Root Cause Problem Solving**   **Date and Location**

Diagnostic Questions:

1. How often are workarounds used instead of investigating and resolving underlying causes of problems?

2. How often do leaders rely on data and analysis to attack a problem versus gut feel, intuition, or impression?

3. To what degree do leaders proceed with changes even though they expect that changes will expose previously unseen problems that cannot be specifically anticipated?

4. How frequently do leaders ask why something happened versus just asking what will we do to get back on track?

5. How many leaders teach and lead problem solving efforts?

6. How well understood and widely used are structured problem-solving tools such as 5 Whys, 8-step problem solving?

7. How frequently do leaders raise their expectations for process performance and tighten process measures in order to uncover the next level of process interruption or problem?

8. In conversation, do employees demonstrate problem-solving, continuous improvement thinking?

Progress			Notes
1	Pre-implementation	Problem solving is only focused on workarounds, not on finding causes of problems. Most employees do not believe problem solving is part of their jobs.	
		Where cause analysis problem solving is used, it is by formally chartered technical teams or designated specialists.	
		Leaders can't describe a problem solving process, or if they can it's not documented.	
2	Beginning implementation	Leaders have begun using visuals to collect problem data but place little emphasis on pursuing cause analysis.	
		The most common response to problems is still to workaround and/or cover the cause with buffers of overtime, extended lead times, temp help, etc.	
		Evidence of one or a few attempts at systematic problem solving. Some leaders trained to teach problem solving.	

Progress			Notes
3	First recognizable state	Leaders beginning to ask why and pursue root causes for major problems. Many leaders teaching structured problem solving, many team members getting involved in problem solving.	
		Workarounds are recognized as such and often referred to as "countermeasures;" evidence of problem solving methods in use to attack them.	
		Interrupters uncovered after process changes still viewed as troubling surprises.	
4	System stabilizing	Many leaders now asking why and pursuing root causes for problems large and small and beginning to use some form of structured problem solving, at least the 5-whys.	
		Leaders expect to surface rocks with process changes and to resolve them at a root cause level.	
		Many leaders seeking to improve their processes by using systematic cause analysis and problem solving methods. Many employees involved in structured problem solving.	
5	Sustainable system	Leaders regularly expect cause analysis and pursuit of root cause solutions for problems large and small.	
		Problem solving tools used routinely to seek root cause solutions. All leaders teach problem solving, all employees involved in problem solving, all in the area involved in problem solving thinking.	
		Process designs and measurements tightened up to uncover next level of problem to attack: stated ultimate goal in the area is to have perfect processes.	

Few < 25%, Some < 50%, Most > 75%, All = 100%

Glossary

Balanced line: A series of workstations, such as an assembly line where the time to do the work is nearly equal in each station within a few seconds. When a line is balanced to takt time, the time it takes to do the work in each station is equal to takt time or very close—within a second or two of takt. *See also* Takt time.

Batch and queue: A method of organizing production. In batch and queue, the focus is on the efficiency of each discrete part of the production operation, such as a machine or a paint shop, as compared with the efficiency of the system as a whole from the first operation to final product. Each operation produces a batch of as many of a particular item at a time as possible, based on a separate production schedule sent to each operation. When the batch is done, it is pushed to the next operation regardless of the type and quantity of item needed by the next operation. The batch sits in queue, waiting for the next operation to get to it. Batch operations typically try to minimize the number of changeovers from one item to the next to maximize their efficiency in, for example, parts produced per machine per minute, hour, or day. *See also* Changeover.

Brownfield: The name given to existing operations, particularly when they are in the process of being converted from batch-and-queue production to lean production. Brownfield operations already have established practices and cultures, as distinct from greenfield operations, which often are literally constructed on what was previously an empty field. Greenfields have no history, no culture, and no preexisting practices.

Changeover: The time it takes to switch production of one product or component to making a different model, style, type of component, or finished product. Changeover time is often associated with machines or other equipment used to make or process components for several

261

different product lines or styles. Changeovers consist of elements, such as shutting down the machine or stopping production, removing the tool, die, or fixture for the first part, inserting the tool to make the second part, removing any remaining first parts and their component materials, bringing in the materials and containers to make and hold the second part, making a second part and checking it against specifications, and resuming production.

Countermeasure: In the Toyota Production System, when a problem arises that cannot be eliminated immediately, countermeasures are put in place to protect the process from the problem. When a countermeasure is in place, the problem is not considered fixed or solved; instead, it is considered just to be a Band-Aid® until a real solution is found that will eliminate the problem instead of simply covering it up. For example, holding inventory to protect against a machine that breaks down often is a countermeasure to be kept in place until the machine's reliability can be improved.

Culture: In a workplace, the sum of habits people rely on to get things done; "The way we do things here." Culture also sums up the things an adult member of a work group needs to know and comply with in order not to be seen as deviant by other members. See Chapter 1.

Cycle time: *See* Work content.

Discipline: What happens when someone breaks the rules or fails to meet expectations. The second meaning refers to adherence to defined processes, such as following the sequence of elements every time in standardized work, or filling in a pitch chart as each pitch cycle is completed. This latter meaning of discipline is especially crucial in a lean system where processes are interdependent and closely tied with one another and failure in any one can quickly bring the entire system to a halt.

FIFO: First in first out. When units move between operations in FIFO order, they maintain their sequence. This can be important when work starts simultaneously, in different areas, on several subcomponents that will come together to form a single unit at the end of the production process. Maintaining FIFO sequence is also important in keeping stored inventory fresh by always using the oldest first.

Five S (5S): Sort, shine, set in order, standardize, sustain. These are five steps to remove unneeded tools, materials, debris, and clutter; thoroughly clean the entire area and everything in it; establish a logical place for each item; mark addresses/locations for each place and the thing(s) that go in it; and establish a system to maintain the cleanliness and order you have established. With 5S, everything has a place, and you can tell at a glance what is supposed to be where, what does not belong in an area, and what belongs, but is missing or out of place. It is one form of basic discipline.

Five Whys (5 Ws): Asking why five times is a basic method of cause analysis. Each successive question is intended to go deeper into the cause of a situation, typically a problem with production. For example: We missed pitch this period. Why? We ran out of parts. Why? The waterspider didn't pick up the withdrawal card. Why? There was no withdrawal card in the container. Why? I took the card home in my pocket by accident and lost it. Why? I didn't put the withdrawal card in the kanban post when I pulled the container in to begin using it. What was the cause? Failure to handle the withdrawal kanban according to the defined process: Put it in the kanban post before using the first part from the container!

Flow: A goal in lean production in which product moves through the steps in a production process with no interruption or waiting between steps. An example of flow is a moving assembly line. The ideal of flow is one-piece flow. In one-piece flow, as work is completed at one workstation, the unit is passed directly to the next with no waiting and a new unit arrives at the first workstation without that operator having to wait for it. In some cases, flow is not one piece at a time, but rather a small batch or lot at a time, such as a pair of arms for a chair or a set of drawers for a storage cabinet.

Flow interrupters: Things that cause production to be halted or slowed below the expected pace, until they can be resolved. Running out of parts in an assembly process is a flow interrupter. So are machines breaking down unexpectedly, and unplanned absences of production team members.

Gemba walk: A Japanese term meaning "the real place," or roughly, "where the action is." In manufacturing, that means the production floor. Gemba walks are one of the primary ways for teaching lean production, and the primary way for teaching lean management. In a gemba walk, a teacher, or sensei, and student walk the production floor. The teacher asks the student to tell what he or she sees and, depending on the answer, asks more questions to stimulate the student to think differently about what is in front of him or her. This includes learning to see what is not there, and learning to see what has been accepted as a given, but should be changed to fit with lean principles. Gemba walks often include assignments to act on what the student has come to see, with follow up on the next gemba walk, typically weekly. *See also* Sensei.

Heijunka: A Japanese term for a visual method used to smooth out demand for production so the demand is level, or stable every interval of time all day long. The intervals can be pitches, fractions of an hour, whole hours, or any other interval that fits a particular production process. In addition to leveling work across intervals, a heijunka system can also be used to introduce the same number and sequence of units of mixed types every interval, reflecting the overall proportions of mixed models to be produced in a given day or other production period. Heijunka leveling can be applied equally well to nonproduction activities, for example, when scheduling work to be carried out by a maintenance group. *See also* Mixed-model line.

Hypothetical construct: An idea or a label applied to an idea that cannot be directly observed. A construct is an abstraction such as market appeal, in distinction to something concrete such as gross operating profit or first year sales.

IT: An abbreviation for information technology, meaning computers, computer automation, and computer networks. IT solutions to information flow and information management are often, but not always, at odds with the visual controls approach in lean production and lean management, where no computer is needed to assess the status of any process. Computer networks can be helpful in lean systems by serving to broadcast or transmit information from one location to another, especially where line of sight communication is not possible or multiple configurations of options make simple visual methods less practical.

Job rotation: *See* Rotation.

Kaizen: A Japanese term meaning "good change." Kaizen is a way of thinking and seeing, of always being alert to the opportunity to make changes for improvement. It typically involves small changes, rarely more than can be accomplished by a team of seven working full time for a week. Many lean organizations include kaizen events as a regular part of their continuous improvement activities. Kaizens are structured events carried out by a team assembled for the task under the direction of a kaizen team leader, where the improvement task is completed start to finish in a week or less.

Kanban: A Japanese term meaning signboard. Kanbans are used to identify and order a specified quantity of parts. They include three kinds of information: the part or item number, the quantity, and authorization either to make parts in the case of a production instruction kanban, or to take parts in the case of a withdrawal kanban. Kanbans are often printed cards, but can also be designated empty containers, or empty spots in a rack or on the floor. *See also* Pull signals.

Layout: The arrangement of equipment and material storage in a production area, analogous to a floor plan for a room or house. Layouts in lean production areas are designed to facilitate flow of material and production, with equipment arranged in the sequence of production steps. *See also* Value stream.

Lean management system: The practices and tools used to monitor, measure, and sustain the operation of lean production operations. Lean management practices identify where actual performance fails to meet expected performance; assigns and follows up improvement activities to bring actual in line with expected, or to raise the level of expected performance. The basic components of the lean management system are standard work for leaders, visual controls, and a daily accountability process.

Lean production: The name for the Toyota Production System popularized by Womack and Jones in *Lean Thinking*. Womack and Jones identify five elements, or principles, of lean production: Definition of value from the customer's point of view, flow production, pull replenishment of what has been consumed, constant emphasis on the reduction of waste, and striving for perfection.

Lot size: Lean practitioners often refer to lot sizes, rather than using the word "batch." In any case, lot size refers to a specific quantity or batch in which parts are produced or procured. Batches, or lots of defined size, are used in lean processes where one-piece flow is not yet possible because of bottlenecks or where resources are shared among value streams. The lot size (and container size) at the point where parts are used, typically in assembly; the lot size in which parts are held in supermarkets; and the lot sizes in which producing work centers make parts need to be in close alignment to avoid adding several potential forms of waste into the system as a whole. *See also* Flow.

Machine balance chart: Shows the load on a machine as a stacked bar chart of the number of hours per week required to produce each type of part the machine makes, including the amount of time it is idle while changeovers from one part to the next are performed, and the amount of time it is typically unavailable because of breakdowns or planned maintenance. The chart reflects the time a machine must run and change over to produce specified quantities of the parts to replenish a supermarket without causing the supermarket to run out of any of the parts produced by the machine. A machine balance chart needs to be produced as part of the work involved in setting up a pull system's supermarket. *See also* Pull system *and* Supermarket.

Mixed-model line: An assembly or progressive build line on which several models of unit are produced, such as two different chair models, each of which can be ordered with different options, or different sizes of similar units like storage cabinets. So, instead of building a single finished good, the line is designed to produce several kinds of finished goods in a way that the mix does not interrupt flow. Heijunka scheduling is helpful for introducing the mix in a stable way that allows the line to maintain flow. *See* Balanced line *and* Heijunka.

MRP: Materials Requirements Planning (MRP) is the planning system for conventional batch-and-queue production systems. MRP forecasts the need for material and components based in part on historical patterns of demand and in part on current orders. MRP schedules work to be performed in batches to maximize efficiency of individual work centers. It is a classic push scheduling system.

Noncyclical processes: Processes not carried out every production cycle (such as every time a storage cabinet is assembled on an assembly line). Noncyclical tasks are those carried out one or only a few times a day, such as cleaning equipment at the end of a shift, or calibrating a process every 100 cycles. Noncyclical tasks can be even less frequent, for example, weekly, monthly, or quarterly maintenance tasks. Compare with *Standardized work*.

Non-value-adding: Tasks that do not transform parts or materials into finished products. Some non-value-adding work remains necessary in many production operations, such as parts traveling on a conveyor through a paint or finishing shop. Applying and curing the finish adds value as it is part of the transformation of materials into products, but travel on the conveyor does not, even though it is necessary in the way the process is set up today. Tasks either add value or do not; people asked to do non-value-adding work are not themselves without value; they are only doing what the current system asks of them. Compare with *Value adding*.

OEE: Overall equipment effectiveness. OEE is a coefficient produced by multiplying three percentages: actual time a piece of equipment was available as a percentage of planned availability; actual yield of good output as a percentage of all output produced; actual speed, or rate of the equipment's operation as a percentage of its designed speed or rate. An OEE of 0.85 is considered excellent. OEE considers six categories of losses contributing to less than perfect (OE = 1.00) performance: waiting for operator, waiting for material, defective outputs, speed losses, minor stoppages, major stoppages.

Pitch: A multiple of takt, first used as a unit of measure in the automotive supplier industry, where units such as door handles or mirrors are produced to order and shipped to assembly plants in standard containers, or packs. The pack quantity (for example, 24 mirrors) is designated as a pitch as a method to manage pace. If each mirror is produced to a takt time of 20 seconds, 24 units would equal eight minutes of work. Instead of having to focus each 20 seconds, pitch allows a leader to check pace every 24 takt cycles in this example. Where standard pack quantities are not used, the concept is still useful. Pitch can be used to designate an interval of time at which to measure whether the actual pace of production equals what was expected. Pitch as a time interval can be an hour, half hour, quarter hour, or other interval depending on the nature of the product and maturity of the process. *See also* Takt time.

Priority board: Part of a pull system for replenishing material that has been consumed by a customer process. Production instruction kanbans that direct a work center to make a specified quantity of a specific part are brought to the work center and placed on its priority board in the order that the cards arrive at the work center. The cards are, in effect, in line waiting their turn. As the work center operator completes a job, he or she takes the first card in line from the next-up position on the board and puts it in a designated spot (often marked "Running") in the work center. The operator or team leader then moves each card up one spot on the board. *See* Figure 4.4 for an illustration.

Process focus: Virtually every process in a lean system is defined, documented, and visually controlled. Each process in a lean system is interdependent with one, several, or many other processes. Failure in any single process can quickly bring the system to a halt. Process focus is the practice and discipline of continually and regularly checking on the status of each process to be sure it is operating normally, or documenting when it is not, and identifying the cause of the abnormal condition and eliminating or preventing it from recurring. Process focus is a principal objective of the lean management system.

Production instruction card: A type of kanban that authorizes the production of a specified quantity of a particular component or part. Production instructions are elements in pull production systems. They typically circulate between a supermarket and the work center where the part or component is produced when the level of that part in the supermarket reaches its reorder point. *See also* Kanban *and* Pull signals.

Progressive build line: Another name for assembly lines where a finished unit is built up piece by piece as it moves from one assembly station to the next. Progressive build does not require a moving conveyor line, only that a unit moves from station to station as it is assembled.

Pull signals, visual pull signals: Pull signals are the devices used to authorize and request the waterspider to pick and deliver a specified quantity of a specific part, or to authorize and request a supplying work center to make a specified quantity of a specific part to replenish what has been taken away from the work center's supermarket. The pull signals are, classically, kanban cards, but can be empty racks or containers, empty spots on the floor or a designated location on a shelf or space in a workstation. Pull signals can be fitted with barcodes to enable scanning and electronic ordering or recording, but for a pull system to remain consistent with a lean philosophy, it must also remain visually verifiable. This means electronic pull signals (appropriate when the distance between supplier and customer is too great to confidently rely on the circulation of cards as the sole signal) and visual signals (the cards) can coexist, but visuals are always a requirement in lean management. *See also* Kanban *and* Supermarket.

Pull, pull system: Used in lean production systems where flow is not practical, pull production is based on replenishing what has been used by a customer, usually the next workstation in a production process but sometimes an actual customer taking away finished goods. Pull production is typically used where a piece of equipment makes components for several product lines or value streams, often where the equipment produces components faster than a single consuming process can use them. Pull systems often involve supermarkets where components are kept in specified locations and quantities. As customers take components away from the market, signals to replenish what has been removed are sent to the producing work center. *See also* Kanban *and* Supermarket.

Queue: Material waiting to be processed is in queue, as in waiting its turn in line. Queues of material between operations are often referred to as WIP, or work in process inventory. Queues of WIP between processes are the inevitable result of producing components in batches as opposed to one at a time. *See also* Batch and queue.

Root cause: The basic source from which a problem grows, as distinct from symptoms that are the visible effects of a problem. By doing a problem solving analysis to find what is causing a problem, it is often possible to eliminate the cause altogether, or to prevent it from recurring. By analogy, if you cut the top off a weed, it is likely to grow back from the undisturbed root. If you dig the weed out by the root, it will not come back. *See also* 5 Whys.

Rotation, rotation pattern: Refers to people moving from job to job at specified intervals or times during the day. Where some jobs involve higher levels of ergonomic stress, rotation might be as frequent as every half hour. In other situations, rotation might be less frequent, such as every hour, two hours, every break, at mid-shift, etc. Rotation serves three purposes: First, it mitigates the risk of repetitive motion injuries, letting people vary the muscle groups and postures from station to station. Second, it provides a broad base of skilled and experienced people able to step into any of several jobs when needed. Third, it provides many people's eyes on each and every job, improving the chances for thinking of and seeing potential process improvements.

Sensei: A Japanese term for one who has gone before, or teacher. The sensei is the master in the master-apprentice learning model for lean management and for much of lean production.

Setup: *See* Changeover.

Standard work for leaders: One of the key elements of the lean management system, standard work for leaders specifies the actions to be taken each day to focus on the processes in each leader's area of responsibility. Unlike standardized work for a production workstation, the elements in standard work for leaders usually are not timed, though some of them take place at specific times during the day, for example, "Lead tier two meeting (6:30 am)." See Chapter 3 for a discussion of standard work for leaders.

Standardized work: Specifications, usually for a production workstation, that include the sequence in which steps or work elements are performed, expected time for each element and the total time for all, takt time, and the quantities of inventory before, in, and after the workstation. Standard work for production operations also can include specific safety information (for example, identifying potential pinch points) and quality checks to be performed during the sequence of operations.

Supermarket: Supermarkets are integral elements in lean pull systems. They are areas where inventory is stored according to specific rules. Each item in the supermarket has a designated address as the only place where it is stored. Each item is stored in specific quantities, typically in a specified maximum quantity of containers. Each container is to hold a specified number of the designated item. The point at which an item is to be reordered, the reorder or trigger point, is clearly designated visually. In some cases, minimum quantities are also designated visually. One should be able to assess the status of a supermarket by using a simple visual inspection: is the stock stored properly, do part numbers correspond to the appropriate address, are maximum quantity limits being adhered to, are there dangerously low levels of some parts, are the kanban cards in the proper locations according to the documented process, etc. *See also* Pull system *and* Kanban.

Support groups: These are technical specialty departments found in most manufacturing plants. They can include engineering, production control [often called production and inventory control (PIC) or materials management], quality control or quality assurance (QC or QA), maintenance, tooling, safety, and human resources.

Takt time: The rate of customer demand calculated by dividing daily demand in units into the time available for production. It is typically expressed in seconds, as in "takt time for the XYZ is 54 seconds." That means a completed unit is due off the end of the line every 54 seconds. Lean systems are designed to produce at the takt rate; thus takt is the basis for pace for the entire lean process.

Team leader: Team leaders are the first level of formally designated leadership in a lean production environment. Where production is done by an hourly workforce, team leaders are typically hourly employees who earn a slight premium for their position. The primary responsibilities of team leaders are to maintain the takt pace of production; maintain and improve on standardized work, including training operators in standard work; and being available for limited (5-minute) fill-in when a team member must leave his or her position in an emergency. Team leaders do not work production except in these situations. Team size is typically five to ten people working in a small area.

Technical lean implementation: Focuses on changes to the layout of the shop floor, the way inventory is deployed and moves, and changes in how and where the production schedule is delivered to the shop floor. Typical areas of focus in technical implementations include establishing flow production balanced to standardized work at takt time, implementing pull systems with kanban signaling for replenishment, establishing waterspider routes, and refining parts presentation and container size, among other things. Technical implementation differs from lean management implementation.

Three-tier meetings: These make up the daily accountability process, one of the three key elements in the lean management system. They are brief, structured, stand-up meetings that take place at or near the beginning of the workday. The first tier involves the work team led by the team leader. The second tier involves the team leaders led by the supervisor. The third tier involves the value stream staff led by the value stream manager. See Chapter 5 for a discussion of three-tier meetings.

Toyota Production System (TPS): Developed over the past 50 years at Toyota, based initially on the writings of Henry Ford. TPS seeks to eliminate waste from production processes. The ideal approach in TPS is for production to operate at exactly the rate of customer demand. This is often expressed as Just-in-Time production, where nothing is produced until there is specific customer demand for it. *See also* Pull, Pull system, *and* Flow.

Tugger: A small, usually electric engine often operated by a driver in a standing position. Tuggers are like small tram engines pulling carts or trailers of material around a production area. In lean production systems, tuggers are often used to deliver materials from supermarkets to the workstations in assembly areas where the material will be used. This is especially true where the distances are too long to walk or the materials too heavy or large to transport by handcart.

Value-adding activity: Anything necessary to transform material on the way to making a finished product. Cutting to size, attaching components, making connections, and applying finish are all examples of value-adding activity. Storing, moving, counting, and reworking are all examples of activities that do not add value to the finished product, even though some of them may be necessary in the current production process. Compare with Non-value-adding.

Value stream: The people and equipment involved in producing a product line or closely related family of products. Value streams usually include each of the operations and pieces of equipment needed to make a product lined up or arranged close together in the sequence of production operations. The intent is to minimize the distance parts have to be moved and maximize the speed of flow through the production process. In a batch-and-queue organization, like operations are typically grouped together in separate departments, such as forming, molding, cutting, sewing, insertion, subassembly, finishing, and final assembly. Batches of parts typically wait, sometimes a long time, between operations and often must be moved long distances from one operation to the next.

Value stream manager: In an organizational structure designed to most fully reflect a lean philosophy, all the support groups related to making a value stream operate would report on a solid line to the value stream manager. This means the value stream would have a dedicated staff group, as well as the typical line management positions, such as team leaders and department supervisors. Especially early in a lean journey, companies may not be ready to make this organizational realignment without creating more turbulence than is worthwhile.

Visual controls: Visual controls are the variety of approaches that make the status of a process visible at a glance. They include production-tracking charts of various kinds that show actual versus expected performance. They also include audit forms for status of safety practices, workplace organization and 5S, compliance with specifications for contents of a supermarket, and number and location of kanban cards. Signs, labeled "parking spaces" on the floor itself, and shadow boards all make it possible to tell where things should and shouldn't be. Strictly speaking, visual controls allow control of processes rather than actually exerting control themselves. *See also* Process focus.

Waterspider: A name often used for the person who circulates between the points where material is consumed and the supermarkets where it is stored. Waterspiders typically have defined routes and defined times, much like bus schedules. They pick up empty containers and kanban cards from the point of consumption, go to the supermarket and use the withdrawal kanban cards as a shopping list to pull full containers from the supermarket shelf or rack, and return to deliver the full containers. Waterspiders sometimes remove finished goods from an assembly area, and sometimes take production instruction kanbans from the supermarket to the producing work center. *See also* Supermarket *and* Kanban.

Work breakdown structure: A basic component in project management, a work breakdown structure is essentially a list of all the steps or subtasks needed to accomplish a larger task. An example is a recipe where the steps are listed in sequence, one at a time, as opposed to simply listing the ingredients and stating, "combine and bake."

Work content: Refers to the total amount of time required to perform all the elements in the standard work for a workstation. This is often referred to as the cycle time for a task. Total work content, also referred to as total cycle time, refers to the sum of cycle times of all workstations' standard work elements. Thus, the cycle times to complete the work elements in each of a series of nine workstations in a progressive build line might be 45 seconds in each workstation (though rarely are workstations perfectly balanced this way). The total cycle time would be 9 stations times 45 seconds for a total work content of 6 minutes 45 seconds.

Work element: *See* Standardized work.

Bibliography

There are many references on lean production. The ones I have listed here provide a good introduction to its concepts and application.

Dennis, Pascal. *Lean Production Simplified*, New York: Productivity Press, 2002.

Imai, Masaaki. *Gemba Kaizen*, New York: McGraw-Hill, 1997.

Lean Enterprise Institute, *Lean Lexicon*, Brookline, MA: Lean Enterprise Institute, 2003.

Liker, Jeffrey K. *Becoming Lean*, New York: Productivity Press, 1998.

Rother, Mike, and Shook, John. *Learning to See*, Brookline, MA: Lean Enterprise Institute, 1998.

Schipper, Timothy and Swets, Mark. *Innovative Lean Development*, New York: Productivity Press, 2009.

Womack, James, and Jones, Daniel. *Lean Thinking, 2nd edition*, New York: Simon and Schuster, 2003.

Index

The Author

David Mann is the author of *Creating a Lean Culture: Tools to Sustain Lean Conversions.* The book was awarded the Shingo Prize in 2006 and is being translated into Portuguese, Chinese, Russian, and Thai.

During his 21-year career with Steelcase, Mann developed and applied the concepts of a lean management system. In his service with the company, he supported 40+ lean manufacturing value stream transformations, following which he developed and for five years led an internal team that completed over 100 successful lean office and product development business process conversions that reduced total cycle time, process time, and rework each by an average of 50 percent. He retired from Steelcase in 2009.

Mann's teaching and coaching experience includes lean transformation in manufacturing, enterprise business processes, and healthcare organizations. His consulting practice includes lean and lean management implementation, troubleshooting stalled lean initiatives, as well as frequent training and speaking engagements on lean management. Mann serves clients in manufacturing, healthcare, and enterprise business processes.

He is a faculty member and consultant for Johnson and Johnson's Ortho-Clinical Diagnostics ValuMetrix Services lean consulting organization. He serves as well on the faculty in the Operations Management program at the Fisher College of Business, Ohio State University, and OSU's Center for Operational Excellence. Mann is a Shingo Prize examiner, an assessor for the Honda Lean Network, and a member of the Lean Transformation Advisory Board for St. Mary's Healthcare in Grand Rapids, Michigan. He is an invited contributor to *Frontiers of Health Services Management*, a frequent contributor to and member of the editorial board of the Association for Manufacturing Excellence's publication *Target*, as well as editor of the *Target* feature: "Single Point Lessons." He serves on the board of AME's Great Lakes Region.

Mann is an organizational psychologist, earning his Ph.D. at the University of Michigan in 1976. He lives in East Grand Rapids, Michigan, with his wife, who is a criminal prosecutor. They have two daughters.

For more information, visit his website at: www.dmannlean.com or contact him at dwmann@comcast.net.